ROUTLEDGE LIBRARY EDITIONS: EDUCATION IN ASIA

Volume 5

CONTEMPORARY CHINESE EDUCATION

CONTEMPORARY CHINESE EDUCATION

Edited by
RUTH HAYHOE

LONDON AND NEW YORK

First published in 1984 by M.E. Sharpe, Inc.

This edition first published in 2018
by Routledge
2 Park Square, Milton Park, Abingdon, Oxon OX14 4RN

and by Routledge
711 Third Avenue, New York, NY 10017

Routledge is an imprint of the Taylor & Francis Group, an informa business

© 1984 Ruth Hayhoe

All rights reserved. No part of this book may be reprinted or reproduced or utilised in any form or by any electronic, mechanical, or other means, now known or hereafter invented, including photocopying and recording, or in any information storage or retrieval system, without permission in writing from the publishers.

Trademark notice: Product or corporate names may be trademarks or registered trademarks, and are used only for identification and explanation without intent to infringe.

British Library Cataloguing in Publication Data
A catalogue record for this book is available from the British Library

ISBN: 978-1-138-30826-8 (Set)
ISBN: 978-1-315-14674-4 (Set) (ebk)
ISBN: 978-1-138-31000-1 (Volume 5) (hbk)
ISBN: 978-1-138-50112-6 (Volume 5) (pbk)
ISBN: 978-1-315-14392-7 (Volume 5) (ebk)

Publisher's Note
The publisher has gone to great lengths to ensure the quality of this reprint but points out that some imperfections in the original copies may be apparent.

Disclaimer
The publisher has made every effort to trace copyright holders and would welcome correspondence from those they have been unable to trace.

Contemporary Chinese Education

Ruth Hayhoe

M.E. Sharpe, Inc.
Armonk, New York

©1984 Ruth Hayhoe
M.E. Sharpe, Inc.
80 Business Park Drive
Armonk, New York 10504 USA

Library of Congress Cataloging in Publication Data
Main entry under title:

Contemporary Chinese education.

  Bibliography: p.
  Includes index.
  1. Education—China—History. 2. Education—
China—Foreign influences. 3. Comparative
education. I. Hayhoe, Ruth.
LA1131.C75   1984   370'.951   84-14057
ISBN 0-87332-297-5
ISBN 0-87332-298-3 (pbk.)

Printed and bound in Great Britain

CONTENTS

List of Tables and Figures

Editorial Preface ... 2

Chart of the Education System ... 4

1. A COMPARATIVIST'S VIEW OF CHINESE EDUCATION ... 7
   Brian Holmes

2. THE EVOLUTION OF MODERN CHINESE EDUCATIONAL INSTITUTIONS ... 26
   Ruth Hayhoe

3. PRIMARY EDUCATION: A TWO-TRACK SYSTEM FOR DUAL TASKS ... 47
   Billie L.C. Lo

4. NEW DIRECTIONS IN SECONDARY EDUCATION ... 65
   Stanley Rosen

5. HIGHER EDUCATION: THE TENSION BETWEEN QUALITY AND EQUALITY ... 93
   Jürgen Henze

6. TEACHER EDUCATION IN THE EIGHTIES ... 154
   Billie L.C. Lo

7. ADULT EDUCATION IN URBAN INDUSTRIAL CHINA: PROBLEMS, POLICIES, AND PROSPECTS ... 178
   David I. Chambers

8. CHINESE-WESTERN SCHOLARLY EXCHANGE: IMPLICATIONS FOR THE FUTURE OF CHINESE EDUCATION ... 205
   Ruth Hayhoe

Notes and References ... 230

Statistical Appendix of Contemporary Educational Provision ... 268

Glossary of Chinese characters for the Chinese terms used in the text ... 273

The Contributors ... 279

Index ... 280

LIST OF TABLES AND FIGURES

Tables

3.1	Teaching Plan for Full-time Five-year Primary Schools, 1982	53
4.1	The Routes Taken by Lower Secondary Graduates in Shanghai, 1964	68
4.2	Students in Various Forms of Secondary Schooling, by Percentage	73
4.3	Secondary Schools and Upper Secondary Students, 1965-1981	75
4.4	Teaching Plan for Full-day Six Year Keypoint Secondary Schools	77
4.5	Teaching Plans for Various Kinds of Upper Secondary Schools	78
4.6	Characteristics of New University Students	80
4.7	New University Students in 1982	82
5.1	Distribution of Institutions of Higher Education by Specialisation (1949-1965)	95
5.2	Enrollment at Institutions of Higher Education by Field of Specialisation (1949-1965)	97
5.3	Entrants into Institutions of Higher Education by Field of Specialisation (1949-1965)	98
5.4	Graduates of Institutions of Higher Education by Field of Specialisation (1949-1965)	98
5.5	Regional Distribution of Institutions of Higher Education (1949-1980)	99
5.6	Regional Distribution of Students at Institutions of Higher Education (1949-1980)	100
5.7	Distribution of Institutions of Higher Education by Specialisation (1971-1976)	106
5.8	The Impact of the Cultural Revolution on the Regional Distribution of Institutions of Higher Education and Students	109
5.9	Estimated Graduates of Upper and Lower Secondary Schools and Entrants into Universities and Colleges (1966-1976)	110
5.10	Graduates of Upper Secondary Schools and Entrants into Higher Education Institutions (1950-1983)	116
5.11	Entrants and Enrolled Students at Institutions of Higher Education by Field of Specialisation (1980-1982)	117
5.12	Number of Enrolled and Graduated Research Students (1949-1983)	117
5.13	Number of Research Students by Field of Specialisation (1949-1980)	118
5.14	Distribution of Institutions of Higher Education by Specialisation (1978-1982)	121

List of Tables and Figures

5.15	Higher Education Institutions, by Administrative Responsibility (1979)	122
5.16	Enrollment at Regular and Specialised Institutions of Higher Education (1949-82)	126
5.17	Enrollment at Regular and Specialised Institutions of Higher Education, by Field of Specialisation (1982)	127
5.18	Requirement and Supply of New Scientific and Technical Manpower in Shanghai, 1979	134
5.19	Graduates of Institutions of Higher Education, by Field of Specialisation (1977-82)	136
5.20	Expenditures in Formal and Nonformal Education of All Types, by Source, 1979	138
5.21	Growth of Recurrent Expenditure, by Type, 1977-1980	139
5.22	Percentage Distribution of Educational Expenditures, by Level of Education	139
5.23	Unit Costs of Education at Different Levels, as a Percentage of GNP/CAPITA	140
5.24	Profile of Higher Education Entrance Examination Candidates 1977-1983	146
5.25	Students and Teachers of Minority Origin at Institutions of Higher Education (1949-1981)	149
5.26	Regional Distribution of Minorities at Institutions of Higher Education	150
6.1	Secondary Teacher-Training School Tentative Four-year Training Programme for Primary School Teachers	164
6.2	Secondary Teacher-Training School Tentative Three-year Training Programme for Kindergarten Teachers	165
6.3	Percentage of Qualified Teachers in Primary and Secondary Schools	168
7.1	Educational Attainment amongst Employees, January 1980	180
7.2	Development of Employee Education Enrollment, 1979-1981	193
7.3	Employee Education Institutions and Performance, 1981	194
8.1	Profile of a Cross-section of Chinese Scholars and Students in USA in 1981-1982	212
8.2	Profile of Three Groups of Chinese Scholars in Germany, 1980-1982	215
8.3	Profile of Chinese Scholars and Students in France, March 1983	218
8.4	Profile of Chinese Scholars and Students in Britain, March 1983	220
8.5	Profile of Chinese Scholars and Students in Canada, 1981-1982	223

List of Tables and Figures

Figures

5.1	Organisational Chart of Shanghai Jiaotong University	130
5.2	Public Expenditure on Education as a Percentage of G.N.P.	141
6.1	The Three-Tiered Structure of Teacher Education	170
6.2	The Organisation and Control of Teacher Education	173

EDITORIAL PREFACE

The main features of China's new social and economic policies are often conveniently summarised by reference to the 'four modernisations' - the modernisation of agriculture, industry, national defence, and science and technology. The need for a serious commitment to economic modernisation in these four areas was first put forward by Zhou Enlai in 1975, and made the keynote of government policy after the demise of the radical 'Gang of Four' which followed closely on the death of Mao Zedong in September, 1976. National conferences on science and education were held in March and April 1978, in which the scientific and educational implications of service to the four modernisation were discussed and the main lines of a new educational policy began to emerge. Parallel to these new developments in education have been changes in the political structure. Provision for the greater utilisation of democratic institutions within the socialist system has replaced the former 'mass-line' approach to socialist democracy and there has been a streamlining and professionalisation of the bureaucracy. The revival of a concern for socialist legality has been another development, highlighted by the passing of a new constitution in 1982 which has important implications for education. Finally, on the economic front, changes include the introduction of a responsibility system which allows local units greater autonomy yet demands of them greater economic accountability and China's increasing economic interaction with the capitalist West. These new developments call for a comprehensive reassessment of the contemporary Chinese education system and its response to the call of service to the four modernisations. This has been the guiding rationale of the book, linked to subsidiary concerns that it should be both comparative and future-oriented.

No further introduction should be necessary in that the first two chapters are both introductory in different ways. In Chapter One Brian Holmes has drawn upon his rich experience as a leading figure in the field of Comparative Education and his specialist knowledge of the Soviet and American education systems to put the Chinese educational experience into a global perspective and discuss how far China's leaders responded in distinctive ways to widely shared problems of the post World War II period. In Chapter Two I have begun from the opposite end of the spectrum - China's own historical experience and her unique educational traditions - and traced the evolution of new educational institutions in the twentieth century which were to meet the requirements of being both modern and Chinese. For the five following chapters which deal intensively with different aspects of the contemporary Chinese educational scene we have been fortunate in finding scholars who have done specialist research, in most cases in recent doctoral work, on the particular level of the education system which they write about.

Billie Lo had the unique advantage of being Chinese and situated at Hong Kong University's Centre of Asian Studies where close contacts with the Mainland were possible. She is thus able to offer sound insights into the vital and interlinked areas of primary and teacher education in the service of the four modernisations. Stanley Rosen also used Hong Kong as a base for his solidly empirical doctoral research on Red Guard factionalism in Canton, which has enabled him to bring depth and penetration to his analysis of the dramatic change in the direction of secondary schooling in the post Cultural Revolution period. Jürgen Henze has collated valuable statistical data on higher education, much of which has only recently become available, and on the basis of this quantitative evidence has addressed himself to the contentious issues of quality and equality in higher education provision over the three decades of China's post-revolution history. David Chambers was able to draw on both his own doctoral research on adult education and recent visits to China to give a clear and incisive picture of present policies and provision for adult education in urban industrial areas, and to set this into the wider framework of the Communist Party's social and economic aims. Finally in the last chapter I have brought together the scattered information which is so far available on Chinese-western scholarly exchange and offered tentative reflections on how this new international stance, unprecedented in Communist China's 35-year history, is likely to affect the educational trends which have been identified in earlier chapters.

Every effort has been made to include in this volume substantial empirical data which will enable our readers to make their own judgements on Chinese educational achievements. I am particularly grateful to Jürgen Henze for preparing the chart of the education system which appears on pages 4 to 5, and to David Chambers for undertaking the demanding task of collating the up-to-date educational statistics which are presented in the statistical appendix. I must express sincere thanks to Ma.Gpe.González-Paredes for her patience, enthusiasm and professionalism in preparing the whole camera-ready manuscript on a word processor. Finally I would like to thank Lu Jiande of Fudan University and Cambridge for the contribution of his Chinese calligraphy.

Chart of the Educational System

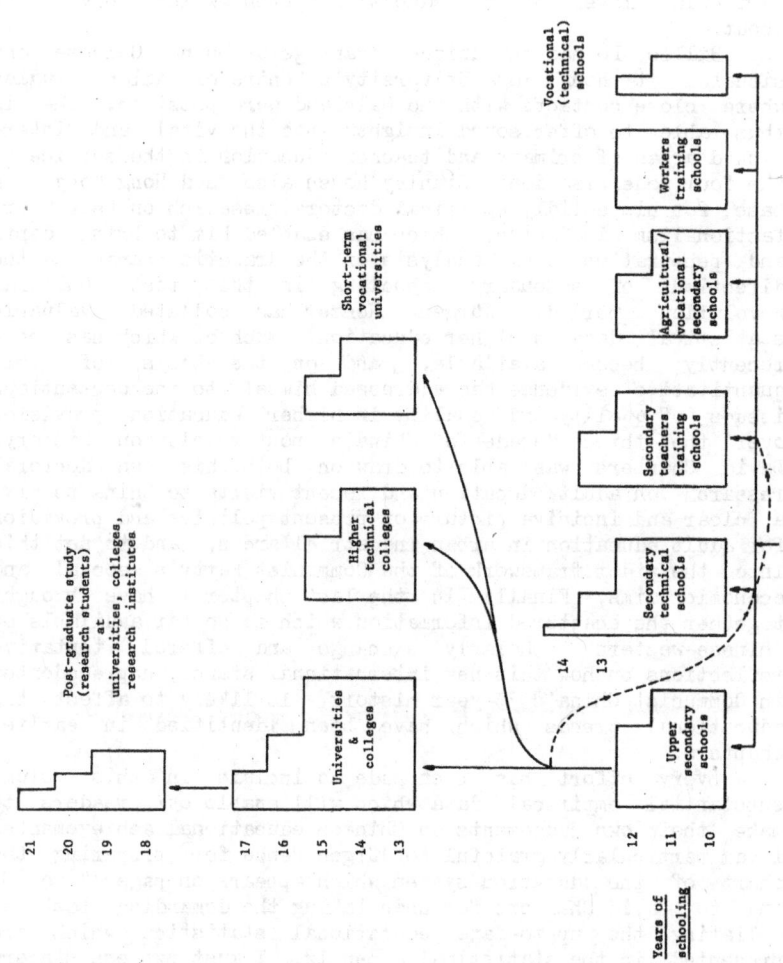

Chart of the Educational System

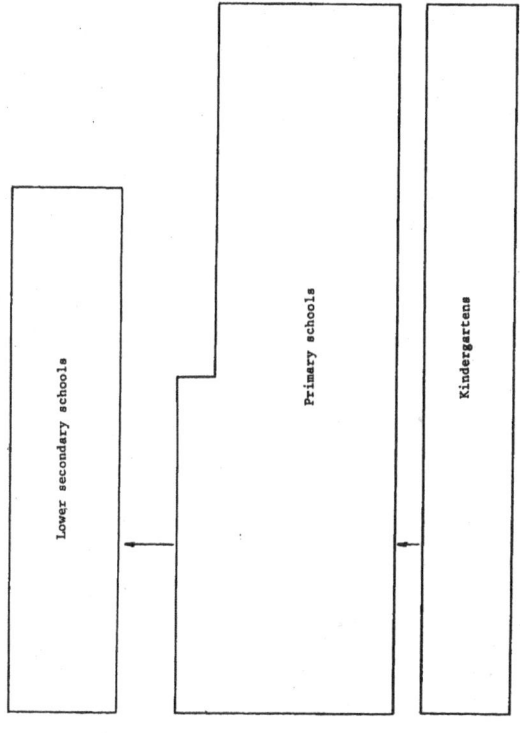

Chapter One

A COMPARATIVIST'S VIEW OF CHINESE EDUCATION

Brian Holmes

Not many years ago I asked a Chinese scholar if he would help me to supervise a potential research student with a degree in Chinese, who wished to investigate some educational problems in China in comparative perspective. He declined graciously, explaining that his field was Chinese philosophy between 500 BC and 400 BC and that because he covered so many years he was already regarded by his colleagues as rather eclectic.

Against this background of monumental scholarship and, until recently, the paucity of first hand information since 1949 based on the observations of foreigners, I have to confess my ignorance of Chinese affairs. Yet for a comparative educationist modern China has a particular fascination, because while the problems its government has faced since 1949 have not been dissimilar to those faced by governments elsewhere throughout the world, policy solutions in China have been based on a borrowed ideology, many features of which are antithetical to traditional beliefs. The strength and persistence of these beliefs and the uniqueness of Chinese conditions ensure that the articles in this book provide not only invaluable information about education in modern China but a case study which illuminates for comparative educationists issues which have been of interest to them for many years.

Consequently, in this introduction I shall place educational developments in China in a comparative framework and suggest that they represent the outcome of unique responses to world wide problems.

SOURCES OF WORLD WIDE PROBLEMS SINCE 1945

Elsewhere I have identified three major explosions which created problems of policy for educationists after 1945. The first of these was the explosion of expectations in the light of which people throughout the world wished to gain political independence, enjoy improved standards of living, live in peace and be granted their basic human rights. A second major problem creating change took place after 1945, when the population of the world began to increase rapidly. Finally scientific inventions and their applications in commerce and industry created unprecedented manpower needs.[1]

Each explosion has implications for education. Among the human rights listed in the Declaration of the United Nations education occupied a prominent place. The achievement of universal primary education soon became a goal towards which governments throughout the world directed their attention. Where it already existed the provision of secondary education for all became an objective. Finally the expansion of higher education took place in response to demands that it should be regarded as a basic human right. Gradually the notion laid down in the UN Declaration that secondary and higher education should be restricted to those capable of benefiting from them was abandoned in favour of the view that lifelong education should be available to everyone. Thus today (1984) central to the aims of education in most countries is the belief that education should be provided for all citizens young and old regardless of gender, mother tongue, race, religion, socio-economic position or place of domicile. In response to these demands attempts were made to re-organise well established systems of schooling by eliminating selection for secondary schools and creating common middle or secondary schools and by expanding higher education provision.

Demographic trends have made the achievement of this goal difficult. Soon after the Second World War birth and survival rates rose dramatically, and by the early nineteen fifties millions of children throughout the world were clamouring for places in school systems which lacked buildings, equipment, teaching resources and teachers. The provision of an adequate supply of teachers was given highest priority in many countries. Less attention was paid to the kind of skills and special knowledge they should possess even in countries where, as in Europe, North America, Japan and some British dominions, levels of provision were already high. Basically class size dominated teacher training expansionist policies.

Meanwhile scientific inventions and their applications were transforming many societies. Consumer goods of all kinds could be produced in vast quantities. Communication systems were revolutionised. Transportation, in the form of air travel, encouraged an unprecedented movement of people within and between countries. In some of them automation reduced the demand for unskilled and semi-skilled workers and created a need for highly trained technologists and skilled technicians. The kind of education which had served societies passing through the first industrial revolution became inadequate in post-industrial societies yet attitudes to worthwhile knowledge and concepts of scholarship did not change much so that curricular change took place relatively slowly.

Detailed policy responses to these changes varied. Traditional European models were abandoned in favour of school structures based on the experience of USA or USSR. Attempts were made to change systems of administration and finance. Highly centralised systems of control were decentralised to encourage local participation. Greater central control and finance was introduced into traditionally decentralised systems in order to equalise provision. As stated, systems of teacher education were expanded and attempts were made, successfully in some cases, to ensure that all teachers received some pre-service initial training. Such training, it was hoped, would be provided in an institution of higher education. In some countries teacher education was incorporated into existing or new universities. In other countries special institutions of higher education were created or further developed in which intending primary and secondary school teachers were trained.

National circumstances influenced policies and the extent to which they were realised in practice. In some cases national independence and autonomous economic development received highest priority. Economic underdevelopment was associated with educational underdevelopment and bi-lateral and multi-lateral technical assistance programmes made many newly politically independent nations dependent on foreign capital and technical experts. The latter inevitably helped to introduce educational institutions patterned on those with which they were most familiar, namely those found in their own countries. Consequently the extent to which, since 1945, national systems of education have developed autonomously or under the influence of foreign experts is a starting point from which a comparative analysis can be made.

Undoubtedly national independence and identity has been a major preoccupation during a period when the pre-Second World War European empires collapsed. Neo-colonialism has persisted and the USA and USSR have competed for the political allegiance of independent nations. Attempts to create new and autonomous national identities have been constrained or thwarted by circumstances. Size, territorial boundaries and internal diversity have influenced the success of attempts to create national unity. Relatively few post-war nations satisfy the 'ideal nation' criteria Nicholas Hans laid down. Few possess populations who speak the same language, accept the same religious beliefs, belong to the same race, or subscribe to one secular ideology. Diversity of language, religion, race and political creed characterise most nations today. Of central concern to most governments has been how to create, and have internalised, a national ideology while allowing for linguistic freedom and racial equality. Deeply held traditions have made the task very difficult. An appeal to tradition might well mobilise feeling of identity but prevent modernisation. On the other hand some traditions reinforce diversity in terms of language and religion.

It is in the light of these general issues that the special case of China and educational developments under the

A Comparativist's View

leadership of Mao and members of the Communist party since 1949 can be usefully analysed. Each chapter in this book deals with a particular issue or stage of education. Together they provide an analysis of the problems faced and an authoritative account of the policies pursued, and the changes in them, since the victory of Mao's forces created a new political situation.

THE POLITICO-ECONOMIC CONTEXT

The Communists took over a country which was economically underdeveloped and politically disunited. Like similar countries, such as India, China's economy was based on agriculture. The vast majority of its population (over 80% are still peasants) subsisted in rural areas although there were both traditional Chinese urban centres and some large cities like Shanghai, Tianjin and Canton, which had been developed as ports by Europeans and used as commercial centres under treaties disadvantageous to the Chinese. Little had been done, except, to some extent in Manchuria, to industrialise the country whose vast size and varied terrain had ensured that the population, even in the rural areas, was very unevenly distributed. The size of the population, at that time, can only be estimated. It was probably around 500 million.[2]

As elsewhere the differences between town and country have persisted. Moreover since 1950 people from the rural areas have moved in large numbers into the urban areas, in spite of governmental efforts to prevent uncontrolled urbanisation. While available figures must be viewed with caution it seems likely that in 1949 the urban population was about 57.5 million and rose to over 89 million in 1956; a majority of the increase was due to immigration from rural areas.

Shanghai has a population of more than 11 million; official figures for 1982 gave the population of Beijing as just over 9 million and Tianjin, Chongqing and Canton have each more than 5 million inhabitants. Since then urban growth has continued, bringing with it problems which have characterised cities elsewhere. An exceptionally high population density in urban areas resulting from overcrowding in buildings, a high proportion of which are deemed unfit for occupation, is a well known phenomenon. Equally common in the cities of economically underdeveloped countries is the presence of many 'dependents' who are not employed in productive labour. Indeed urban unemployment and underemployment remain extremely serious problems. However hard life is in rural areas and however squalid it is in urban areas the latter attract in large numbers people hoping for a better life.

Over-riding the uneven distribution of population are general demographic trends. Since the Communists came to power the population has more than doubled, having reached by 1982 a figure of over a billion. Again population rises of more than 2 percent per annum have not been unusual in countries in Africa,

A Comparativist's View

Asia and Latin America since 1945. Birth rates have risen and survival rates improved dramatically. In the case of China these phenomena have been accentuated by family traditions which have continued to inform behaviour in spite of government attempts to curb population growth. Stern measures to restrict family size regardless of gender may well have provoked the reputed increase in female infanticide. The government has set birth and natural growth rate targets by 1985 at considerably less than half the estimated rates for 1979. Major educational problems are associated with the extremely rapid growth in population and the uncontrolled drift of peasants to the urban areas along the eastern seaboard.

Politically China offers an interesting case study of an economically underdeveloped country. It has many features in common with the countries of Africa and Asia, whose indigenous leaders struggled successfully after 1945 to gain freedom from the European powers. Throughout the ages and particularly during the nineteenth century Europeans attempted to influence Chinese affairs, and Buddhism became popular in periods when the central authority of the Confucian school broke down. Traders and missionaries penetrated the country as they did in Africa and Asia during the nineteenth century. Britain, France, Germany, Japan and Russia competed in a scramble for concessions and special privileges. Attempts by these powers to establish spheres of interest and influence were probably intended as precursors to formal annexation. By 1928 China seemed to be making progress towards emancipation from the 'unequal treaties', by which time Britain, France, Japan, the United States and some other foreign powers were involved. Before formal arrangements could be finalised the Japanese seized cities in Manchuria - their sphere of interest - and embarked on what in 1937 became a life and death struggle between China and Japan.

Many countries in Africa and Asia became part of a European empire. China did not. Competition between the powers helped to prevent its colonisation. China's officials remained hostile to 'foreign devils' and refused willingly to accord their representatives diplomatic rights. At the turn of the nineteenth century Christians were persecuted in an attempt to rid the country of foreign influence. The Boxer Uprising and the empress dowager's order that all foreigners should be killed represent extreme examples of the traditional approach of the Chinese to autonomous development. Confidence in it was, and is, based on the strength and richness of the Chinese cultural heritage and the administrative system which had evolved over centuries. These two features of Chinese history are well exemplified in the scholar official in whom erudition and administrative expertise were combined.

The movement towards complete political independence in China is characterised, as elsewhere, by indigenous revolution. The revolution of 1911 which brought Sun Yat-sen to power gave

A Comparativist's View

rise to a republican constitution. Subsequently the Guomindang was outlawed in 1913 and a warlord government emerged. After World War One internal squabbles prevented the unification of the country but gave rise to two movements - nationalism and Chinese Communism - which were in conflict until 1949. This conflict was not always overt. The Communists, for example, urged an end to the civil war with the Nationalists under Chiang Kai-shek, in order to form a united front against the Japanese and events conspired to bring this about. Thus as in the case of the Hindus and Moslems in India, the Tamils and Singhalese in Ceylon and the Ibos and Yoruba in Nigeria members of rival groups were prepared, for the time being, to forget their differences in order to fight a common foreign enemy.

In the case of China the Nationalists and Communists accepted two distinctly different ideologies both of which ran counter, in some respects, to Chinese experience. Sun Yat-sen, the founder of the Guomindang, emphasised much of China's old learning as the foundation on which his Three Principles could be built. These were, in translation, 1) nationalism to achieve national emancipation and racial equality, 2) democracy to achieve political rights for the people and 3) livelihood to ensure economic welfare. Conscious of the bases of China's cultural greatness, Sun Yat-sen nevertheless accepted that in building nationalism, democracy and the economy the Chinese people should go out and learn what was worthwhile from the West. The leaders of the new government of the People's Republic found in the ideology of Marx, Lenin and Stalin beliefs and policies which they hoped would mobilise the people of China to strive for the development of a modern, industrial nation. During the period 1952-57 China depended heavily on the USSR for know-how and plant. The Great Leap Forward was associated with the departure of Soviet specialists and a subsequent period of reduced agricultural and industrial production. Mao Zedong launched the Cultural Revolution in 1966. After his death and the purge of the 'Gang of Four' government policies have been directed towards modernising agriculture, industry, national defence and science and technology.

Fluctuations in educational policy since 1949 reflect not only internal differences of opinion within the Communist Party but the very real dilemmas which face governments wishing to create a national consciousness based on new ideals and a modern and developing economy without either overtly doing violence to cherished traditions or arousing the opposition of those who have a vested interest in these traditions. Success depends upon the ability of political leaders to create an ideology in which radical and conservative beliefs are reconciled and to establish a political system which allows for circulation of members from the masses into the elites and between the governing and non-governing elites. Under these circumstances education is expected to play many roles. It is expected to promote national consciousness, increase political understanding and contribute, in China, to the Four Modernisations. Under conditions of linguistic and ethnic diversity, vast differences between the rural and urban populations and traditional commitments to family, classical scholarship and suspicion of foreigners, it has been no easier in China than elsewhere to establish education as a human and universal right and to use it to modernise the economy.

IDEOLOGY

Member of the Chinese Communist Party and Government leaders were initially willing to adopt Soviet policies. Central to the aims of education in the early days of Soviet power was that education as a human right should emancipate indiviudals from the 'false consciousness' they or their parents had acquired under capitalism. A major task in the process of emancipation was the removal of illiteracy by providing all children in the USSR with an education in their mother tongue. Fundamental to Marx's view of education was the link he made between education and productive labour. Hence central to Soviet theories of education is the polytechnical principle which, when realised in practice, enables workers to understand the social implications, (including relationships among workers and between them and the means of production), and the practical applications in the productive life of a socialist society of the principles learned in school. Polytechnical education is designed to contribute to the all round development of individual pupils as new socialist men and women and through their proper understanding of society and production to the development of that society.

In practice Soviet policies included the creation of a common, universal ten year school in which pupils received instruction in the language chosen by parents; the development of specialised vocational and technical schools to supply industry with skilled workpeople, and the expansion of institutions of higher education - universities, polytechnics and pedagogical institutes - to meet the need of the country for technologists and professional personnel. Members of the Communist Party are responsible for the formulation of policy on the basis of research undertaken by academics associated with the Academy of Pedagogical Sciences and its research institutes. Educational policies are adopted after wide discussion with teachers and put into practice through a system of administration in which each autonomous Republic is responsible in association with local authorities, for its schools. On the authority of Lenin all the socio-political experience of mankind, properly interpreted as the outcome of a ceaseless conflict between capitalists and workers, should constitute curricula in schools. In effect this principle meant the continuation in Soviet schools of an encyclopaedic curriculum favoured by Western Europeans and the inclusion of Marxism-Leninism as the all pervading basis of political education. Teachers are well versed in this philosophy and by intention all intending teachers should receive training in an institution of higher education and subsequently should return as serving teachers for refresher courses.

Soviet policies imply radical changes in Western European systems of education. Selection for secondary schools on the basis of ability to benefit has been abandoned. Higher education, including university courses, are in principle open to all through full time, evening and correspondence arrangements. The traditional two track system in which a few carefully selected pupils entered general academic secondary schools and then went on to universities while the rest completed elementary schooling or trained for jobs in vocational schools has been slowly abolished by postponing differentiation and introducing virtually the same curriculum throughout the period of compulsory attendance in schools throughout the country. Classical languages have been downgraded. Mathematics has retained its pre-eminent position but the importance of the pure and applied sciences has been greatly stressed. Attitudes to pure knowledge and research are being transformed.

Platonic theories about inherited inequalities, the nature of the just and stable society, leadership by philosopher kings and how knowledge of permanent 'ideas' by intuition and reason can be acquired have all been challenged by Soviet educationists. Many theories similar to those of Plato are found in the Chinese classics and have been institutionalised in family, community and school practices. Consequently the educational ideology imported from the Soviet Union differed in many respects from orthodox Chinese educational ideology. Since, in this context, I am using the term ideology to mean a system of beliefs and values which motivate behaviour it is apparent that serious opposition to the imposition of Soviet ideology in China was inevitable. The strength of this opposition was related to the ability and willingness of Chinese intellectuals to propose alternative educational policies or to prevent Communist Party policies from working.

At the same time it would be unwise to assume that an analysis made from an occidental perspective can do full justice to the complicated politics of educational development in China since 1949. In judging the extent to which education has contributed to the creation of national consciousness it might not be sensible to accept the criteria laid down by Nicholas Hans as measures of an 'ideal nation'. Unity of language, religion and race within an identifiable territory and political system might not be necessary before nationalism can be successfully promoted. Economic growth along Western European and North American lines may not be the most appropriate way of modernising Chinese agriculture and industry. The abandonment of traditional Chinese family and community structures in favour of European and North American nuclear families and urban societies may not be a necessary feature of social modernisation. Finally occidental concepts of democracy may need to be revised if Chinese educational policies are to be devised. It is apparent that Mao was very conscious of the differences between Marxism-Leninism and the kind of ideology he wanted to create in order to modernise China. Some of the dilemmas examined in this book are associated with the differences between ancient Chinese, modern Soviet and Mao's own ideology.

IDEOLOGY AND EDUCATIONAL POLICIES

A question of some interest to a comparative educationist is the extent to which in the evolution of education ideology has played a major role. It is frequently assumed that in socialist countries particularly, educational policies are based exclusively on ideology and are in no significant way a response to the problems arising from the three postwar explosions previously mentioned. As in the case of many economically underdeveloped countries the communists wished to improve China's economy and embarked upon a programme of industrialisation. Mao acknowledged that such a programme would involve the movement of millions of peasants into new cities and factories. In the immediate post-Second World War period the modernisation of industry was accepted as the major goal of policy. It had implications for education and the distinction drawn in China between urban and rural schools until 1966 is indicative of the role schools were to play. The primary schools were to be the 'foundation of the foundation' of industrial development. Some schools were to prepare some pupils for higher education and the professions, other schools were to prepare workers for the labour force. In the two track system urban primary schools were academic, rural schools were work-study schools. Rural parents objected to the lack of opportunities rural schools provided. 'Walking on two legs' meant that the state supported high standard urban schools while rural communities were responsible for rural schools.

Belief in industrialisation was widely shared. Socialist and capitalist governments took the view that economic growth depended on the creation of an industrial base - socialists tended to favour investment in heavy industry and communication, capitalists favoured an increased in consumer goods. Traditionally secondary schools, usually located in towns, were along the French model - state maintained - while local primary schools were run by communities.

Rural development as a way of promoting economic growth and raising standards of living was an alternative strategy advocated by Gandhi for India. Fundamental education in which the vocational activities of the village were the core of primary school curricula was recommended by some of the founders of Unesco. It resembled Gandhi's Wardha scheme and India's National 'basic education' policy.

Planners have oscillated between a commitment to industrialisation and to rural development as the most appropriate way of promoting economic growth. Educationists have moved uneasily back and forth between primary school policies designed to inculcate traditional forms of literacy - the 3 R's - and fundamental or basic education in which functional literacy is an important by-product of vocational activities.

Prior to 1966 the Chinese school system was designed to promote industrialisation and to reduce extremely high levels of illiteracy. Ideological commitment to the universalisation of education as a human right seems to have played a minor role. The urban primary schools inculcated basic literacy and numeracy. The secondary schools and universities were selective and favoured the children of intellectuals. In short during this period experimentation of the kind which took place in the USSR during the nineteen twenties did not occur. The system remained elitist, favoured those who could pass examinations and overtly recognised differences between urban and rural schools. Differentiation at the second level of education was legitimised in terms of school type and streaming within schools. The Chinese system of education up to 1966 showed most of the characteristics of pre-war Western European systems and few of the features advocated by Soviet educationists. Primary schooling was not universal and lasted only five to six years. An enrolment rate of 90% in rural areas disguised an attendance rate of 60% and a passing rate of 30%. Very few communities had popularised primary education which for a vast number of pupils was the only education they received.

It would be unwise to compare educational provision in China today with levels achieved after more than seventy years of Soviet power. Fluctuations in policy occurred in the USSR during the first decade with a consolidation during the nineteen thirties along traditional lines. Attempts under Kruschev radically to transform education to bring education nearer to life were frustated by a combination of forces among which the power of teachers to carry on as before was very influential. Marxist-Leninist principles of policy have been retained but in practice the system of education in the USSR has probably changed less than observers, who claim for ideology a decisive role, imagine.

The frequently made assertion that the members of the Chinese Communist Party imported Soviet know-how takes little account of the inertia of educational systems in general and the fact that prior to 1966 policies and practices in China did not reflect those consistently advocated by Soviet politicians and educationists. It is necessary only to review the development of education during the Cultural Revolution from

1966 to 1976 to demonstrate the correctness of Mao's judgement about the revisionist nature of educational policies at the time he initiated the revolution. The popularisation of educational provision was the key. The two track system and selection for secondary and higher education on the basis of academic achievement were abolished. While Chinese statistics should be viewed with caution, as indeed should the statistics issued by all governments, the impression those published give is of a massive expansion during the decade 1966-1976. The number of pupils in lower secondary schools rose from 8 to 43.5 million and the number in upper secondary schools from 1.3 million to nearly 15 million and while for a period of four years the universities were effectively closed their re-opening was based on a policy of expansion, admission being on the basis of appropriate work experience and political activism which would not make it possible to exclude workers and peasants in favour of members of the intelligentsia.

Institutionalised selectivity represented by the promotion of key schools during the pre-Cultural Revolution period was to be abolished, again in line with earlier Soviet policies. Key schools were favoured in terms of resources and admission to them, while based on academic achievement and political acceptability, was clearly related to class origin and place of residence. These features, overtly or covertly, characterised traditional Western European selective school systems and indeed schooling in Nationalist China. Central to the policies pursued during the Cultural Revolution was a desire to eliminate inequalities between schools and students. Radicals, who promoted the Revolution, objected to the benefits bestowed on children of intellectuals and on the products of the key point schools. These objections to selectivity within school systems were voiced by radicals and left wing politicians throughout the world after 1945. Their objective was to abolish secondary schools whose major function was to prepare young people for admission to a university and vicariously to initiate them subsequently in to high status positions, well paid jobs and positions of political power. There is every reason to suppose that Mao and his radical supporters recognised that between 1949 and 1966 the system of education, far from breaking the political and economic power of the intellectuals, was reinforcing it. The abolition of the two track system and the keypoint schools was vital to the achievement of equality and the universalisation of educational provision as a human right.

Circumstances in the USSR made it possible immediately after the Revolution to stress equality of provision and to make the elimination of illiteracy the key to educational progress. Experiments, under conditions of post-revolution chaos, during the nineteen twenties were designed to break down the elitist Czarist school system and to emphasise the individual needs of children in their upbringing. Undoubtedly

A Comparativist's View

there was tension between the child-centred educationists and those, like Makarenko, who emphasised the role of the collective in the education of children for society. It was not until the nineteen thirties, however, that as a result of Stalin's apprehension about Hitler's intentions, selectivity, specialisation and during the Patriotic War single sex schools were re-introduced to build up cadres of specialists who could strengthen the industrial base of the country and defend it against anti-Bolshevist aggression. The Chinese experience has been somewhat different, although the educational policies pursued after Mao's death are not dissimilar to Soviet policies in the nineteen thirties. As indicated, policies in China prior to 1966 were far less radical than those adopted in the Soviet Union immediately after the Revolution.

The content of education and the way schools are administered also have a bearing on equality of provision. As a matter of principle Soviet educators have consistently attempted to extend the period of general education and to introduce a common compulsory curriculum for all pupils in ten year schools. For nearly twenty years emphasis was placed on the elimination of illiteracy. Only when this had been achieved in the mid nineteen-thirties was it possible to see a slow but steady rise in the length of compulsory education. Until recently, Soviet policy was designed to ensure that pupils in urban and rural areas completed ten years of education in a general polytechnical school, thus reducing differentiation into academic and vocational schools at the second level of education. The survival of a very large number of specialised technical schools reflects the difficulties associated with this historical dichotomy. Prior to 1966 in China the two track system perpetuated differences between general and vocational training and the number of vocational schools grew.

During the Cultural Revolution attempts were made to remove the differences between urban and rural schools and between general academic and vocational schools. Prior to 1966 primary schools had two functions to perform: the provision of a literate labour force for society and the preparation of an adequate number of qualified students for the institutions of higher learning. In the event during the decade of the Cultural Revolution enrollments in primary schools had reached 90 percent by 1976. By 1968 there was a single track five year system of primary schools in which rural and urban children received the same education. Technical and vocational secondary schools were transformed into ordinary secondary schools and access to universities was no longer based on examinations geared to test academic achievement. As in the Soviet Union in 1958, work experience became a pre-requisite for admission to a university. In short this period was one in which policies now similar to those consistently held in the Soviet Union were adopted in China. Emphasis was on a general education for all pupils in which appropriate knowledge of and attitudes towards productive life in a socialist society would be inculcated. This involved integrating education with productive labour by not legitimising the distinction between specialised vocational schools and schools with a more academic form of education, which would ensure future leaders possessed a correct socialist consciousness. The dangers of allowing political training to go by default were recognised and political education as a separate study was introduced.

Administratively the extent to which the Communist government in its early years in China drew sharp distinctions between urban and rural schools and delegated to the localities responsibility for running local schools was not a policy pursued with any vigour in the USSR. Special attention was paid in the Soviet Union to literacy campaigns in rural areas and among adults living in those areas. Mother tongue instruction, written into the Constitution, was designed to ensure that children would not be denied the opportunity to read and write by being compelled to learn in the imperial language of the Czars - Russian. Members of the Communist Party were responsible for the formulation of national education policies and while in the Constitution each of the Republics was responsible for its own system of education, after the early period of post-revolution chaos attempts have consistently been made to equalise opportunity throughout the country. In particular boarding schools for rural children provide them with the chance either to learn a trade or to prepare for admission to a prestige university.

The local funding of rural schools and the view taken that each locality should solve its own educational problems by providing an education relevant to local needs have historical and present day support. In most Western European countries during the nineteenth century it proved impossible adequately to support rural primary schools on the basis of resources raised locally. Only in the USA indeed has it been possible to retain a system of local funding, and even there an increased proportion of expenditure on the schools is provided from State and Federal funds. It is not surprising consequently that holding local communities responsible for the funding of primary schools in China has not made it possible to equalise provision between urban and rural schools.

Moreover there is evidence that in China, as in other economically developing countries, parents see schools as a way of helping their children to escape from rural areas. As the British found out in their nineteenth century colonial schools, parents find few advantages in sending to and keeping their children in vocational schools. Indeed the help children can give to their parents in a peasant or subsistence economy makes it difficult to reduce the percentage of pupils who drop out before completing primary schools. Not surprisingly Chinese rural parents resist attempts to turn local schools into agricultural schools or to vocationalise the content of general education. For them the function of the schools is to promote social mobility and they recognise the value of an academic education which will enable their children to compete for admission to high status universities. In many countries national policies encourage rural people to think in these terms in spite of the rhetoric which insists that schools and their curricula should be relevant to the needs of the community.

Locally determined curricula, another notion to which in theory credence is given in the USSR, create rather than reduce inequalities and indeed it is difficult to see how in any country in which there are major differences between the urban and rural areas equality can be promoted except through substantial national financial support for the less well off communities and central control of the curriculum. In practice these requirements have been recognised in the USSR. In China since 1976 there has been a move towards centralised control and funding which may go some way to reducing the inequalities of provision between provinces and between town and country.

Linguistic diversity remains an obstacle to the creation of a democratic society in which the masses can actively participate. Attempts have been made, in many countries, to identify one of the indigenous languages as the national language. In the Moslem world Arabic is the favoured language even though it is not the mother tongue of some inhabitants. The newly independent Indian government chose Hindu as the national language. The hope was that it would provide a way of developing a national consciousness among people speaking many different languages. In many cases the choice of an indigenous language was designed to eliminate the influence of foreign imperialism. English and French were widely used in the colonial empires of Britain and France. While the motivation to unite these nations through one indigenous language was strong the outcomes have been variable. Choice of one language rather than another has given rise to conflict. The economic value of a world language is very evident and the claim that children learn more successfully in their mother tongue has made it difficult for governments to promote nationwide instruction in the national language. Broadly speaking the choice lies between one indigenous language to promote national unity, a major foreign language to further economic modernisation and mother tongue teaching to ensure that all children become literate.

The dilemmas in China are longstanding. Traditional solutions in an elitist political and educational system were possible through the ideograms and the use of Mandarin as the official imperial spoken language. In a largely rural country with a peasant economy relatively few members of the population had the need to communicate with others except in their local community. The administration of the country was in the hands of scholar-officials and a system of selecting from among young villagers boys who could be trained as scholars and administrators ensured that admission to the elite was not simply on the basis of an inherited position. As in many countries the written language and a selected indigenous spoken language became, not the national language, but the official language, access to which was undoubtedly restricted.

As in Russia so in China the new Communist governments did not face the task of eliminating a foreign language as the lingua franca of the academic, economic and political elites. They faced the tasks of modernisation and of creating a literate population who spoke many mutually incomprehensible languages. Policies in the two countries have differed. In the Soviet Union a commitment to mother tongue instruction for the many minority groups was introduced and has been consistently followed. In China the massive investment of cultural capital in a knowledge of the thousands of Chinese characters probably dissuaded the authorities from following similar policies. Some restriction of the number of characters used in newspapers and other publications for popular consumption was necessary but proposals to introduce new occidental scripts received short shrift. Basic literacy in terms of reading implies that children can recognise and grasp the meaning of around 2,000 characters. Perhaps an ability to draw a similar number of characters represents basic writing literacy. Instruction, except in designated areas where non-Han linguistic minorities live, is in Mandarin, now called *Putonghua* (the common language). The cost of making all school materials available in minority languages inhibits governments everywhere but Chinese policy has been less overtly committed to mother tongue teaching than in several countries, for example USSR and India, where a multitude of mother tongues are spoken.

It is indeed the massive investment in scholarship, reflected in classical Chinese texts, which gives to Chinese educational problems a unique character. Both during the pre-1966 period and after Mao's death diversity was recognised in terms of primary school policies. Local communities were, and are, responsible for running schools which meet local economic and cultural needs. The goals and standards established for primary schools consequently differ according to locality, and since emphasis during these periods has been placed on preparing young people for work a variety of school types have been developed. In some cases the academic year is divided into seasons - the Very Busy Farming season, the Quite Busy Farming season, the Not-so-busy Farming season and the Not Busy Farming season. This way of categorising the year is a clear acknowledgement of a problem which has faced educators in many developing countries where the economy is heavily agricultural. How can schools ensure that pupils will attend regularly when their parents want them at certain times of the year to help on the farm? Recognition by the authorities of the difficulties of ensuring regular attendance indicates a realism on their part which has little to do with ideology. The two track system is also a recognition of the limited direct role primary school education can play in the modernisation of society.

The issues are more complex at the level of secondary and higher education. Elitism in the secondary school system has been mentioned. Prior to 1966 secondary schools were, as in the traditional systems of Europe, designed to prepare in vocational schools workers with special skills and to prepare a minority for higher education. During the Cultural Revolution the emphasis was on quantitative expansion so that the debate has been less about equalising provision in rural and urban areas and more about the type and quality of education to be provided for more and more young people.

QUALITY AND EQUALITY IN HIGHER EDUCATION

Higher education in China always served a practical purpose. It prepared young men for the civil service and as teachers. The system, although allowing capable youngsters to achieve promotion on the basis of their abilities, was nevertheless a selective system. Selection was based on scholastic achievement within a very traditional framework. Specialisation and high quality were the hallmarks of that scholarship. Individuals who attained these high levels of scholarship would either pass on their knowledge to the next generation or apply the general principles of administration and government which they had acquired to administer the law, rules and regulations. Of importance in an analysis of debates about higher education are the extent to which it was available, the concepts of scholarship which informed it and the power enjoyed either vicariously as teachers or directly as officials, by those who had gained recognition as scholars.

The perpetuation of a scholarly elite through the power knowledge bestows is a well known phenomenon. In most countries alliances are formed between members of the political and academic elites. In France, Germany and the USSR, to mention only some examples, academic success has traditionally been an important criterion in gaining access to positions of political power either in elected governments or bureaucracies. In few countries has scholarship played such an important role in the formation of a political and administrative elite as in China. Consequently Mao took over a country where scholars possessed enormous power and were in a position to thwart attempts radically to change the organisation and control of education.

Initially, in contrast to policies for primary and secondary schools, Chinese higher education policy was based on de facto practices which had persisted in the USSR from Czarist days. A system of general universities, polytechnical institutes and technical institutes was envisaged. This pattern was very different from the pattern of comprehensive universities in the USA and Britain. The intentions of Chinese leaders were laudable. One hope was that there would be no distinction in terms of status between them. A second expectation was that the number of institutions preparing engineers, agriculturalists, medical doctors and teachers would be increased to meet the needs of industrial construction. Growth, particularly in professional subjects, was the criterion of success as in many countries. Clearly between 1949 and 1965 the policy met with some success, the percentage of general universities declined, the number and proportion of science and technology institutions and teachers colleges rose dramatically, and there was overall a modest rise in the percentage of institutions devoted to agriculture. Enrollments showed similar trends particularly in engineering. In terms of numbers, the overall expansion was impressive, emulating rates which occurred elsewhere during the postwar period. Entrance however was still based on college entrance examinations but some attention was paid to regional inequalities, and to the class origin, professional status, ethnicity and gender of applicants. Prior to 1965 attempts by Mao to combine education with productive labour and to select students on the basis of their class largely failed through the power of academics to ensure students were admitted to universities on the basis of academic achievement rather than political commitment. No pronounced success in terms of ironing out regional inequalities can be discerned during this period. In short the development of higher education in China during the fifties and early sixties follows trends which were apparent in most countries during a period when university age cohorts increased considerably.

During the Cultural Revolution a model for universities and other institutions of higher education stressed the importance of establishing a proletarian world outlook among students so that they would be able effectively to combine education and productive labour. Central to the aims of the revised system was the politicisation of students so that they could contribute to socialist, rather than capitalist, forms of modernisation. Workers' universities were to meet the nation's necessary manpower needs but these were conceived to be different in kind from those which had previously informed policy. It was a radical proposal which went far beyond recommendations made in 1958 by Khruschev to bring education in the USSR nearer to life or higher education policies elsewhere. Central to Mao's policy was that the products of higher education should be fully developed morally, intellectually and physically as persons with a socialist consciousness.

To transform officials to scholars who would understand relationships in industry and be able to develop them in accordance with Communist ideology is an enormously difficult task. It involves not only providing them with new forms of knowledge (which the Soviet and Chinese systems could no doubt accommodate) but internalising in teachers and students radically different forms of knowledge and their relevance to

A Comparativist's View

social and economic life. Mao, and his radical supporters, doubtless appreciated that this transformation of internalised beliefs in the value of knowledge was crucial to the modernisation of China along socialist rather than capitalist lines. It is an issue which confronts socialist governments everywhere. Few of them have so boldly attempted to resolve it in ways which were attempted during the Cultural Revolution, when admission policies based on academic achievement were abandoned, workers and others were involved in the running of universities in ways which did violence to concepts of academic freedom and university autonomy. Subjects to which tradition accorded high prestige were downgraded and preference was given to the children of workers, peasants, and youths who had returned to their village and had three or more years of practical experience. This last policy was in line with that included in the 1958 Soviet Law Bringing Education Nearer to Life. It did not work in the USSR and was soon abandoned after Mao's death in China.

Given the power of scholars brought up in Confucian traditions and socialised into a belief of their role in society, a question of some importance to comparative educationists turns on the possibilities in China that modernisation in all its aspects can be successfully achieved without transforming traditional and deeply held beliefs about the academic importance of the knowledge contained in the Chinese classics. One possibility is that honest bureaucrats well versed in this literature can administer policies which will transform the economy and the political system. How far they will be able to change values central to Confucian ethics which motivate relationships between members of a family, between older and younger people and between the sexes is more doubtful. On the other hand concepts of modernisation have too frequently been legitimised not only by the rhetoric of occidental economic growth but in the light of what has happened, for example, to the family and to human relationships under capitalism. Whether or not the path followed by the Soviet leaders and the policies they have attempted to implement are appropriate to the modernisation of China is also a question of some importance to comparative educationist who wish to use their expertise to evaluate educational policies. The similarities between European theories of man, society and knowledge from the time of Plato and Chinese theories are too obvious to be ignored. The difficulties of translating alternative European theories based on the writings of Marx and interpreted by Lenin into practical policies in China are equally daunting. Fluctuations in policy in China reflect not only the struggle for power within the Communist party but a real dilemma. Platonic theories are less alien than those of Marx and Lenin to Chinese scholars. Socialist modernisation demands that the leaders have not only accepted the rhetoric of socialism but have internalised its central values about the worth of productive labour. Can the leaders of China achieve their goals of modernisation without the assistance of scholars whose commitment to traditional forms of knowledge is very deep? And if they have to depend on those scholars for leadership and to train future cadres of professionals and specialists can their hope for socialist modernisation be realised in the foreseeable future?

The evidence from the USSR suggests that the creation of a 'new Soviet man' will take generations in spite of Breshnev's optimistic assessment of the success of the educational system in achieving the goal. Given the resistance of Chinese scholars, this creation of 'new Chinese men and women' may take even longer in view of the cultural investment in knowledge which under their patronage is bound to reproduce so many features of society rather than to transform them. The Soviet model is useful insofar as it makes clear the kind of problems communist educators in China are likely to face. The difficulties of maintaining the integrity of a Chinese intellectual heritage while transforming the economy into a modern socialist one are immense. On the other hand, within a different ideological framework and through the pursuit of different economic policies the leaders of Japan have succeeded in retaining central features of their culture while promoting economic growth in accordance with a North American/Western European model.

Clearly the chapters in this book provide an analysis of some the problems faced by educators in China and describe the attempts made to solve them. It is difficult in any country to anticipate future events but the unique responses made in China since 1949 to problems of development which have been experienced everywhere suggest that the transfer of policies and practices from any or several foreign countries will only succeed if they do not do violence to classical Chinese concepts of knowledge and do not threaten the power of the scholar officials who have for so long guided the destinies of a country, if not a nation, with such a rich and prized culture.

Chapter Two

THE EVOLUTION OF MODERN CHINESE EDUCATIONAL INSTITUTIONS

Ruth Hayhoe

INTRODUCTION

Two paramount issues have faced Chinese educators in this century: the need for a new Chinese ideology which could support modern educational institutions, and the difficulty of adapting attractive features of western educational patterns to the Chinese context. In relation to the first issue, Chinese scholar and educator Liang Qichao made the following comment in 1922:

> It is almost ten years since the success of the 1911 revolution but all that we have hoped for has proven vain, item by item. As we have gradually thought back, in our disappointment, we have realised that a social culture is a whole unit, and as such it cannot make use of new institutions with an old psychology. By degrees there has grown up a demand for a reawakening of the whole psychology.[1]

With simple profundity he expressed the search for a modern Chinese 'psychology' to replace Confucianism as a framework of values within which modern educational institutions could take shape. The 'Three Principles of the People', 'People's Nationalism', 'People's Rights' and 'People's Livelihood', put forward by Sun Yat-sen, represented the first coherent step in this direction. These were formulated by this father of the 1911 Revolution, published in the early twenties, and taken up as the guiding ideology of the Nationalist regime established by Chiang Kai-shek and the Guomindang Party in 1927.[2] The second coherent modern Chinese ideology, the Thought of Mao Zedong, was formulated during the years of Communist guerilla struggle, as Mao and his supporters applied Marxism-Leninism to the realities of a Chinese peasant-based revolution, culminating in the Communist Liberation of 1949.[3] These two ideologies remain the main reference points for an understanding of Chinese educational development over this century.

The second issue, the adaptation of western educational institutions to the Chinese context, might best be considered by starting from the perceptive remark of a distinguished British educator, speaking in the year 1900 when educational borrowing was a common phenomenon:

> We cannot wander at pleasure among the educational systems of the world, like a child strolling through a garden, and pick off a flower from one bush and some leaves from another, and then expect that if we stick what we have gathered into the soil at home, we shall have a living plant. A national education system is a living thing, the outcome of forgotten struggles and difficulties, and of 'battles long ago'. It has in it some of the secret workings of national life.[4]

With this statement Michael Sadler began a debate over the viability of the transplantation of educational institutions from one socio-cultural environment to another which has absorbed theorists of Comparative Education ever since. In this regard the Chinese case is of rivetting interest because of the otherness of the Chinese socio-cultural context, both its rich traditional thought and its modern ideologies, and because of the ambitious scale on which Chinese leaders over this century have engaged in the borrowing of foreign educational practices. Japanese, American, European and Soviet institutional patterns were all tried in succession over the years from 1898 to 1966. The Great Proletarian Cultural Revolution of 1966 might be interpreted as a passionate rejection of these foreign implants, as well as a repudiation of persisting Confucian educational values.

Most studies of Chinese education have proceeded within a framework which Comparative Educationists might label 'Hansian'. It was Nicholas Hans who built upon Sadler's insight an approach to educational research which focused on the classification of a range of societal factors which he saw as shaping a national educational system, making it a distinctive and unique organism which can function only within this environment.[5] The thorough historical orientation of his work in the analytical study of these factors has proven a salutary restraint on researchers tempted to make facile comparisons among educational institutions in different societies, and on policy makers tempted to make the even more dangerous assumption that an educational practice which produced desirable results in one country can be counted on to do the same in another. Therefore Sinologists have had good reason to treat the Chinese case as unique and to seek an understanding of Chinese education in relation to China's socio-cultural and political context,[6] giving only secondary attention to the problems arising out of the persistent cultural borrowing that has marked this development. The Chinese context is one of such complexity and richness that it has inspired a rigorous and sophisticated body of Sinological scholarship which must be taken into account. Furthermore, in both traditional and modern China, the education system has had an even lower autonomy from the political and economic systems than in the West, making a study of the context of vital importance.

However in this chapter it is the deliberate intention of the writer to focus on the issue of cultural borrowing, and to examine carefully the interaction between Chinese educational values and practices on the one hand and, on the other, the various foreign institutional patterns and their concomitant values which have been introduced into China over this century. Of all the Comparative Education theorists, Brian Holmes has dealt most exhaustively with the problem of cultural borrowing in his methodological approach. He makes a distinction between normative and institutional patterns in education, and has developed techniques for operationalising these in the form of ideal types.[7] He pioneered an approach to the analysis of neo-colonial educational influence in which problems are seen as arising out of the dislocation between the normative values expressed in legislation or mental states resulting from deeply internalised traditional values of a people and educational institutions transplanted from another culture, which easily give rise to consequences quite different from those intended.

In this chapter concise ideal types will be sketched out of the traditional Confucian education system, and the modern Maoist system forged in Yanan as the only fully developed modern Chinese system which owed little to western educational patterns. Although the institutional structure of the Confucian system collapsed with the abolition of the Imperial Examinations in 1905,[8] Confucian values have persisted. Similarly, Maoist educational values will continue to shape Chinese education,[9] in spite of widespread agreement that the Cultural Revolution institutions which embodied them were a failure. It is into this normative context that a whole series of foreign educational institutions have been introduced. The Japanese system was emulated in the first two decades of this century, as Chinese leaders felt it could offer modern institutions already adjusted to the framework of oriental culture.[10] Then in the twenties American influence was strongly felt, with a new generation of young Chinese returning from study in the United States to man the education system.[11] From the early thirties European influence had its effect on national education policy, with a study made by a League of Nations Mission of Educational Experts recommending

Evolution of Modern Educational Institutions

European solutions to the problems of China's educational system.[12] Finally with the success of the Communist Revolution in 1949, Chinese leaders looked to the Soviet Union for ideas about educational institution-building that would serve socialist modernisation.[13] The Cultural Revolution could be interpreted as a reaction to this last and most thoroughgoing transplantation of foreign higher education structures to Chinese soil.

In this chapter each of these educational experiments will be depicted in a few bold contrastive lines in order to provide a framework for reflection on the options available to Chinese policy makers today, and the constraints within which they operate, as they turn from the xenophobia of the Cultural Revolution and attempt once again to implement Mao's guideline of letting foreign things serve China.

THE CONFUCIAN WAY

Chinese traditional education was dominated by the imperial examination system, which had roots in the 2nd century B.C., became fully institutionalised in the Tang dynasty (618-907 AD), and continued to operate until 1905.[14] Within this system the most valued knowledge was that enshrined in the Classical Canons, which focused on human relationships, beginning with the family and embracing the whole empire. Knowledge of the principles and techniques of benevolent government, gained by the scholar through years of study and preparation for a rigorous series of examinations, could finally be demonstrated when he achieved official position and could put this knowledge into action in the practice of government.[15] Applied politics was therefore a central theme of the Confucian curriculum, one which can be found explicitly dealt with or implicit in most Chinese classical texts.

The examination system was an integral part of the bureaucracy. Aspiring scholar-officials could in theory come from any family which could spare a productive member.[16] They had to go through a gruelling series of examinations held at the levels of county, prefecture, provincial capital and imperial capital. Those successful at the lowest level, popularly known as *xiucai* (cultivated talent), gained a high social standing in their locality and were considered well able to teach, although they did not qualify for an official position. Those who passed the provincial examination were given the title of *juren* (recommended person), and were eligible for official positions in the lower echelons of the bureaucracy. Finally, those who gained the crowning distinction of *jinshi* (promoted scholar) at the examinations held in the capital qualified for the highest official positions in accordance with their standing in these examinations. A quota system ensured that all provinces were represented in the tightly-knit community of scholar-officials bound together through ties forged in the climb to success. Relations among successful candidates and between student and examiner remained life-long bonds, ensuring close cooperation within the community. The highest examiner was the Emperor himself, who received the successful candidates into the imperial family as sons of the Empire.[17] Although fully integrated into the bureaucracy, the scholar-official community had some autonomy as guardians of Confucian orthodoxy, providing a kind of counterbalance to Legalist tendencies in the imperial system, which found expression through the Emperor's retinue of eunuchs, clerks and experts of various kinds.[18] Scholar-officials were ritually expected to express criticism of imperial policy through petitions and admonitions, also through the Censorate. This was a criticism that came from within, based on the Confucian teachings.[19]

All other educational activities in traditional China were subordinate to the imperial examination system, so there was nothing one could describe as a schooling system in the western sense. There were government 'schools' which were more like bureaux of education at the county, prefectural, provincial and imperial levels. Although some of these had once been genuine centres of scholarship, by the time of the Qing dynasty they had no teaching function. They were merely offices administering the complex series of examinations and carrying out ceremonies related to the Confucian temples to which they were attached.[20] However the importance and prestige given to learning within such a system meant that independent educational institutions of all kinds flourished, and there was a very fertile environment for learning, not only in the classics, which remained the central focus of educational activity, but also in mathematics and various areas of the applied sciences.

The highest type of independent institution was the *shuyuan*.[21] These were scholarly societies which started mainly as private organisations, often located in remote areas and identified with Buddhist temples in their earliest period, the Tang dynasty. They carried out many functions, operating as libraries and as centres for the collating and publishing of scholarly texts. They also offered a venue for scholarly debates and discussions, for the organisation of competitions in essay writing that would encourage aspiring young scholars, and even for lively exchanges on political issues in certain periods. Only gradually did these come more and more under public control, and become shaped into teaching institutions for the express purpose of preparing candidates for the imperial examinations. Even in the late Qing dynasty, a few had resisted this trend and remained vital centres of independent scholarship.[22] However this was an independence won by the individual institution. The *shuyuan* could not be regarded as an independent system of schools interacting among themselves and setting communal scholarly standards as had the medieval universities of Europe. They differed greatly in different localities and periods, and their scholarly reputation was more often established by one great scholar than by a community of scholars. Leading scholars in these *shuyuan* might be retired officials or officials on leave because of the three year mandatory mourning period for their parents' death. In China those who reached high levels of scholarship seldom remained simply teachers all their lives. However at times the *shuyuan* provided refuge for scholar-officials who had fallen into disfavour with the Emperor or who were withdrawing from imperial service as an expression of protest.

Below the *shuyuan* in academic level were a variety of schools, from the family school where one scholar taught the children of a single family to clan schools, community schools or charity schools, all of which provided basic teaching in literacy and elementary classical studies. These schools adjusted their rhythm to agricultural demands, with flexible hours according to the needs of planting and harvest, and an individualised teaching style in which a child would learn the required text, then recite it to the teacher, who gave correction and explanation. The central moral and political content of the curriculum, expressed in its simplest form in the ubiquitous 'Three Character Primer', was uniform throughout the country. Otherwise curricula varied greatly in different localities. There was a whole range of simple morality literature, which teachers might deem suitable for classroom use, and in addition a huge selection of popular literature, including vernacular novels, ballads, songs, drama, amusingly illustrated and suitable for the newly literate child. One recent study suggests that the level of literacy among ordinary Chinese in the nineteenth century may have been much higher than had been thought due to the proliferation of these traditional schools. Below the level of the elite scholar-official class there was a wide sector of public employees with adequate literacy for clerical work. Also literate employees were required by merchants for their commercial ventures.[23]

Another whole area where learning flourished and reached remarkably high levels was in the applied sciences, evidenced in the outstanding achievements of ancient and medieval Chinese technology, in civil works such as irrigation and bridge building, in trades such as printing, clock making and metal work, in the application of herbal and chemical knowledge to medicine. These fields of applied science were developed mainly through apprenticeship relationships, and the intellectual stimulation responsible for them arose from the Daoist rather than the Confucian world view.[24] However the popular stereotype of the Confucian scholar-official as a man of letters absorbed in the dry minutiae of classical scholarship, who enriched himself and his family by his official position yet was unwilling the dirty his hands with practical work, may be seriously distorted. In fact many of these scholar-officials had broad intellectual interests which included curiosity about science and mathematics and their applications. They often drew technicians of various kinds into their *mufu* (secretariat) and encouraged research in applied science and its application to local engineering projects which they were overseeing.[25] The fact that this kind of knowledge was not included in the examination syllabus did not preclude its very rich development.

To sum up, in traditional China the central focus of the curriculum was on the principles and techniques of good government, derived from the classical canons and demonstrated in action in the practical work of government. This was inextricably linked with the personal cultivation of the scholar as a *junzi* (superior man). It was the outward expression of his inner benevolence. The imperial examination system ensured that the highest scholarly talents were absorbed into the bureaucracy where criticism of imperial policy could be offered only from within orthodox Confucian teaching. All other areas of knowledge and types of schooling were subordinate to this system, and its scholars offered supervision to historical and literary scholarship, to the applied sciences and technology, as well as to literacy studies on the local level. The extreme decentralisation and local orientation of all these arenas of learning stood at the opposite pole to the rigid centralisation of the examination system, and the uniform orthodoxy imposed by the classical curriculum. The teacher qua teacher had a high status in local society, but in the wider society of the Empire was regarded merely as a scholar who had failed to reach officialdom and demonstrate his knowledge in action.

THE YANAN WAY

The Yanan style of education was forged in conscious reaction to western education systems which had been imposed on China for some decades with uneven success. In their educational experiments in the Border Regions under their control before and during the Civil War, roughly from 1936 to 1949, the Communists were clear as to why a western style education system would not suit their needs. It could only be sustained by a highly developed economy, which China did not have, it was ideologically unsuitable as the tool of capitalism, it was an urban oriented education, not suited to the needs of the countryside, and a peace-time education inappropriate to the war-time conditions in which China found herself.[26] They also consciously set themselves against certain aspects of traditional Chinese education: the feudal content of classical teaching which had persuaded the people to subjugate themselves to the old imperial order, the separation between mental and manual labour, and the limited availability of education mainly to those who were to become part of the ruling elite. On the deepest level, however, the Yanan way may have owed more to certain central values of the Confucian way than its leaders would admit.

In Mao's thinking, knowledge was to arise out of the people's historical experience and express itself in service to the people. In addition to literacy, the mastery of the language, it encompassed two main areas: knowledge of natural science gained in the struggle for production and in scientific experimentation, and knowledge of social science, gained in the experience of class struggle. By mastering these two areas of knowledge, the people could improve their material lives and liberate themselves from the bondage of the old society, but it was a mastery to be gained primarily through revolutionary action, not through book learning. Theory was to arise out of practice and be refined by further application to practice in both production and class struggle.[27]

In fact, of course, Communist educators were not in favour of creating a situation where the wheel had to be reinvented, but did depend on basic textbooks for scientific theory. They also depended on Marxism-Leninism as the basic theory that would enable the peasants to transform their social and material environment. Mao's writings, adapting this theory to the Chinese situation, were widely used for educational purposes, although at this time they had not reached the status they were later to attain in the Cultural Revolution, when they became as sacrosanct as the Confucian canons. There was a genuine attempt to use Marxist theory creatively and adapt it to the realities of the Chinese situation rather than imposing it as dogma. The central focus on the application of authoritative knowledge, which left little space for the freewheeling imagination or for areas of study not directly related to the needs of the Border Region, was probably a necessity in the difficult conditions of the time, but it was also deeply Chinese as the foregoing analysis of traditional Chinese educational values has shown.

The Yanan system had two main goals, cadre training for the urgent needs of their expanding administration, and mass education which should enable peasants to take part fully in the revolutionary struggle.[28] It was the peasants themselves who rejected early attempts to impose a regularised schooling system for all children on the grounds that both the content and timetabling were unsuited to their needs. From this situation arose the idea of *minban* (people-run) schools organised by the peasants themselves under their village leaders, with the government only helping by supplying limited funds and sending a teacher where necessary. The peasants were to decide the content of education according to what suited their needs, and the timetabling. This meant flexible arrangements such as half-day schools, winter schools, and evening classes, adapted to the rhythm of agricultural life. Occasionally the difficulty arose that some peasants decided the Confucian classics were what they wanted as the content of education for their children, in which case persuasion had to be used.

If mass education could be carried out in a totally decentralised locally oriented way, as it had been in traditional China, cadre training required a more regularised system. Thus secondary education was to train first level cadres to work at the county and district level, and higher education was to train mid-level cadres working at the military district or border region level, a hierarchy with some echoes of the traditional system.[29] At the secondary level, teacher training was the central focus, then other types of vocational and general education. Higher education, as exemplified in Yanan University, provided several kinds of training in the College of Administration, College of Natural Sciences, Lu Xun Arts School and Medical Department. A fairly structured set of courses were laid out, with 30 percent of the time being given to common courses, including studies of Marxist-Leninist theory and of Border Region legislation and bureaucratic practice. Yet there was a built-in flexibility in timing which meant that courses varied in length from 3 years in the sciences to one or two years in other areas, and classes were time-tabled in such a way as to allow teachers and students to be substantially involved in productive labour.

There was a close integration between the university and both the government bureaucracy and the army, with some of the teachers being government functionaries who gave a part of their time to teaching and with practical work arranged for students within the main government departments. In the teaching and learning process great emphasis was placed on self study, and group study in small collectives, rather than on classroom teaching. There were no written examinations, but all assessment was carried out by mutual evaluation among students and between teachers and students. On graduation all students were assigned posts within the bureaucracy, in non-military tasks in the army, or in teaching.

The main features of this modern Chinese model of education may be summed up as follows. Knowledge encompassed both the natural and social sciences, but applied politics, based on Marxist-Leninist theory, was a requirement for all students and had a guiding and shaping role for other areas of knowledge. Only when false consciousness had been dispelled and people gained a true understanding of the class nature of society could all other forms of knowledge have a sound basis and be directed towards valid ends. In the institutional structure of education, there were two clear levels. Mass education was initiated in cooperation with village leaders who controlled its organisation and curriculum content, and was addressed to the perceived needs of the local community. Cadre training was very closely linked with the civil and military bureaucracy, so that students were educated through close practical involvement with various government departments and were assigned jobs at the appropriate level on graduation. Free discussion and criticism of government policy was acceptable but only from within the fundamentals of the Marxist-Leninist world view.

The Yanan way had taken some of the features of traditional Chinese education - an effective integration of education with the bureaucratic system, the commitment of all to the study and application of the principles and techniques of good government, the informal lively patterns of teaching and learning found in the *shuyuan*[31] - freed them from the rigid hierarchical structure of the examination system and turned them towards the service of a new revolutionary society. Scholars were now not only involved in administration but were prepared to dirty their hands in productive labour. Applied science which could solve production problems was added to applied politics in the formal curriculum. Attempts were made to link the schools with local political and productive movements through student and teacher participation, ensuring a strong accountability to the community. Mao's version of Marxism-Leninism found institutional expression in educational patterns that had some parallels with aspects of the Chinese past, even though Confucian values had been repudiated.

THE JAPANESE INFLUENCE

When the earliest attempts were made to build a modern schooling system in China, the normative context was still strongly Confucian. It is not surprising then that the Qing imperial government should look to Japan for a suitable pattern and adopt the Japanese model almost exactly. Here they hoped to find the best of western education already adapted to an eastern worldview, a suitable tool for national self strengthening. Between 1902 and 1908 the number of Chinese studying in Japan rose from 271 to 17,000,[32] providing a steady stream of young Chinese who had received a modern education to form a teaching cohort for the new school system. They were aided by a small number of Japanese teachers who were hired by the Chinese government.

The structure of the new public education system was laid down in legislation passed in 1903: five years of lower primary school at the village level, four years of higher primary school at the county level, five years of secondary school at the prefectural level, leading to a *xiucai* degree. Three years of higher school at the provincial level, leading to a *junen* degree, and four years of university at the national level, leading to a *jinshi* degree. The length of schooling envisaged is not surprising in view of the marathon to be covered in the curriculum, which included both Chinese classical learning and a European encyclopedic curriculum, filtered through the Japanese system: morals, Chinese Classics, Chinese literature, foreign languages, history, geography, mathematics, biology, physics, chemistry, civics, economics, drawing, and physical education, with appropriate variations at different levels. The aims, expressed in legislation of 1906, remained strongly traditional: to inculcate loyalty to the Emperor, the veneration of Confucius, public spiritedness, a martial spirit and practical learning.[33]

The problems of this adaptation of the Japanese model to Chinese needs were considerable. Although the imperial examination system was abolished in 1905, the main outlines of its administrative structure were used for the new public education system. Education officials appointed by the imperial government to serve at each level, county, prefectural provincial and national, were political appointees with no professional knowledge of modern education. Many of them saw their function in terms of the traditional system, where the main task of education officials was to register and organise candidates for the imperial examinations and to conduct appropriate ceremonies, rather than to provide practical facilities for the teaching and learning process. Often funds earmarked for education were appropriated by the provincial governor or county magistrate and the education officials lacked either the power or the will to prevent this. With a curriculum as ambitious as the one laid down, it was difficult to find suitable teaching materials, and there was a tendency for the old recitation methods used in Chinese classical learning to be extended to the learning of modern subjects, so that the study of these bore even less relation to actual life than the classical learning. To an even greater degree than before, education became a ritual for the gaining of appropriate degrees that should open doors into officialdom for the successful few who reached the top of the ladder.

Up to the revolution of 1911, this 'modern education system' remained largely an empty shell in the absence of any substantial input on the part of a beleaguered imperial government. The considerable achievements that were made must be credited mainly to enlightened gentry such as Zhang Jian whose celebrated Nantong cotton mills and the system of normal, secondary and primary schools they sustained provided a widely emulated exemplar of what might be done on the basis of local initiative. In 1909 it is estimated that there were 35,787 modern schools at all levels in China, with 1,006,743 students. Of these schools, 72 percent were established and funded by private individuals or local groups, and only 28 percent by the national or provincial government.[34] These figures must be seen against the background of a population that had already reached a roughly estimated 331 million by 1910.[35]

After the Revolution of 1911 important changes were made in educational aims and institutional arrangements. In legislation of 1912, the aims were formulated as 'to emphasise moral education, support this with utilitarian and military education and complete it with aesthetic education.'[36] In this year also the system was shortened to 18 years in all, Chinese classical learning was removed from the curriculum, and the traditional degrees were abolished. Statistics give evidence that genuine progress was made in the decade after the revolution, with an estimated 6 million children in public primary schools by 1921 and 165,000 in secondary schools.[37] However progress was uneven and still depended greatly on the individual initiative of certain enlightened governors or educational officials. One such was the Governor of Shansi Province, whose remarkable achievements in developing educational institutions in his province were often cited as an example for other provinces.[38] Much also depended on the initiative of provincial education associations mainly made up of progressive gentry with a strong commitment to modern education. A sustained effort to introduce vocational education was begun in 1917 under the leadership of Huang Yanpei,[39] who had been inspired by American ideas. In the same year, Peking University, the main national university, was revolutionised under the direction of Cai Yuanpei who had just returned from Germany deeply impressed by the German accademic tradition. He was determined to transform this decadent institution, which was functioning mainly as an antechamber to officialdom, into a genuine centre of higher learning.[40]

The Japanese educational system provided a model for China's first modern schooling system, yet its adoption within the Confucian normative framework, and its assimilation to traditional Confucian structures meant that it offered little of substance to China's educational development. Most actual educational progress in the period was achieved through the energetic efforts of enlightened gentry, and a new breed of professional educators such as Huang Yanpei, many of them returned from overseas, who were prepared to commit themselves to the development of a modern Chinese education system. Japan's infamous 21 Demands of 1915 and her manipulation of western powers prior to the Treaty of Versailles inspired such widespread antagonism in China that Chinese leaders were eager for a new educational model to emulate by 1919, and for this they turned to America. The other significant change which turned the minds of Chinese educators from Japan to the West was the definitive rejection of the Confucian framework of values that took place in the May Fourth Movement of 1919, and the beginning in earnest of a search for that new 'psychology' which Liang Qichao wrote about in 1922.[41]

THE AMERICAN INFLUENCE

Of all the foreign influences that impinged on Chinese education in this century, the American one came at the most auspicious period for the shaping of a new 'psychology' that should provide the normative framework for a modern education system. Between 1910 and 1924 the number of Chinese students studying in America increased from 600 to 2,200, and many were returning to serve in China's education system.[47] A whole series of monographs appeared on Chinese education which represented the work of Chinese research students in American universities such as Teachers College, Columbia, New York University, and Stanford University.[43] Extended visits by such American educators as John Dewey, Paul Monroe, Helen Parkhurst, and George Twiss strengthened the impact of American values and institutions on Chinese education.[44]

The remarkable openness of Chinese educators to the forging of a new worldview was evident in this period. In 1919 representatives of the provincial education associations held their 5th annual meeting where, under American influence, they formulated new aims for education to replace those of 1912, which they considered excessively militaristic and nationalistic. They recommended that the government adopt the aims of 'fostering healthy character and a republican spirit'. Although this suggestion was not accepted, they were satisfied with the 1922 legislation which stated that no firm educational aims could be laid down in a changing environment, but that the following 'standards' should guide educational development: adapt to the evolution of society, give full play to the spirit of education for the common man, seek the development of individuality, take into consideration the strength of the national economy, pay attention to education for life, universalise education, and be flexible in giving space for local initiative.[48]

The legislation of 1922 also reflects a number of other recommendations made by the provincial education associations which had held their 7th annual conference in 1921 with Paul Monroe as technical advisor. In order to strengthen local and provincial educational administration and ensure both adaptation to local needs and continuity in educational policy and funding, boards of trustees were to be established at county, provincial and municipal levels. This was a bid to wrest educational decision making out of the hands of the politicians. The boards were set up, yet their members were not elected by provincial educational associations and professionals as the 1921 conference had recommended, but appointed by the Ministry of Education on nomination by the local or provincial governor, a compromise between the American and the Chinese way.[47] Their role was to determine local policy, to raise funds, and to discuss all aspects of educational work.

The basic structure for the education system established in the 1922 legislation followed American lines very closely: six years primary education, three years lower secondary, three years upper secondary, and four years college. The curriculum was reorganised along the lines of the American pragmatic curriculum, focusing less on academic subjects than on skills for citizenship and the service of society. At primary level it covered the following areas: conversation, reading, composition, penmanship, arithmetic, hygiene, citizenship, history, geography, nature study, gardening, industrial arts, imaginative arts, music and physical education.[48] At secondary level the credit system was used to facilitate some diversification of courses and the integration of practical and vocational studies into the curriculum, specially for the majority who would not go on to higher education. New textbooks were prepared with an emphasis on the development of the individual child and the fostering of a practical understanding of society and its workings. Experimental teaching methods such as the project method and the Dalton plan were tried out in order to break away from the rigid and ceremonial recitation style of teaching that had been so common in Chinese classrooms.

Tremendous enthusiasm and energy went into this American inspired burst of educational development which took place in a period of unparallelled political and ideological freedom due to the declining power of the corrupt warlord government. However in the Chinese context two of its central ideas, individual initiative and local self management, degenerated into chaotic activism and anarchic indiscipline, as a contemporary Chinese historian reflected wryly.[49] Chinese schools had neither the material resources nor the intellectual atmosphere for the individualised learning and the social orientation intended within the pragmatic curriculum. Secondary school students, however, were only too easily encouraged to express their concern for society by organising mass demonstrations on national issues which led to continual disruption of the learning process, and in some cases, to the closing of schools for prolonged periods. When there were no burning national issues to arouse them, these students turned their attention to internal school politics and fought battles to oust unpopular teachers and strengthen student control over school decision making.

Evidence suggests that the American model may have been most successful at the college level, where the philosophy of pragmatism proved attractive to some Chinese intellectuals, providing a framework for lively experimentation and innovation in the development of new courses in such applied social sciences as journalism, library science, rural sociology, and various types of professional training suited to local needs. At the college level student political involvement took a more responsible form than in the secondary schools, and China's college students made a serious contribution to the second great revolution, the Northern Expedition of 1926-27, which overthrew the warlord regime and established a new Nationalist government centred in Nanjing.[50] It had a coherent Chinese 'psychology' in the 'Three Principles of the People', a soul which gave direction to its policies such as the warlord government had never had. In spite of the Nationalist government's continued political rapprochement with America, Chinese leaders and educators now turned to Europe for ideas about institutional structures able to harmonise with the normative patterns expressed in the Three People's Principles, which enjoyed wide popular support in the early years of the Nationalist regime.

THE EUROPEAN INFLUENCE

When the Guomindang came to power in 1927 and held its first national education conference in 1928 there was perfect clarity about the aims of education: to realise the 'Three Principles of the People' in administrative style, educational provision and curriculum.[51] Here was finally an ideology both modern and truly Chinese. The first principle, 'People's Nationalism', was a concept unknown in imperial China, and Chinese leaders regarded its inculcation as an urgent educational task if China was to stand up to foreign aggressors. The second principle, 'People's Rights' or democracy, was also unknown in the benevolent absolutism of Confucian society. It was interpreted by the Guomindang as an increasingly broad political participation under Party tutelage as the people were educated to a level where they could take responsible part in representative democratic institutions.[52] The third principle, 'People's Livelihood', involved the idea of economic growth through improved agricultural productivity and the development of modern industry and commerce. This stood in contrast to Confucian notions of restraint in the use of agricultural produce and contempt for commercial activity.

For appropriate institutional patterns to realise these new aims of education, Chinese leaders now looked to Europe where more centralised organisational patterns seemed to offer a useful tool for unifying the country behind the Guomindang. Between 1927 and 1929 an attempt was made to reorganise educational administration along the lines of the French university district system with one university in each educational district exercising supervision over all secondary and primary education. This was intended by educators such as Cai Yuanpei to ensure both university autonomy and a scholarly jurisdiction over all aspects of educational development.[53] Although it failed, the European influence was reinforced in other ways, particularly by the visit of the League of Nations Mission of Educational Experts in 1931, and the exhaustive study and recommendations for reform which they made. They specifically attacked certain aspects of the American influence - the fragmentation of the curriculum brought about by the use of the credit system, the unnatural division between lower and upper secondary school, and the emphasis on individual choice in a situation where resources could barely provide the minimum needs and often vocational and practical subjects were neglected. They suggested a unified six year secondary education with a strong emphasis on the basic academic subjects for all in the early years and for those going on to university in the higher years, also a more effective vocational training at higher levels for the rest.[54]

Although the basic structure of the system was not changed, the influence of these recommendations can be seen in Chinese educational legislation of the thirties: the return to a more regular academic curriculum, similar to the one borrowed from Japan in the early years of the Republic, the abolition of the credit system at secondary level, and the introduction of province or city-wide examinations at the end of both lower and upper secondary school testing only academic subjects. The list of examination subjects for upper secondary school was citizenship, Chinese literature, mathematics, physics, chemistry, biology, history, geography, and foreign languages.[55] On the basis of results in these examinations a more rationalised selection process could be enforced for higher education, and better academic standards maintained. That was the argument at least.

The results of this European inspired legislation in the Chinese context were devastating. Academic subjects with the promise of examinations to be passed and higher echelons to be reached dominated the curriculum more and more, crowding out the vocational subjects which were just beginning to come into their own after many years of devoted efforts by men such as Huang Yanpei. The most talented students were drained from the vocational schools that did exist. The persistance of values related to the Confucian examination ladder meant that Chinese students were very good at passing examinations and striving to reach the rarefied atmosphere of restricted higher levels of education. However after their gruelling struggle up the ladder most were greeted not with the prize of officialdom but with the grim prospects of unemployment in a country devastated by war. The academic disciplines at which they excelled made them unemployable in terms of the practical needs of China's productive system.

Perhaps the most serious educational problem of the National government arose out of the well-intended efforts of Cai Yuanpei to draw a clear line between the university and politics, and ensure that university student organisations were not manipulated by political parties, not even the ruling Guomindang Party. In his many years at the University of Leipzig, he had come to admire the German notion of academic freedom. However this notion was not well understood in the Chinese context, and Cai's attempt to legislate for it had disastrous results for the Nationalist government. Instead of mobilising the powerful National Union of Students in support of the Guomindang, Cai saw that it was abolished, and student activities were restricted to the individual campus and to academic and cultural fields.[56] This alienated the Chinese student population from the Guomindang Party, which they had supported heartily in the revolutionary struggle of the Northern Expedition. They disregarded the Nationalist ban on student politics, and their activities in inspiring resistance to Japan were one of the strongest challenges which the hard-pressed Nationalist government had to deal with. Their intolerance of government corruption and their organised resistance to government policies contributed to the Communist victory.[57]

At the end of this brief review of China's pre-Liberation experiments with foreign models of education it must be stressed that these educational practices adapted from Japan, America and Europe never touched more than superficially the enormous rural population and the needs of rural education. Secondary education was exclusively an urban phenomenon and public primary education never reached more than a small percentage of rural inhabitants, in spite of grand schemes for providing compulsory education in planned stages, inspired by such international organisations as the League of Nations. What did touch the rural population effectively were the various mass education projects initiated and carried out by the few who felt that China's future lay with the rural masses, men such as Liang Shuming,[58] Tao Xingzhi and Yan Yangchu (James Yen).[59] Successful as there were within limited areas, they never succeeded in being generalised, perhaps because they depended on resources and leadership from outside rather than the initiative of the people themselves, or perhaps due to the chaos of war-time conditions. When Liberation came in 1949 it was estimated that 80-90 percent of the population were illiterate, and only a small proportion of school-age children were in school: 24,391,000 in primary schools, 1,497,000 in secondary schools, and 117,000 in higher education[60] in a population estimated at 576,409,000 in the census of 1953.[61]

NEW CHINA AND THE SOVIET INFLUENCE

Most studies of modern China emphasise the aspect of change more than that of continuity in the immediate post-Revolution period. This is probably a correct balance in view of the freshness which the Communists brought to their way of dealing with many of China's age-old problems. However in the area of education possibly more can be understood in terms of continuity than change in the early years. The structure established under American influence in the twenties, six-three-three-four, was maintained except at the tertiary level where many programmes were extended to five years. The curriculum at primary and secondary levels had a similar encyclopedic content organised around academic subjects as that used in the Nationalist period, with Communist teaching replacing Nationalist in the slot for citizenship or politics.[62] At the secondary level the school system still largely served urban areas and prepared students for the enormously increased intakes of higher education. Meanwhile the educational principles developed by Mao at Yanan were drawn upon to build a supplementary system with large numbers of rural schools and part-time schools linked to factories and other enterprises. The main change then which took place in the first decade of China's educational work was an enormous expansion of provision at all levels, and a dedicated struggle to wipe out illiteracy by all means.

The one radical systemic discontinuity was in the sensitive area of higher education. Here the Chinese carried out a total reorganisation of all existing institutions, many of which had been comprehensive along American lines, including pure and applied sciences along with arts and social sciences in their curriculum. The Soviet model adopted in 1952 dictated that there should be one 'comprehensive university' devoted to pure theoretical studies in the arts and sciences in each region. This was surrounded by a cluster of polytechnical, normal and monotechnical institutions.[63] The curriculum emphasis in these was on the applied sciences needed for a rapidly expanding socialist economy, and there is little doubt that the system was remarkably effective in producing large numbers of experts who contributed to the great success of China's industrial expansion.[64] Communist leaders were little more eager than Nationalist ones had been to maintain the tradition of student radical activism which had contributed to the success of the 1949 Revolution and the absorption of student energies in equipping themselves to serve national reconstruction proved a healthy and satisfying alternative for a time at least. However it cannot be mere coincidence that the most wide-reaching political upheaval China has seen in this century, perhaps in its entire history, the Great Proletarian Cultural Revolution of 1966, began with an outbreak of student activism in the universities, activism on a scale such as the most radical students of the Nationalist period could barely have dreamt of. It resulted in the overthrow and death in tragic circumstances of China's President, Liu Shaoqi, and the downfall of many of her most respected cadres at all levels.[65]

THE CULTURAL REVOLUTION

There are many ways of interpreting the Cultural Revolution, but in terms of the foregoing analysis it might be seen as an attack on the whole 'regular' schooling system with its American, European and Soviet components, and on the very notion of a university which fostered values of pure scholarship and 'expertise in command'. These had combined with reactionary elements of persisting Confucian values such as the separation of mental and manual labour, and were vigorously criticised on the basis of Maoist values. The whole system was to be revolutionised along the lines of the Yanan model. As had happened in the victory of guerilla warfare in 1949, the countryside was to take over the cities in educational leadership, and young people were to learn correct political attitudes from the peasants, so that all the knowledge they gained could be shaped to serve the people. All levels of education were to be integrated with productive labour, either by schools setting up their own small factories and farms, or students and teachers being sent for extensive periods to farms and factories. All learning was to take place through practice in productive labour and class struggle, followed by the study of basic theory in natural and social science, then the refinement of theory in further practice.[66] The principle of 'politics in command' ensured that Mao Thought provided a guiding role for all other areas of knowledge, and in some cases it was even accredited with inspiring new inventions in the applied sciences, a claim that went beyond any ever made for the Confucian Canons![67]

The university, often regarded as the pride and flower of western learning, had no parallel in the educational patterns of traditional China and over and over it has proven a subversive institution in the Chinese context. Apparently Mao and other radical Chinese leaders saw no great loss therefore in the closure of China's major universities from 1966 to 1970 while alternative higher education structures closely linked with China's political and productive system were being forged to take their place.[68] Nor was Mao the first Chinese thinker to see the abolition of the university as necessary for a healthy development of Chinese education, although he was the first to have the authority to carry it out.

A Chinese historian writing in 1934-5 and already seriously concerned about the pernicious 'academicism' beginning to infect Chinese education under European influence offered his solution also in terms of the abolition of the university. He recommended the establishment of a genuinely Chinese education system with seven years of primary schooling for all, a variety of secondary programmes ranging from four to nine years, none academic but all offering different types of professional training combined with productive labour and related to the actual needs of national construction, and at the top research centres for the few capable of dedicated scholarly research at high levels.[69] Unfortunately for them, Guomindang leaders were far more interested in the recommendations of European advisors than these suggestions made by a Chinese scholar deeply versed in traditional scholarship and thoroughly loyal to the Three Principles of the People.

It can easily be demonstrated how inimitably Chinese were the values of the Cultural Revolution. Equally there is no doubt about the wide appeal of these values, so passionately egalitarian, so unequivocally oriented towards the practical service of society. No wonder they reverberated through university campuses all over the world in the heady years of the late sixties. Yet the unpleasant fact is that Cultural Revolution institutions were not capable of serving the needs of a socialist society far more complex than that of the utopian Yanan years, nor could they meet China's need to keep up with international developments in science and technology. That at least is the judgement of China's present leaders.

Post-Mao changes in educational policy have seen the reemergence of the old 'regular' system with its residues of foreign models and its acceptance of inegalitarian gaps between those institutions whose main task is to raise quality and strive for international scholarly standards and less prestigious locally oriented institutions. Also many new channels for interaction with the West are opening up which can hardly fail to exert an influence. Over 15,000 Chinese scholars and students, are studying or doing research in European, American and Japanese universities. Several hundred western teachers are teaching in Chinese institutions. Sister relations established between Chinese and western educational institutions have encouraged a great flow of scholarly visits both ways, and much informal consultation over educational policy.[70] There is also a flood of information about all aspects of western society including western educational systems which is being intently studied by Chinese scholars of Comparative Education.

In light of the almost certain influence of western educational values and institutions on the future of Chinese education, it is clearly important to reflect on the results of past Chinese experiments with western models. Now that China has become established as an independent socialist nation with a dignity that derives as much from the admirable achievements of over 30 years of socialist modernisation as from the renown of her traditional culture, are Chinese educators in a better position than ever before to 'digest' these western influences and turn them to the service of Chinese goals and priorities? Or is interaction with the West likely once again to introduce values that are explosive in the Chinese social context, or institutional patterns that are unsuited for the achievement of Chinese modernisation goals?

This question could be considered in a number of ways. One could look at the present value system to see what new constellation of Maoist and traditional values is emerging, and whether it has any common ground with the educational values of the western countries now interacting with China. National legislation is often a useful barometer of widely shared values, and the new state constitution passed by the National People's Congress in 1982 bears close examination. Article 24 gives Chinese education a far wider brief than the previous service to proletarian politics and combination with productive labour set down in the 1975 and 1978 constitutions:

> The State strengthens the building of socialist spiritual civilisation through spreading education in high ideals and morality, general education and education in discipline and the legal system, and through promoting the formulation and observance of rules of conduct and common pledges by different sections of the people in urban and rural areas.
>
> The State advocates the civic virtues of love for the motherland, for the people, for labour, for science and for socialism; it educates the people in patriotism, collectivism, internationalism, and communism, and in dialectical and historical materialism; it combats capitalist, feudalist and other decadent ideas.[71]

Secondly, one could examine the new institutional patterns that are being adopted, and reflect on how appropriate they are to the Chinese value system. To what extent do they represent the revival of previous patterns introduced from the West, how effective were these in the past, and what new combinations are being formed which may resolve some of the contradictions of the past? Alternately will these be exacerbated by present experiments? A third approach would be to look at present economic trends and consider the ability of the economy to sustain the patterns that are now being developed and to absorb the kind of graduates that are now being produced. In this regard the conditions of the rural majority are of crucial importance. Will the present responsibility system succeed both in improving their own lot and enhancing their contribution to the national economy, and will rural education policies be found which are appropriate to these conflicting aims? Will the economic motivation now being encouraged succeed where the ideological motivation of the Cultural Revolution period failed? Agricultural prosperity remains the fundamental basis for the success of modernisation tasks in other areas, yet rural education is not given high priority by the central government, nor is interaction with the West likely to contribute much to it. It remains to be seen whether the traditional patterns of local self-reliance, and self-provision in education will serve the educational needs of rural youth and contribute to rural prosperity. These questions are no more than a starting place for reflection on some of the issues facing Chinese educators in the eighties.

Chapter Three

PRIMARY EDUCATION IN CHINA:
A TWO-TRACK SYSTEM FOR DUAL TASKS

Billie L.C. Lo

INTRODUCTION

Post-1977 Chinese educational policies show clearly the authorities' intention to develop primary education on a two-track basis with urban academic schools on one hand and rural work-study schools on the other. This is, however, not an innovation but a return to an ancient tradition. Limited educational resources in a vast country like China have always meant that the government could only support urban schools. The education of rural children has always been a responsibility of rural communities. The Chinese have had a long tradition of village schools supported by local resources. Relatively well-to-do families hired teachers for the education of their children. Other sent children to attend a school run by a local teacher, whose well-being was looked after by the parents of his students.[1] This two-track tradition has continued throughout the Communist regime except for the years of the Great Proletarian Cultural Revolution.

In 1949 when the Communists took over the country, they had the people-run schools in the rural areas on the one hand, and the urban schools inherited from the Nationalist Government on the other. The 'Decision on the Reform of the Education System' issued in 1951 acknowledged the existence of two tracks of education.[2]

On November 11, 1953, the State Council issued a 'Directive Concerning the Reorganisation and improvement of Primary Education'. It stressed the importance of developing education in cities and industrial and mining areas to meet the demands of industrialisation. As for rural areas, it was merely stated that "the principle of voluntariness and need should be the basis upon which to promote the operation of primary schools by the people."[3]

An editorial of the People's Daily at the end of 1953 further confirmed the authorities' intention to concentrate resources in the urban schools. Entitled 'Reorganise and Improve Primary Education Step by Step', it called for an increase in the development of urban schools to counter the 'rapid but blind development' in the rural areas.[4] The government's emphasis on 'selective development' meant that rural people had to take up the responsibility of educating their children. Expenses for maintaining people-run rural schools had to be raised by the masses themselves.[5]

The period 1955-1957 saw full implementation of the policy of 'walking on two legs', the one leg being the state supported high standard urban schools and the other being people-run rural schools. In December 1955, the Ministry of Education announced a plan to achieve 7-year education that was compulsory and universal. This was to be done through the strength and support of the masses.[6] The government's policy of relying on the masses to develop education in the countryside can also be seen in later official documents such as 'Report of the Third National Educational Administrative Conference'.[7] In 1956 and 1957, there was a big increase in primary school enrollment because of the mushrooming of people-run rural schools.[8] In 1957, a state directive on rural people-run schools was issued.[9] Since then, the distinction between rural work-study programmes and urban academic schools has been made even clearer.

Chairman Mao, however, disapproved of the distinct rural urban differences in educational provision, attacking particularly the urban academic schools for their 'bourgeois' tendencies.[10] In 1962, Liu Shaoqi justified the situation by his theory of 'two kinds of labour and two kinds of education systems'.[11] He argued that if the country was to quickly turn out qualified experts for modernisation, it was necessary to concentrate the limited resources on a number of 'key' schools to train a selected group of talented young people. Until the economic situation of the country had improved sufficiently to provide better educational facilities on a large scale students in the other track had to take whatever form of education their 'objective local conditions' allowed. The two tracks of educational provision were equally important, Liu maintained. While one was mandated to train experts to serve economic development, the other was given the important responsibility of producing a generation of literate successors with correct socialist consciousness.[12]

The two track system continued until 1966 when Chairman Mao launched a full attack on the educational front. What started as a 'Socialist Educational Movement' turned into the Great Proletarian Cultural Revolution which affected practically the entire nation in all aspects. Education at all levels came to a halt for two years. In 1968 when schools were re-opened, primary education became a single-track five-year system in which children in rural and urban areas were to be educated alike.[13]

Primary Education

The post-1977 period has seen serious efforts to raise the quality of education for the modernisation of the country. In an effort to develop education efficiently and economically, the educational authorities have once again called for local responsibility for the provision of the first level of education. The two-track structure in education has slowly returned. The argument that Liu Shaoqi used to justify the two-track system in the early sixties has appeared again in newspaper and journal articles. It is exactly the same argument: for China to modernise quickly, a large number of experts are needed; to quickly turn out these experts at a time when resources are limited, it is necessary to concentrate limited resources on a few 'keypoint' schools. These 'key' schools are for the training of experts while the 'non-key' schools are for raising the cultural level of the masses.[14] With the posthumous rehabilitation of Liu Shaoqi and the restoration of his two-track theory of education,[15] the two-track phenomenon has once again become a prominent feature in the Chinese educational scene. It can be seen both in the distinction between state-run urban schools and people-run rural schools, and the distinction between 'key' and 'non-key' schools within each system.

AIMS AND DUAL TASKS OF PRIMARY EDUCATION

Education after 1977 has been assigned the arduous task of training competent people for the realisation of the country's modernisation goals.[16] While education itself is seen as the foundation of all scientific and technological advancement, primary education is regarded by the authorities as the core of the foundation.

In a call for popularising primary education, People's Daily, [12 August, 1979] discussed the importance of primary education to the Four Modernisations as follows:

> To achieve China's grand goal of realising the Four Modernisations before the end of the century, science and technology are the key, and education is the foundation, while primary education is the foundation of the foundation. Primary education is the point of departure in raising the scientific and cultural level of the entire nation.[17]

The Central Secretariat expressed similar views on primary education.

> An important measure to realise the Four Modernisations is to raise the cultural and scientific level of our nation; and the foundation of raising our cultural and

> scientific level is primary education.
> Primary education is the foundation of a
> person's development; it is a key to the
> early discovery and development of talent; an
> important stage of a person's moral and
> spiritual development; the foundation of the
> whole educational system; and the starting
> point for raising our nation's cultural and
> scientific level.[18]

Thus, the aim of primary education is to lay the foundation for the preparation of future citizens with socialist morality and advanced scientific knowledge.

In terms of specific tasks, primary and secondary education are to fulfill the dual tasks of 1) supplying educational institutes of higher levels with well-qualified students for the training of expertise in various fields and 2) providing a literate labour force for society.[19] Educational writers in China have repeatedly elaborated on the theme of the dual tasks, emphasising that both tasks are equally important for raising the scientific and cultural level of the nation.[20]

In reality, only about two percent of China's youngsters have the opportunity to receive a higher education.[21] The rest have to join the productive labour force. In order not to raise hopes for further education, the second task - that of training potential good workers - is stressed more often. Teachers and parents are encouraged to take this task seriously and not to feel that it is less honourable or less important than the first task.

A TWO-TRACK SYSTEM FOR DUAL TASKS

The 'dual tasks' for Chinese primary schools find expression in a two-track schooling system. In theory, all primary schools are assigned both tasks.[22] In practical implementation, there is a clear 'division of labour' as to which schools are to carry out which tasks. Schools with 'immature conditions' are not expected to fulfill the first task of training talent for higher level educational institutions.[23] They are to strive to fulfill the second task of training competent labour reserves for society as a whole. These are mainly schools in the rural areas. The task of training candidates for institutions of higher learning is assigned to schools with better facilities, mainly those in the cities.[24] Among these schools, those with the best facilities and teachers are designated as national key schools for the sole purpose of raising educational standards and preparing talent for higher education. By February, 1978, twenty such key schools were put under the direct charge of the Ministry of Education to ensure that they would be run well.[25]

A common practice in other stratified educational systems is for students who excel in primary school to be transferred to better primary schools in which chances for promotion to the next level of education are greater. In this way, the best students are selected and given the best opportunity for further education. In China, very few such transfers occur. When such transfers do occur they occur within the same educational district. Transfer across the rural urban boundary is made almost impossible for several reasons. Firstly, academic standards for rural and urban schools are very different. Most rural schools are 'incomplete schools'. Secondly, primary education is meant to be local. Each educational district supports its own schools for children of the district. The recruitment of talented students from other educational districts is not encouraged.[26] Thirdly, unlike American parents who can move to more desirable educational districts so that their children may attend better schools, Chinese parents have no such mobility. In China, the change of residence has to be in the interest of the state and has to be officially approved. Hence, there is very little chance for a rural primary school student to be transferred to an urban primary school.

The educational authorities have stated explicitly that different primary schools are to carry out different tasks. This can be seen in the circular of the Draft plan for a Ten Year Full-Time Teaching System promulgated in early 1978. The circular states that there should be full-day schools, work-study schools and spare-time schools. It is stated clearly that among these three types of schools, some will be charged with the task of improving the quality of education and furthermore the Draft Plan was designed for the use of these schools.[27]

The circular acknowledges openly that most schools in the country-side operate on a combined nine-year basis. The task of these schools is not to supply higher institutions with high standard students but to train competent workers. No national draft plan has been designed for these schools. Their teaching programmes are to be formulated by the respective local educational authorities.

In mid-1978, the existence of the two tracks of primary educational provision was further confirmed by an Education Ministry spokesman.[28] In 1979, a conference was convened announcing plans for the development of part-farm, part-study and part-work, part-study schools.[29] In January, 1982, the Vice-Minister of Education Zhang Chengxian spoke of the authorities' decision to implement two different teaching programmes. According to him, with the reorganisation of the structure of education in the future, not only two, but a few teaching programmes will have to be designed in the near future.[30]

This two track educational system with little provision for inter-track transfer is antithetical to the traditional

Chinese perception of education as a means to upward social and economic mobility. A consequence of this is that parents of the majority of children who do not have much much hope for higher education tend to withdraw children from school before primary school graduation. This will be discussed later.

URBAN ACADEMIC SCHOOLS - FOR THE RAISING OF EDUCATIONAL QUALITY AND PREPARATION OF TALENT FOR HIGHER EDUCATION

The concept of universal primary education in China has been stated as a situation in which "over 95% of the local school-age children are able to go to school, complete the 5-year course and basically arrive at the cultural level of a primary school graduate provided for in the teaching programme".[31] Only in twenty-five percent of the populated areas in China has primary education been made universal.[32] These are mainly urban areas in which China's best primary schools can be found. Schools in these areas are to fulfill the task of raising educational quality and training talented students for institutes of higher learning.

Schools in these areas are mostly full-day state-run schools. They have on the whole achieved a reasonable academic standard, although they also differ among themselves in material conditions and educational quality. They are the ones which follow official directives and policies closely for they have the necessary conditions to do so. Usually, new policies and teaching strategies are first tried out in selected schools in these areas before they are advocated for broader implementation.[33] Thus these schools also serve as a testing ground for new policies of primary education in the country.

All state-run urban schools were five-year schools before 1980. Children entered primary school at the age of seven or above. In July, 1978, Vice-Minister of Education Li Chi announced that six-year-olds in the cities would be eligible to start school at the beginning of the fall term.[34] Subjects taught in these primary schools include Chinese, arithmetic, elementary knowledge of nature, a foreign language (chiefly English), politics, physical culture, music and drawing. Elementary knowledge of nature and politics are for students of the third grade and above. A foreign language is taught only in some of the best schools.[35] Table 3.1 indicates the way in which these subjects are distributed by the number of class hours and level.

At the end of 1980, Beijing took the lead to lengthen the period of primary education from five to six years. Curriculum for these six-year schools remains similar to that of the five-year schools with two changes: the subject of politics is to be gradually replaced by training in ethics; history and geography classes are to be reintroduced.[36] Other provinces such as Liaoning Province followed suit to transform some of their five-year schools into six-year schools.[37]. In 1982, the

Table 3.1:

TEACHING PLAN FOR FULL-TIME FIVE-YEAR PRIMARY SCHOOLS, 1982

Subjects	First Grade	Second Grade	Third Grade	Fourth Grade	Fifth Grade	Total Class Hours	%
Ideological and Moral Education	1	1	1	1	1	180	3.9
NATIONAL LANGUAGE -TOTAL	11	12	11	9	9	1,872	40.3
-Speaking and Reading	10	11	8	6	6		
-Composition			2	2	2		
-Writing	1	1	1	1	1		
Mathematics	6	6	6	7	7	1,152	24.8
Foreign Language*				(3)	(3)	(216)	
Natural Science			2	2	2	216	4.7
Geography				2		72	1.6
History					2	72	1.6
Physical Education	2	2	2	2	2	360	7.8
Music	2	2	2	2	2	360	7.8
Art	2	2	2	1	1	288	6.2
Labour				1	1	72	1.6
TOTAL Class Hours per week	<u>24</u>	<u>25</u>	<u>26</u>	<u>27</u>	<u>27</u>	4,644	
EXTRA-CURRICULAR ACTIVITY							
-Self-Study	2	2	2	2	2		
-Scientific,Technological & Recreational Activities	2	2	2	2	2		
-Sports Activities	2	2	2	2	2		
-Class Meetings & Group Activities	1	1	1	1	1		
TOTAL School Hrs/W.	<u>31</u>	<u>32</u>	<u>33</u>	<u>34</u>	<u>34</u>		

* A Foreign Language is offered only in schools with the necessary resources.

Source: This teaching plan has been translated from an official document issued in January, 1982. I am grateful to Lau Wing Fong of the Chinese University of Hong Kong and Professor Stan Rosen of the University of Southern California for providing this document.

Primary Education

State Council made the decision to gradually extend the full-time five-year primary school system into a six-year one.[38] The transformation will take time, but the tone is set for a longer period of primary schooling.

Extension of the period of schooling is regarded as a means of raising the quality of education. Running key schools in another means to the same end. The authorities wish to raise the standard of the most capable students in the shortest possible time by concentrating them in a number of better facilitated schools. It is a measure to train talented students at an early age. Moreover, key schools are to act as models to guide the development of education.[39]

The administrative system for key schools is a rather complicated one. At the national level, there are twenty key schools under the direct supervision of the Ministry of Education.[40] At the lower educational administrative levels, provincial and municipal educational bureaux, as well as prefectural educational offices are authorised to run key schools under their own jurisdiction, thus producing an overlapping administrative arrangement. The provincial educational bureau can run key schools on an all-province basis or within prefectures. Prefectures in turn can run key schools on an all-prefecture basis or within counties. Counties run their own local key schools; but communes within the counties can also run key schools.[41] According to a Ministry guideline issued on November 11, 1978, five or six key primary schools are recommended for each county or city district.[42] By the end of 1979, the number of key primary schools in the whole country exceeded 7,000, accomodating more than 5,100,000 students.[43]

Not all of the key schools are of the same standard. In accordance with the local control and generally wide variability of Chinese primary schools, there is considerable variation among even the key schools. For instance, a commune key school is not to be compared with a key school at the national level. A commune key school simply means that it is the best school found in the commune.

The rationale behind the running of key schools - that of concentrating resources on the best students - has become very popular. This is manifested in yet another practice that has been revived within the schools, namely, intra-school streaming. Schools (non-key as well as key) group their students at each grade into 'key', 'fast', 'average', 'slow', and 'remedial' classes.[44] The argument behind this practice is that students differ in their intellectual ability. By grouping students of the same intellectual ability together, teachers can teach each group accordingly.[45] In this way, students can learn and develop at a rate most suitable to them. This is seen as the best way to meet the individual needs of the students.

In actual implementation, the pressure to produce high standard students is so great that schools only concentrate on the 'key' classes. Students, as well as teachers of these 'key' classes are under the heavy burden of extra lessons and excessive homework.[46] It has been reported that many primary school students can only sleep five or six hours per day. In still worse cases, there is no winter or summer vacation and no rest on Sundays. Classes are conducted on 365 days of the year.[47] Students in the 'slow' or even the 'average' classes are, on the contrary, neglected. As a result, students in these classes lose confidence and give up hope in themselves.[48]

The effect of intra-school streaming has proven harmful to students. The Minister of Education Jiang Nanxiang expressed his concern as follows:

> What merits our attention is the present situation in the slow classes. Students there often give themselves up as hopeless and drift along. Even among the students in accelerated classes, there are also many ideological problems, even signs of law and discipline violations. We must not turn a blind eye to this situation. We must adopt effective and timely measures to cope with the situation.[49]

Complaints from the public against the situation of putting too much pressure on a small group of students but neglecting the majority has increased. The authorities first appealed to the schools to give attention to the entire student body. This appeal did not improve the situation. The authorities then called for a gradual abolition of intra-school streaming. The rationalisation was that streaming was only necessary immediately after the fall of the Gang of Four because students' standards differed widely under the pernicious influence of the Gang of Four. It was an "emergency policy under some special historical conditions". With the reorganisation of the educational system, such extremes in educational standards would not occur and hence there would be no need for more intra-school streaming.[50] Schools were encouraged to abolish streaming from grade one and, step by step, eliminate the practice all together. This has received support from municipalities and provinces. Changchun Municipal Educational Bureau issued a decision on November 6, 1981, stating that no primary and middle school in the city is allowed to classify students into 'key', 'fast' or 'slow' classes. Schools are not allowed to enroll superior students or repeaters from other schools.[51] Sichuan Province issued a similar decision on November 10, 1981.[52] Linyi prejecture of Shanxi Province abolished the practice of intra-school streaming as early as 1978. The practice was abolished across Shanxi Province in the fall term of 1981.[53] By January 1982, the practice is reported to have been abolished in all of

Primary Education

Beijing's primary and lower secondary schools.[54] With further discouragement from the government and more public pressure, the practice of intra-school streaming is expected to gradually disappear from the primary educational scene.

Key schools are, however, meant to continue. There is a tendency for key schools to be even further strenghened. Vice-Minister of Education Zhang Chengxian quoted Beijing's example to explain how the practice of intra-school streaming can be slowly eliminated at the same time maintaining that the running of key schools is a correct and necessary policy. He suggested that key primary schools (zhongdian xiaoxue) can be called central primary schools (zhongxin xiaoxue); but whatever they are called, "there should always be a group of better-run primary schools to take the leading role".[55] Another educational official gave a lengthy discussion on why intra-school streaming should be abolished; but when asked if key schools should also be slowly eliminated, his answer was a definite 'No'. "Key schools should be continued, and should be run better and better... Grasp key schools to lead the development of education. This is an objective law of educational development. It is a guideline most suitable to our country's situation in education."[56]

RURAL PEOPLE-RUN SCHOOLS - FOR THE TRAINING OF COMPETENT LABOUR RESERVES

While urban primary schools are run more or less uniformly on a full-time five or six-year basis, rural primary schools vary from place to place in form and structure. This is a result of the government's call for the adaptation of national policies to suit local conditions.[57] As China is a vast country with extreme variations in local conditions, national policies concerning primary education find expression in broadly diverse ways within rural communities.

It must, however, be pointed out here that local variations of rural primary education are only variations in forms of educational provision which unfortunately still all follow an academic curriculum. The authorities have talked about designing a separate school programme for rural schools, as mentioned above. But up to now, no such programme has been designed and rural schools use various indigenous ways of following the standard curriculum. Local variations are therefore variations in form of educational provision and level of attainment in relation to a standard academic curriculum.

The vast variation in standards of rural primary schools is not a major concern of the educational authorities at the moment. The chief goal for rural education in the immediate future is the popularisation of the five-year primary school system, in whatever way appropriate to and affordable by the local authorities.

In most rural areas in China, primary education is still

not 'popularised'. The situation in most rural areas is described as the 'three-six-nine situation'. That is: although the enrollment rate is over 90%, the average attendance rate is around 60%, and the passing rate is only 30%.[58] The average attendance rate for even Beijing's rural areas is only 75%.[59] Very few rural communes have successfully 'popularised' primary education.

The educational authorities recognise the difficulties that rural communes encounter in striving to popularise primary education. They advise that primary education should be popularised stage by stage. The official plan is for primary education to be popularised in the economically more advanced areas by 1985. Other areas can proceed to popularise primary education step by step and hopefully by 1990, primary education will have been popularised throughout China.[60]

The principle of 'people-run, state-assist' is stressed in the provision of rural education:

> In view of the fact that the state is still unable to finance the operation of all the schools, it remains necessary to encourage the communes and production brigades to run their schools largely at their own expense, namely, to practise the traditional method of "having people run schools with government subsidy".[61]

Rural educational authorities at the commune level finance the schools, interpret national policies to teachers and parents and decide how the commune will implement these policies. Besides directives and suggestions, they receive little or no assistance from educational officials at higher levels.

The prefectural level educational officials have a more direct effect on the development of education in the communes. They can more directly finance the implementation of certain policies and put pressure on communes to adopt or abolish certain practices. Beyond the prefectural level are the provincial bureaux of education and the Ministry of Education. These two formulate policies and point out the general direction of development. Their assistance and/or interference in educational provision in the rural areas is minimal.[62]

Thus, rural communes have a lot of local autonomy in terms of whether and how certain national policies are to be implemented. Local autonomy also means responsibility. Communes have to bear the cost for almost all educational provision. A result of this local autonomy is a whole range of local variations in educational provision and quality. Communes which devote more to education have better educational facilities. Communes which place their priorities in other areas have little reserved for the development of education.

Primary Education

The variations in form and quality of rural primary education are really quite fascinating. There are full-day schools, half-day schools, half-farm, half-study schools, spare-time schools, double-session schools, 'incomplete schools', slack-season schools, winter-schools, mobile schools and special literacy classes etc. In terms of quality, at one end of the spectrum are key rural schools[63] whose successful experiences have been widely publicised. At the other end of the spectrum, there are rural schools in extremely poor condition: school buildings are in a critical condition; there are not enough desks and chairs; there is no newspaper and no school clock for classes to go by.[64] Unfortunately, the majority of rural schools are at the latter end of the spectrum. Many schools are still striving to attain the minimum condition of having "a safe building for every school, a classroom for every class and a desk and a chair for every student."[65]

On the whole, many of these people-run rural primary schools are make-shifts of one kind or another. Improvements remain slow and there is little hope that these make-shift improvisations will eventually become part of the regular full-time stream. The authorities accept the situation and in fact approve of the many forms of rural educational provisions. After all, the main task of rural schools is to turn out workers who are literate and competent. If rural schools in their many different forms manage to teach rural children some rudimentary skills in the three Rs, the task is fulfilled.[66] Rural schools are urged to recognise the fact that their task is different from that of the full-time schools. They are not expected to reach the standard of full-time primary schools.[67]

The post-1977 agricultural responsibility system makes it all the more necessary for rural primary schools to be operated on a make-shift basis. When more labour means more income and when it is clear that rural primary education does not lead to social or economic mobility, peasants are quite reluctant to let children go to school, once they become old enough to assist production. Since the implementation of the new agricultural policies, enrollment and attendance rates in many rural areas have reportedly dropped.[68] To avoid conflicts and to adapt educational policies to suit local conditions, rural primary schools change their schedules and operate only at times when farming is not busy. Slack-season schools, winter-schools and evening schools are some of the forms adopted by rural schools. Some schools divide an academic year into the Very-Busy Farming season, the Quite-Busy Farming season, the Not-So-Busy Farming season and the Not-Busy Farming season. School hours vary according to the season. In the Very-Busy Farming season, schools are closed for students to assist in farm work. In the Quite-Busy Farming season, classes are run only in the mornings. In the Not-So-Busy Farming season, individual students are allowed to take leave of absence and teachers will give them make-up lessons afterwards. In the Not-Busy Farming season, students study full-time in schools.[69] This has been advocated as a flexible and very effective way to popularise rural primary education without jeopardising the agricultural responsibility system.

A rural school practice which has been revived and is increasingly receiving attention and encouragement is 'double-session teaching'. In sparsely populated rural areas where there are too few children to justify a class for each grade, children of two or more grades are put together in one classroom and taught alternately by one teacher. This saves human and material resources as fewer teachers and classrooms are required. 'Little assistants' are chosen from among the students to help discipline and tutor other students while the teacher is teaching another grade. In Fujian Province, about half of the rural schools are one-teacher or two-teacher schools. These schools all use 'double-session teaching'.[70] This practice has been increasingly recognised as something most suitable to China's rural conditions. A conference on 'primary-school double-session teaching' has been convened; 'double-session teaching' programmes have been designed and 'little assistants' have been trained.[71] There are indications that in the near future, the practice of 'double-session teaching' will become increasingly popular.[72]

To summarise, it is intended that local educational authorities shoulder the entire responsibility of providing rural primary education. As mentioned above, the principle is 'people-run, state-assist'. In actual operation, government assistance is minimal. The central authorities stress local initiative and responsibility. They encourage every single indigenous educational improvisation that works to provide some kind of education to rural children. "Good schools rely on their own resources to develop and grow", stress the educational authorities.[73] The intention to shift as much responsibility to the lower levels as possible is clear and understandable. As the very limited funds available for education have to be spent first on training experts in higher education institutions and second on urban full-time schools, rural areas have to finance their own educational provision.

Since the introduction of various new agricultural policies, drop-out rates in rural schools have reportedly increased. The following have been noted as some of the main reasons for the high drop-out rates:

1) Peasants cannot or are unwilling to pay tuition. Education is by no means free in China. The amount and ways in which tuition is paid vary from place to place. Peasants who now have to invest in agricultural production under the agricultural responsibility system find tuition increasingly a financial strain.

Primary Education

2) The rural school curriculum is not compatible with the requirements of life and production in the rural areas. No agricultural or technical knowledge is included in the curriculum. As a result, schools are seen as nothing more than a place to acquire basic literacy. Once students finish grade three and have acquired basic literacy, peasants see no point in keeping their children in school.

3) The agricultural responsibility system makes it more rewarding for parents to send children to work in the fields than to send them to school.

4) The opinion that girls should not study still persists in rural communities. Drop-out rates among girls are particularly high.

5) Peasants have lost faith in education as a means of providing social and economic mobility to their children. They would rather have their children learn some useful skills at home or under apprenticeship than send them to school.[74]

The urban rural differences in primary education are likely to become even more distinct. With the central educational authorities designing totally different school programmes for rural schools in the future, rural and urban schools will drift further apart.

The implication of this is significant. Broadly, the single most important criterion for selection will be the geographical location of a child's registered permanent residence over which he has neither choice nor control. A child of an urban area in which schools have better human and material resources has a much better chance of receiving a further education. A child of a rural area in which schools are make-shift educational improvisations has practically no chance of advancing himself educationally. The differences between rural and urban schools in terms of school facilities and especially the quality of teachers are enormous. Thus, to require a student of a rural school to come up to the same level of achievement as an urban student before promoting him to the next level of education is simply denying him further educational opportunities from the start. The result of this is clear. There will be a rise of urban elites in China.

POST-1977 INNOVATIONS

A significant difference between primary education today and primary education in other periods of the Communist regime is in the area of political-ideological education. A core subject of the curriculum for many years, politics had been the study of Chairman's Mao's quotations, the study of the evils of imperialism and the singing of revolutionary songs. Today, politics is a subject of the primary school curriculum only for students of the third grade and above.[75]. Moreover, it is to be gradually replaced by training in ethics.[76]

Political-ideological education in primary schools today stresses the development of good morals and good behaviour more than anything else. "Lessons in good morals and good behaviour are lessons in politics in primary schools."[77] In March 1981, the Ministry of Education announced that all primary schools were to introduce ideological and moral education which emphasised:

- The lofty ideals of communism to realise China's modernisation;
- Ardent love for the Communist Party and the socialist motherland;
- Readiness to give whole-hearted service to the people and to safeguard the people's interest;
- Fondness of labour and fostering of diligence, honesty, modesty, hard work and plain living;
- Discipline and respect for the law and public order, concern for public property and pleasure in helping others.[78]

Compared to the study of politics in the earlier periods which was concerned mainly with the eradication of bourgeois tendencies by studying quotations of Chairman Mao and current events as transmitted by official agencies, this shift of emphasis to developing good morals and good behaviour is quite a big contrast. "...... (today) revolutionary values call on students to study diligently, observe discipline, love labour, take pleasure in helping others, work hard and dare to fight the enemy courageously."[79]

Another aspect of today's ideological-political education supports the authorities' efforts to run primary education on a two-track system. Besides the good morals and good behaviour mentioned above, ideological-political education today also stresses the honour of becoming labourers with socialist consciousness and encourages students to enter the labour force willingly. The authorities call upon teachers to do a good job in ideological-political work among students by pointing out to them explicity that only a small number of primary and middle school graduates will be able to pursue advanced study; the majority of students will have to work after their primary or secondary schooling. This aspect of ideological-political education is perhaps not unique to the post-1977 period, but is certainly emphasised to a greater extent than before. A very important task of ideological-political education today is to "teach the young people that it is an honour to be a cultured labourer with socialist consciousness, so that they can become useful construction personnel and contribute to any undertaking of the socialist motherland."[80]

Compared to other periods of the Communist regime, this period of the Four Modernisations places much less emphasis on the use of productive labour as a means to instil correct consciousness in primary school students. To help students acquire the "viewpoint of the labouring class", primary schools used to operate small factories and farms for students to work on. According to one report, primary schools in the whole country in 1959 operated 490,000 small factories and 400,000 small farms.[81] Regular work in agricultural or industrial production was an integral part of elementary education. Some schools allowed as much as half of the school time for productive labour. Other schools set aside entire days for work.[82]

The authorities now believe that the practice of laying too much emphasis on manual labour in the past was erroneous. Productive labour as a subject in the curriculum is now only for students of the fourth and fifth grades. The period required is half a month every year.[83] However, because of heavy academic pressure, even this greatly shortened period of productive labour is overlooked. Some schools have even abandoned the subject altogether.[84]

When productive labour as a subject is overlooked or removed from the regular primary school programme, students of full-time primary schools which are concentrated mainly in the urban areas will have little experience with productive labour. In contrast, rural educational policies guarantee the participation in productive labour by rural primary school students not as a school subject, but in the real sense of assisting production. This again points to the widening gap between urban and rural primary education.

CONCLUSION

In sum, Chinese education in the post-1977 period follows a two-track tradition with government schools concentrated largely in the urban areas and people-run schools mainly in the rural areas. This two-track system is to fulfill the dual tasks of supplying talented students to institutes of higher learning and training competent labour reserves.

A likely trend is for this two-track system to become, in effect, a major mechanism for stratification in China. Urban government schools with better human and material resources will turn out students much better qualified for the next level of education. As primary education is intended to be local, the geographical location of a child's registered permanent residence becomes the most important variable in determining his chances for further education. It is perhaps not stretching the evidence too much to say that, by and large, educational stratification begins as early as a child's birth and is confirmed after he completes his primary education.

In a vast developing country like China, urban-rural differences in education are to be expected. In fact, it seems quite rational for the Chinese to point out that local variations in education are the best way to meet local needs. Yet what I object to is that so far local variations still unfortunately all follow an academic curriculum. Local variations therefore result in variations in levels of attainment in relation to a standard academic curriculum instead of variations in curricula to better meet local needs. Thus, students of rural primary schools are urged to join the labour force eagerly upon completing their primary education but are taught subject matter which is intended for students who will continue their education. It is not surprising that one of the objections made about primary education in the rural areas is that the curriculum is irrelevant to local needs.

Localising primary education will be more meaningful if the authorities concerned take the trouble to look into local needs and organise local school programmes accordingly. At present, localising primary education simply means the shifting of responsibility to local educational authorities who struggle with limited resources to offer a watered-down version of an academic curriculum intended for students going on for further education. Such localisation of education can hardly be regarded as beneficial to children of the local communities. Bearing in mind that primary education is a complete education to most rural children, rural study programmes should be very different from those of the urban schools.

As mentioned before, localising educational provision is not an innovation in the communist regime. The Chinese have always had a fine tradition of village schools supported by local resources. Village schools existed long before governments paid any attention to education in the rural areas. They were quite well-established before 1949. Thus, today, to call for local responsibility for education in the rural areas is not a problem.

Problems exist in the designing of appropriate programmes for rural schools: there is an urgent need for ingenious ideas from the grassroots level to develop primary schooling programmes to suit the rural economy. Unfortunately, the best educators from whom these ideas should come have been transferred either to secondary schools or to urban schools.[85] The majority of rural teachers are non-qualified teachers. It is, however, precisely in the rural schools where resources are limited, the quality of students is poor and school programmes have to meet local needs that the best teachers are required. It is much easier for a teacher to teach an assigned curriculum to a group of selected students in an urban school with all the required facilities. Therefore, to improve primary education in the rural areas which accomodate more than 80% of China's primary school students, a strong force of primary school teachers is most necessary.

Unfortunately, more than 50% of China's primary school teachers are unqualified.[86] In China, there is in fact not a shortage of primary school teachers but a surplus. In some of the bigger cities, there is a surplus of 10,000 primary school teachers. The task is therefore not to recruit more primary school teachers but to raise the quality of these surplus teachers for rural primary schools.

Like other levels of Chinese education, primary education is going through a transitional period when the authorities concerned are searching for ways to best suit China's situation. With regard to primary education, the Chinese are doing all that one could expect at this point. There is room for optimism. The fine tradition of local responsibility for education, the increasing number of enlightened educational cadres and the awareness of the need for more suitable programmes for rural schools are all reasons for optimism.

That primary education is to be run on a two-track basis to meet the dual tasks is a concept already well accepted by the Chinese. The next step forward would be for the authorities to design more practical and achievable primary school programmes to develop human resources in ways beneficial to the rural communities. The official position is as follows: "It is always a small number of middle and primary school graduates who can go to college to pursue advanced study. The majority will mostly join the socialist labour force and engage in various undertakings of socialist construction."[87] Students have to be prepared not only motivationally to accept this fact; more importantly, they have to be equipped technically to take up the tasks assigned to them because of this fact.

Chapter Four

NEW DIRECTIONS IN SECONDARY EDUCATION

Stanley Rosen

INTRODUCTION

The Chinese educational system has undergone great change since the death of Mao Zedong and the political demise of his radical associates (September-October 1976) led to the repudiation of the Cultural Revolution (1966-1976). The present leadership is moving toward the mid-1980s with a good deal of confidence. Educational plans - including enrollment projections - have been drafted for the Sixth 5-Year Plan (1981-1985), with published projections for higher education down to 1990. The polemics that often made educational questions appear as zero-sum issues played out between 'moderate' and 'radical' forces in the Chinese leadership have disappeared from China's newspapers. The current emphasis is on both expansion and quality. Target dates for the universalisation of primary education have been set, while the number of regular college students will increase by 53% between 1983-1987, and the number of other (nonformal) college students will increase by 270% over the same period. There is one area, however, over which the effects of the Cultural Revolution persistently linger. In this area debates, now less ideological though no less political, have remained heated and sometimes public. The issue is the structure and future development of secondary education.

That secondary education should continue to prove so contentious is not surprising. The universalisation of primary education - considered basic education by both radicals and moderates - has long been a relatively non-controversial, if elusive, goal. The restoration and development of higher education became the top priority of a post-Mao leadership whose policies, conveniently summarised as the 'Four Modernisations' require the rapid training of high level and specialised personnel.

The functions of primary and higher education are therefore clear. The tasks to be performed at the secondary level, however, as a recent Chinese publication put it, are simultaneously "the most crucial and most complex".[1] Stated simply, "secondary schools should train both qualified students for institutes of higher learning and good labourers for society."[2] In practice, the desirability of a university degree and the small numbers permitted to enter university have made the contest mobility function of secondary schools of overriding importance both before and after the Cultural Revolution. Several scholars have argued, in fact, that this competition to enter university was the major source of tension in many pre-Cultural Revolution secondary school classrooms and a prime contributor to Red Guard factionalism during the first stage of the Cultural Revolution (1966-1968).[3]

Moreover, the effects of the Cultural Revolution have been greatest at the secondary level. The long-term impact of the Cultural Revolution on primary and higher education, despite obvious dislocations, was not fundamental. The 'ten years of catastrophe' brought with it an expansion in primary schooling from 116 million enrolled students in 1965 (70% enrollment ratio) to 150 million in 1976 (over 90% enrollment ratio). While changes at the university level were far more controversial - because of the diminished role of entrance examinations in favour of recommendations, the necessity of engaging in several years of manual labour prior to submitting an application, the enhanced importance of class origin as a factor in selection, and so forth - university enrollments had always been kept small. In 1965, there had been 674,000 university students; in 1977, before the restoration of the entrance examinations, there were 625,000 university students. Even by 1979, under the new policies, the enrollment ratio for higher education had crept from the 1.4% of 1965 only to 1.6%, still well below the ratios of most developing countries.

In contrast, the changes introduced at the secondary level constituted a structural transformation of major proportions. Attempts by the post-Mao leadership to jettison the Cultural Revolution reforms and return to the structure of the mid-1960s have introduced a set of new controversies which will be discussed below. Before turning to these current problems, it is helpful to examine the structure of secondary education in the 1960s and its Cultural Revolution replacement.

THE SECONDARY SCHOOL STRUCTURE BEFORE THE CULTURAL REVOLUTION [4]

Secondary schooling before the Cultural Revolution was distinguished by its diversity. Students were presented a variety of options, with the major selection decisions made after primary, lower secondary and upper secondary graduation. In larger cities, lower secondary education was universalised by the mid-1960s, so a student's decision as to future career could be put off until lower secondary graduation. At that point, a variety of options were available. There were regular secondary schools which prepared one for university entrance;

specialist (technical) schools which trained middle-level professional personnel, such as accountants and nurses; workers' training schools which trained middle-level technical workers, such as carpenters and welders; and vocational schools which trained workers with special skills, such as chefs, tailors and photographers. In the countryside, there were agricultural secondary schools.

Within these categories were further distinctions. Some schools were full-day and some were half-work, half-study. Some regular schools were 'keypoint' schools, in which financial and pedagogical resources were relatively concentrated, and at which the country's most promising students could be trained. Most of the regular schools were 'ordinary' schools which, although less well funded than the keypoints, were expected to perform similar functions. The number of students in upper secondary was kept deliberately low - nationally, only 9.1% of all secondary school students in 1965 were in regular upper secondary - to coordinate with the needs of higher education and the labour force. By 1965, the enrollment ratio of upper secondary graduates to university enrollees was about 46%. Table 4.1 reveals the choices made by students in Shanghai in 1964.

The decisions as to which students would be allowed to further their education during the 1960s were also carefully monitored. Advancement through the educational system depended on three criteria: academic achievement, class origin, and political manifestation. While these criteria varied from year to year, academic achievement was generally accorded greater weight as one moved up the educational ladder. The system was clearly a compromise, incorporating the divergent views of both radicals and moderates, with the year to year changes in part reflecting the shifts in the balance of political forces. For example, in 1964 it was exceedingly difficult for students whose parents had been capitalists, landlords, or rich peasants to gain entrance to a university, even with outstanding examination results. In 1962, a student's class origin had hardly been a factor in determining university enrollment.

The Cultural Revolution, with its purge of moderate elements in the leadership, enabled the radicals to reshape the complex educational structure of the 1960s. Far from acknowledging the benefits of such a varied system, the radicals objected that the prime beneficiaries of this kind of educational structure were the children of intellectuals. The wide variety of options available were not options at all, but were simply levels of an educational pyramid. In this hierarchy, the best schools were the keypoint schools. These schools received the most funding, had the best teachers and facilities, and had their pick of the country's most desirable students. In effect, this meant that a disproportionate number of students at the best keypoints were children of intellectuals, recruited because of outstanding academic

Secondary Schooling

Table 4.1

THE ROUTES TAKEN BY LOWER SECONDARY GRADUATES
in Shanghai, 1964

Route Taken	Number of Students	% of Total Graduates
Entered Regular Upper Secondary Schools	26,700	35%
Entered Secondary Specialist Schools (including Teacher Training Schools)	8,869	12%
Entered Workers' Training Schools	6,617	8.7%
Entered Vocational Schools	11,614	15.3%
Took Other Routes (1) Entered Schools for Further Tutoring (2) Joined Army (3) Waited for Job Allocation	22,128	29%
Totals	76,018	100%

Source: The Secondary Education Structural Reform Research Group of the East China Normal University Educational Research Centre, 'A Study of the Structural Reform of Secondary Education in Shanghai' in *Jiaoyu Yanjiu*, No. 8, August, 1981, p.25.

ability. Many of the students chosen by the country's best universities were products of these keypoint schools. In like manner, regular schools were considered superior to work-study, vocational, or workers' training schools. From the perspective of the radical reformers, those with the fewest options were the children of workers and peasants since they could not match the academic achievements of those from intellectual families. Nor did the educational advantages that accrued to children of 'good' class origin necessarily favour those of worker-peasant background. Just as their academic achievements were often inferior to those from intellectual homes, their class origins, as calculated by educational decision-makers, were considered a cut below those born into families of party or military officials.[5]

THE CULTURAL REVOLUTION REFORMS [6]

In June 1966, most of China's schools shut down as students divided into antagonistic Red Guard factions. By 1968, when the schools began reopening, a different secondary school structure emerged. As the main features of this new structure have frequently been described in the literature, they need be mentioned only briefly here. The new system sought to eliminate the inequalities of the old. A major object of the reforms was to eliminate the distinctions between schools and between students. Not only was the division between keypoint and ordinary schools to be abolished, but divisions between work-study and full-day schools also disappeared. In fact, almost all academic distinctions that had divided one school from another and one student from another were eliminated. For example, entrance examinations for secondary school and university were abolished, removing the most important advantage possessed by children from intellectual homes. Moreover, all students were expected to spend at least two years after graduation from secondary school performing manual labour before becoming eligible for university. With this break between secondary school and university, the raison d'etre of the keypoint system evaporated. To ensure equality between students and between schools in the urban areas, virtually all lower secondary schools and technical, vocational, and work-study schools were transformed into ordinary secondary schools with lower and upper sections. Enrollment in secondary schools went from 14.4 million in 1965 to 68.5 million by 1977. The length of primary and secondary schooling was reduced from the original twelve years to nine or ten. Within the schools, teaching materials were revised to stress practical over theoretical learning. No students were to be held back, none were to skip grades, nor was there to be division by ability (streaming) within each grade. Some teachers were transferred from the former keypoint schools to the newly established schools. The entire pre-Cultural Revolution educational system and the 'bourgeois academic authorities' who were alleged to have been in control of that system were incessantly vilified in this period.

The structural reforms of the Cultural Revolution removed many of the inequalities the radicals had found most intolerable. Prior to the Cultural Revolution, regular secondary schools had competed with each other to send their graduates on to university; a school's ranking depended on this competition, although an open ranking system was officially discouraged. Those that had become keypoints were essentially the schools with the highest promotion rates. Elimination of the entrance examinations for university and secondary school admission, and enactment of the minimum two year work requirement, deprived secondary school administrators of their basis for ranking. With students attending school in their neighbourhoods and then going off to the countryside or to a factory job on graduation, there was no clear differentiation between the schools. Thus, the competition between schools to recruit and train outstanding students disappeared. Cultural Revolution recruitment to university was based more on recommendation from one's work mates and approval by political authorities than on examination results.

But the removal of these inequalities carried their own substantial costs. In a sense the baby had been thrown out with the bath water. While the disappearance of the competition between school administrators was viewed positively, the reaction of secondary school students to the new structure was more problematic. The diverse, hierarchical school structure in the 1960s had produced some students who were more fiercely competitive (in many of the keypoint schools) and others who eschewed political activism entirely (more common in average or poor schools). The egalitarian structure produced not only a decline in activism but also a disinterest in academic study. Students no longer saw a direct relationship between their behaviour and their future. Not academic achievement nor class origin nor political manifestation determined one's job assignment in this period. Decisions regarding urban and rural job assignments for upper secondary graduates depended primarily on the number of siblings already given rural postings. Since a student's job prospects were fixed by his or her family situation, many sought to spend as little time in school as possible. In the 1960s there had been intensive competition to move from lower to upper secondary school; it is ironic that in the egalitarian atmosphere of the 1970s, in which an attempt was made to universalise upper secondary in many large cities, many students petitioned to be given job allocations directly upon lower secondary graduation, since upper secondary was perceived as two years wasted. Finally, despite pronouncements that the new system for recruiting university students would favour children of worker-peasant background, it was an open secret, recently confirmed, that the system - one that relied heavily on recommendation by party officials - worked primarily to the advantage of children of cadres.

SECONDARY EDUCATION AFTER MAO: QUALITY OVER QUANTITY

The death of Mao Zedong and the removal of his radical supporters led to a total repudiation and dismantling of the Cultural Revolution educational reforms. At the secondary level, the new leadership found the stress on quantity over quality and the elimination of distinctions between schools most objectionable. A return to the 'golden age of education', as some were now referring to the period before 1966, was deemed necessary. But such a transformation could not be accomplished immediately. The changes wrought by the Cultural Revolution had been too great. For example, in 1965 there had been 18,102 regular secondary schools; by 1976 there were 192,152 such schools.[7] Since 1977, the transformation process had had a dual thrust, corresponding to short and long-term priorities. The most immediate need was to convince educators, teachers, students, and intellectuals generally that the pursuit of academic excellence would be duly recognised and rewarded, that the Chinese Communist Party was committed to restoring an educational system capable of training specialised and high-level technical manpower. Also of importance, although less immediate, was a return to the 'balanced' educational structure of the 1960s, with regular, specialist, vocational and agricultural secondary schools again providing options for students and training a variety of skilled personnel.

To meet the first priority - the pursuit of quality - the keypoint school system was restored, and made more hierarchical and competitive than it had been in the 1960s.[8] Although most of the newly designated keypoints were merely reinstated from the 1960s, administrative control was now more complex. Twenty of the best primary and secondary schools around the country were to be run directly by the Ministry of Education as national keypoints. In addition, medium and large cities could run key schools both on an all-city basis and more narrowly within their individual districts and suburban counties. Each district was allowed to run two or three key secondary schools, subject to local discretion. Provincial education bureaux were authorised to run key schools on an all-province basis and more narrowly within individual prefectures and counties. Prefectures and counties also were allowed to run their own key schools.[9] These overlapping administrative relationships had the potential to be a much more hierarchical system than previously. With keypoints at county, prefectural, municipal and national levels, a much tighter rank order of school quality could be maintained. Moreover, so that no school would feel completely slighted, it was announced that ordinary schools should be run according to the same requirements as key schools, with those that were successful to be gradually accepted into the key school fold.[10] Key schools that were poorly run risked the loss of such status. The most important indicator of a school's performance was its promotion rate to university. Teachers and administrators were praised and often given financial remuneration when their efforts led to promotion rate increases. Students (and their parents), fully aware that entrance to a key school greatly enhanced the possibility of university entrance, returned to their books, motivated once more. By the end of 1979, there were 5,200 key secondary schools in the country, containing 5,200,000 students, about 8.63% of all secondary school students.[11]

Teachers and administrators at the more than 180,000 ordinary schools did their best to duplicate key school conditions by dividing students by ability and devoting attention primarily to those in the 'keypoint classroom'. The consequences - particularly the social costs - of this restratification of the regular secondary schools will be discussed below.

Of equal importance in the long run is the restoration of balance to the secondary school structure. Just prior to the Cultural Revolution the issue of balance had been raised, leading to a great expansion in vocational schooling in 1964 and 1965, as is shown in Table 4.2. Although such schools were not considered as desirable as regular upper secondary schools or specialist schools, the increasing threat of rustication faced by urban youths who had finished regular lower or upper secondary and could go no further helped fill even vocational school classrooms.[12] Thus, 31% of all secondary school students in 1965 were in vocational and agricultural secondary schools as compared with the 65.2% in regular lower and upper secondary. By 1977 a miniscule number were in vocational schooling, while 99% were in regular lower and upper secondary. In absolute numbers the change was even more striking. In 1965, just over 8 million students were in lower secondary and 1.3 million in upper secondary. By 1977 there were close to 50 million in lower secondary and 18 million in upper secondary. Considering that secondary graduates already had experienced difficulties in finding urban employment by the mid-1960s, it is not surprising that the enormous numbers of secondary graduates in the late 1970s should have been temporarily unemployable, particularly since urban youths were no longer being compelled to rusticate, the large majority of the 17 million youths who had gone to the countryside in the 1960s and 1970s had returned to the cities and been given priority in job placement, and around 14 million urban workers had been recruited from the countryside over this period.[13] In Shanghai, 85% of the 1977 secondary graduates were, to use the Chinese euphemism, 'waiting for work' (daiye). Of the 1978 graduates, 72% waited for work; in 1979, the equivalent figure was 61%.[14] The waiting period was around two years.

As Table 4.2 reveals, the restoration of balance is likely to be a slow process. By 1982, fully 96.3% of all secondary school students were still in regular, academic track schooling. The greatest change has been in the declining numbers of upper secondary students. In 1977, upper secondary students constituted 26.3% of all students in secondary schools; by 1982 the percentage had dropped to 13.6% with the forecast for further decline over the next few years. From a high of 18 million in 1977, the number of upper secondary students has dropped to around 6.4 million. In contrast, although the absolute numbers of lower secondary students is also dropping - from just under 50 million in 1977 to 41.4 million in 1981 - the percentage of students at the lower secondary level is increasing. By 1982, over 82.7% of all

Table 4.2

STUDENTS IN VARIOUS FORMS OF SECONDARY SCHOOLING, BY PERCENTAGE
(Each unit represents 10,000 students)

Year	Lower Secondary Students		Upper Secondary Students		Secondary Specialist Students		Agricultural Secondary & Vocational sch. Students	
		%		%		%		%
1949	83.2	65.6	20.7	16.3	22.9	18.1	--	--
1957	537.7	76.0	90.4	12.7	77.8	11.0	2.2	0.3
1960	858.46	58.0	167.49	11.3	221.59	15.0	230.20	15.6
1961	698.40	67.4	153.30	14.8	120.30	11.6	61.77	5.9
1962	618.83	74.3	133.90	16.1	53.49	6.4	26.66	3.2
1963	638.03	76.2	123.52	14.7	45.14	5.4	30.78	3.7
1964	729.28	71.5	124.67	12.2	53.16	5.2	112.34	11.0
1965	802.89	56.1	130.80	9.1	54.73	3.8	443.34	31.0
1976	4352.9	73.7	1483.6	25.1	69.0	1.1	--	--
1977	4979.9	72.7	1800	26.3	68.9	1.0	--	--
1979	4613.0	76.3	1292.0	21.3	119.9	1.9	23.5	0.39
1980	4538.29	79.9	969.79	17.1	124.34	2.2	45.36	0.8
1981	4144.58	82.6	714.98	14.2	106.90	2.1	48.09	0.99
1982	3887.97	82.7	640.52	13.6	103.94	2.2	70.36	1.5

* For a more complete picture of enrollment in secondary specialist and regular secondary schools from 1949-82 which, however, does not break the figures down by lower and upper secondary, see Statistical Yearbook of China 1981 (Chinese Edition), p.511.

Sources: For 1960-1965, see Gu Mingyuan, 'Lun zhongdeng jiaoyu di renwu he jiegou', Beijing Shifan Daxue Xuebao, No.5, 25 August, 1982, p.7.
For 1949, 1957, 1976 and 1979, see Zhongguo Baike Nianjian 1980, pp. 536, 544.
For 1977 see Zhongguo Qingnian Bao, 24 June, 1982, p.1 and Statistical Yearbook of China, 1981 (English Edition), p.451.
For 1980, see Zhongguo Baike Nianjian, 1981, p.471.
For 1981, see Zhongguo Jingji Nianjian, 1982, p. V-389.
For 1982, see Zhongguo Baike Nianjian, 1983, p.595.

secondary school students were in lower secondary, the highest percentage since the founding of the People's Republic. During this transitional period, educational opportunities beyond lower secondary have become greatly constricted. Since 1977, many upper secondary schools have been shut down, transformed into lower secondary schools, or had individual classrooms converted to vocational schooling. While school closures have been common, particularly in the countryside, vocational and specialist school expansion has been slow, and subject to numerous restrictions. For example, many provinces have issued orders forbidding the construction of any new vocational schools. Nor is the state willing to allocate much funding for vocational and technical education; the money is to come from local budgets or out of the financial plans of enterprises. Nor will the state assign jobs to graduates from vocational schools.[15] The decline in the number of secondary schools, particularly at the upper secondary level, is documented in Table 4.3.

SECONDARY SCHOOLING AS EDUCATIONAL SELECTION: CURRICULUM AND EXAMINATIONS

While secondary schools are frequently admonished to train good labourers for society as well as qualified students for institutes of higher learning, in practice the two functions have not been treated as co-equal. With as many as 12 million students currently graduating from lower secondary schools, only 3 million of whom move on to regular upper secondary schools, out of which 300-350,000 go on to university, the competition throughout one's secondary school years can be relentless. This competitive atmosphere is exacerbated since over 95% of the students are in regular, academic track schooling. University entrance is the prize, one that provides an 'iron rice bowl', since university graduates are assigned jobs by the state. Once a position is allocated, an individual is virtually assured of retaining his job until retirement. Moreover, because of the widespread practice of giving preferential treatment to children of retiring employees when hiring new workers in state factories, offices, commercial units, and universities, to some extent the iron rice bowl can even be passed down to the next generation.[16]

Promotion within the educational system is dependent on examination performance. Unified examinations at the municipal or county level determine who will move from primary school to lower secondary and lower to upper secondary. A nationally unified examination determines who will go on to university. The secondary school curriculum is unified and fixed by the Ministry of Education. Both the curriculum and the teaching plan have been arranged with the promotion examinations in mind. For example, university candidates are divided into two major examination groups: liberal arts and science and

Table 4.3

SECONDARY SCHOOLS AND UPPER SECONDARY STUDENTS, 1965-1981

Year	Total Number of Secondary Schools*	Regular Secondary Schools (Lower and Upper)	Upper Secondary Schools	Upper Secondary Students
1965	80,993	18,102		1,308,000
1976	194,595	192,152		14,836,000
1977			65,000	18,000,000
1979	147,266	144,233		12,920,000
1980	124,760	118,377	31,300	9,697,900
1981	112,505	106,718	24,447	7,149,800
1982	107,829	101,649	20,874	6,405,200

Source: For 1965, 1976 and 1979, see Zhongguo Baike Nianjian 1980, pp.535-536.

For 1977, see Zhongguo Qingnian Bao, 24 June, 1982, p.1.

For 1980, see Zhongguo Baike Nianjian 1981, p.471.

For 1981, see Zhongguo Jingji Nianjian 1982, p.V-389.

For 1982, see Zhongguo Baike Nianjian 1983, p.595.

* The following schools are included in the category of secondary schools: secondary technical schools and teacher training schools, regular secondary schools, and vocational and agricultural secondary schools.

engineering (including agriculture and medicine). All candidates take politics, Chinese language, foreign language and mathematics. Liberal arts candidates add history and geography; science and engineering candidates add chemistry, physics and biology. For 1983, the examination weights were as follows: Chinese language and mathematics, 120 points each; biology, 50 points; all the rest, 100 points each.[17]

Although there are local variations in teaching plans, with working drafts of several plans circulated by local education bureaus, the variations are not great. One fairly standard arrangement divides upper secondary students planning to apply for university into liberal arts and science programmes. This division commonly takes place during the second and third year. Table 4.4 shows one proposed teaching plan for keypoint secondary schools in Guangzhou in 1982. Keypoint schools, however, are a small minority of all secondary schools. Most of the students are in ordinary secondary schools, with many slated to become vocational and agricultural schools in the future. Students in ordinary schools and even vocational programmes are also eligible to sit for the university exams. Table 4.5 compares proposed teaching plans for keypoint upper secondary schools, ordinary upper secondary schools not yet converted to a three year programme, and vocational/agricultural classrooms/schools.

FROM PRIMARY SCHOOL GRADUATION TO UPPER SECONDARY:
RECRUITMENT UP THE EDUCATIONAL LADDER

One of the major themes of this chapter is the transitional nature of arrangements at the secondary level. As China seeks to reduce the number of students in regular schooling and promote vocational education, looks at factors other than examination scores in promotion decisions, strives to guarantee quality through concentration of resources in keypoint schools, secondary school enrollment policies have become rather complex. In this section we will examine lower and upper secondary recruitment patterns. Since most cities have relatively similar policies, to avoid confusion we will take one city - Guangzhou (Canton) - as an example, using data from 1981 and 1982.[18]

Students graduating from primary school in 1981 took three examinations, in Chinese language, mathematics and English. Those who scored around 240 points (out of a total 300 points) could register for keypoint schools, of which there were six. They would also list 'reference choices,' of which there were four, one in each district of the city. These reference choices had been listed as district keypoints prior to 1981, the name change coinciding with the decision in 1980 to concentrate resources in a small number of key schools (see below). Those not accepted by a keypoint, which had first choice, or a reference school, would be allocated to an ordinary school

Table 4.4

TEACHING PLAN FOR FULL-DAY SIX YEAR KEYPOINT SECONDARY SCHOOLS
(Working Draft, January 1982 - Guangzhou)

Course	Lower Secondary			Upper Secondary (hours per week in class)					Total time in Class Programme	
	1	2	3	1	2A	2B	3A	3B	A	B
Politics	2	2	2	2	2	2	2	2	384	384
Chinese Language	6	6	6	5	7	4	8	4	1,208	1,000
Mathematics	5	6	6	5	3	6	3	6	906	1,086
Foreign Language	5	5	5	5	5	5	5	4	960	932
Physics		2	3	4		4		5	292	560
Chemistry			3	3	3	4		4	288	432
History	3	2		3			3		350	266
Geography	3	2			2	2	3		328	234
Biology	2	2			2			2	200	192
Hygiene			2						64	64
Physical Education	2	2	2	2	2	2	2	2	384	384
Music	1	1	1						100	100
Fine Art	1	1	1						100	100
Hrs/wk. in class	30	31	31	29	26	29	26	29	5,554	5,734
Labour Training	2 weeks			4 weeks					576	

NOTE: (a) Programme A in Upper Secondary 2 and 3 is for those who select a liberal arts speciality; Programme B is for those who select a science speciality.

(b) During the labour training period, there are 4 classes per day in Lower Secondary and 6 per day in Upper Secondary.

* I would like to thank Lau Wing Fong of the Chinese University of Hong Kong for making his collection of primary and secondary teaching plans available to me.

Secondary Schooling

Table 4.5: TEACHING PLANS FOR VARIOUS KINDS OF UPPER SECONDARY SCHOOLS (Working Draft, January 1982 - Guangzhou)

Course	Keypoint schools (hours/week in class)								(hrs/wk. in class)				
	Classrooms not divided by coursework			Classrooms divided into Arts & Science students					Ordinary Schools		Vocational and Agric. Schools		
	1	2	3	1	2A	2B	3A	3B	1	2	1	2	3
Politics	2	2	2	2	2	2	2	2	2	2	2	2	2
Chinese Language	5	4	4	5	7	4	8	4	4	4	5	4	4
Mathematics	5	5	5	5	3	6	3	6	6	6	5	5	5
Foreign Language	5	5	4	5	5	5	5	4	3	3	2	2	2
Physics	4	3	4	4		4		5	4	4	4	4	
Chemistry	3	3	3	3	3	4		4	3	3	3	3	
History	3			3			3		2				
Geography		2			2	2	3			2			
Physical education	2	2	2	2	2	2	2	2	2	2	2	2	2
Biology		2			2			2					
Elective Courses		4	4										
Vocational Classes									6	6			
Specialised Technical Courses											8	8	16
Labor Training	4 WEEKS			4 WEEKS					2	2	2	2	2
Hrs/wk in class	29	30	30	29	26	29	26	29	34	34	33	32	33

NOTES: (a) Programme A in Upper Secondary 2 and 3 is for those who select a liberal arts speciality; program B is geared for those who select a science specialty.
(b) During the labour training period, there are 6 classes per day in Keypoint Schools; Ordinary and Vocational Schools can arrange labour training in accordance with their regular vocational or specialised courses.
(c) The physics and chemistry textbooks for vocational schools are geared to a 2-year programme, and are the less rigorous of the two levels of textbook available.

close to home. Since primary schools were in transition from a five to a six year programme, only 70% of primary school students were allowed to advance to lower secondary. The remaining 30% would stay behind for a sixth year. Lower secondary students applying for regular upper secondary, middle-level teacher training schools, and vocational schools, took exams in politics, Chinese language, mathematics, physics, chemistry and English. The promotion rate from lower secondary was around 70%, with those unable to continue their schooling enrolling in street or school run tutorial classes, or vocational training classes. Those below the age of 17 could try to gain entrance to upper secondary the following year. At the lower secondary level, 1,440 of the 16,704 new enrollees entered keypoint schools (many simply moving from lower to upper secondary at the same school).

In 1982, there were some important changes. First, the municipality had restored its unified promotion examination, with primary and lower secondary graduates listing three choices in order of preference. Those not accepted by any of their choices would be allocated to a school in their neighbourhood. The examinations for lower and upper secondary remained the same, although in fairness to primary school graduates from districts or schools where English teaching was not up to standard, the English exam scores were weighted only 50% of the math and Chinese exams. Since many upper secondary schools had not yet reverted to a three year programme, it was decided that the highest scoring 53.3% of the lower secondary graduates would go to schools with three year programmes, with the rest moving on to two year programmes. Primary and lower secondary graduates seeking admission to keypoint schools had to take a special test in physical education. Recruitment of lower secondary students by municipal and county keypoints was restricted to their localities, although they could range more broadly, as in 1981, for their upper secondary recruits. Special provision was made for those who had particularly distinguished themselves. For example, lower secondary graduates who had been designated 'three-good students' (good in academics, morality, and athletics) at national, provincial, or municipal levels were allowed to move on to teacher training schools, vocational schools, or upper secondary at their own schools (including keypoint schools), without sitting for the unified exams. There were 40 such lower secondary graduates in 1981. Those in ordinary schools with similar distinctions seeking entrance to keypoint upper secondary schools had ten points added to their exam scores. This accounted for an additional 28 students. Those who had distinguished themselves in individual or team athletic contests at provincial or municipal level had ten points added to their exam scores. There were 124 primary school graduates and 54 lower secondary graduates so rewarded. To put this in perspective, over 41,000 students had applied for lower or upper secondary schooling in

Secondary Schooling

Guangzhou in 1982, so the number benefitting from factors other than exam score was small indeed. Finally, it should be noted that teacher training and vocational schools had still not become popular with students; such schools attracted only 2,000 applicants.[19]

INEQUALITIES IN SECONDARY EDUCATION

Considering the importance accorded university entrance in China, as well as the radical critique of the pre-Cultural Revolution educational pyramid, it is interesting to examine how much inequality has crept back with the return to quality, diversity and student options. While comprehensive statistical data is lacking, the more forthcoming Chinese press of recent years provides some answers.

Entrance to university. Selected data on university enrollees for 1979-1981 are provided in Table 4.6. These figures require explanation. China lags behind most socialist countries in the proportion of female university students. One reason is a prevalent attitude in China that girls develop more quickly than boys, but begin to decline in ability by the last years of lower secondary. One explanation given by Chinese educators to a visiting scholar attributed the decline to the smaller brain size of women. At least partly because of this apparently widespread belief in China, women often have to score higher than men to gain entrance to the best upper secondary keypoints and universities. Although such discrimination has at times been criticised in the press, the practice has continued.[20] It should also be noted that the moderate increase in female

Table 4.6

CHARACTERISTICS OF NEW UNIVERSITY

STUDENTS (in percentages)

Year	Women	Children of workers and poor and lower-middle peasants	Members of Communist Youth League	National Minorities
1979	22.52%	54.31%	79.23%	3.63%
1980	23.57%	55.58%	82.96%	4.28%
1981	25.12%	56.90%	86.39%	4.77%

Source: Zhongguo Baike Nianjian 1982, p.537.

enrollment from 1979-1981 may not have made up for a drop in their enrollment over the 1976-1979 period.[21]

The figures on children of workers and poor and lower-middle peasants are a welcome improvement over recent statistics that, for example, claimed that 97.4% of the 1977 freshman class was from the families of workers, peasants, armymen, cadres and intellectuals[22] and that over 99% of freshmen recruited in 1979 were from families of workers, peasants, and other labouring people.[23] One would still like to know how many children of peasants are able to enter the best urban universities,[24] what percentage of successful peasant children are actually from well-off suburban areas or keypoint schools in county towns, how many of those designated peasant are actually 'urban rusticated youths,' and so forth. As we will see in Table 4.7 below, the Chinese press is beginning to address such distinctions.

The high percentage of Communist Youth League (CYL) members gaining entrance to university is not surprising, nor should it be interpreted to mean that ideo-political criteria for university entrance have once again become important. In fact, as I have argued elsewhere, it may be an indication of the reduced importance of such criteria in admissions decisions.[25] It apparently has become common for upper secondary schools to recruit virtually all students with the potential to pass the university entrance exams into the CYL. Whole classrooms of students in some keypoint schools have become league members.

Six percent of China's population consists of national minorities. There are ten institutes of higher learning considered 'nationalities institutes,' at which minority cadres are trained. In 1981, these institutes enrolled 2,345 students, many of whom would be national minorities. Thus, perhaps 10-15% of China's national minority enrollees would likely be at these nationalities institutes.

Additional data has recently been provided for 1982 enrollees. This data is summarised in Table 4.7. Once again, some interpretation is necessary. First, the success rate of 16.34% represents only those who actually took the examination. Most provinces have a preliminary exam to screen out those upper secondary graduates considered unlikely to pass the actual entrance exam. According to press reports, this preliminary exam, combined with 'persuasion' by school authorities, has convinced many mediocre students to forgo their studies long before the exams.[26] Surveys in some districts in Beijing showed that 52% of upper secondary students felt they had no chance of entering a university.[27] The ratio of graduating upper secondary students to university enrollees was only 9.12%.[28] It is also interesting to note that only 55.79% of the 1982 entrants were current year graduates, as were just over 50% of 1983 examinees. In 1980 and 1981, around 70% of the applicants were current year

Secondary Schooling

Table 4.7

NEW UNIVERSITY STUDENTS IN 1982

TOTAL: 305,000

	%
Promotion Rate of Those Taking The Examination:	16.34
(increase of 5.41% over 1981)	
Current Year Graduates of Urban Secondary Schools:	21.40
Current Year Graduates from county Towns:	18.76
Current Year Graduates from Rural Areas:	15.63
Urban Rusticated Youths and Returned Village Youths:	20.93
Workers, cadres, Transferred and Demobilised Soldiers and Others:	23.28*
	100.00

Source: Shanghai Wenhui Bao, 3 November, 1982, p.1

(* Most of the successful university enrollees in the last category on Table 4.7 would likely be former upper secondary graduates repeating the exams, since only 2.4% of all university applicants in 1981 were workers, cadres, or demobilised soldiers.)

graduates.[29] Moreover, as late as 1979, 71.79% of the enrollees had been current year graduates.[30] This reflects a trend the leadership regards as serious. In their efforts to increase promotion rates to university, schools - and often county education bureaux as well - frequently interrupt schooling well before term's end to bring together those with the greatest potential to succeed on the entrance exams for extensive review sessions. Participants include current year as well as previous year graduates. Published figures from some districts show these review classes to be almost double normal class size (70 students instead of 40).[31] Although provincial education bureaux have taken strong measures to stop this practice, the results have yet to be effective. Nor is this practice limited to suburban and rural counties. Individual schools in urban areas run their own tutorial classes to prepare prior graduates for the examinations. Under these conditions, it is impossible for schools to adhere to the annual study outline. In particular, courses not being tested on the exams will be ignored.

Finally, using statistics provided by individual Chinese

educational institutions some scholars have argued that students from families of intellectuals and officials now predominate in many of the best tertiary institutions. For example, at Zhejiang University, 25% of the students were reported to be from a peasant background, 15% from workers' families, 23% from the families of officials and other administrative employees, and 28% from intellectual families.[32]

The Debate Over Keypoint Schools.[33] Among the most controversial of current policies is the continued existence of keypoint secondary schools. When the keypoint system was restored in 1978, these schools were responsible for accelerating the development of talented students for the universities. From 1978-1980, the 5,200 keypoint secondary schools competed with each other and with ordinary schools to prove their worth by registering high university promotion rates. This competition led to some serious side effects; since the main criterion for measuring the performance of secondary schools was university promotion rate, both keypoints and ordinary schools devoted attention only to 'promising' students. By autumn, 1980, it was decided that, despite the side effects, the keypoint strategy was correct. To allow the very best keypoints to concentrate more on cultivating talented students and less on constantly competing with lesser keypoints and ordinary schools on the annual university entrance examinations, around 700 of the nation's best schools were singled out for priority investment. In addition, many keypoint universities began to 'establish links' (guagou) with the best keypoint secondary schools in their area. Through such links, national keypoint universities outside Beijing hoped to draw some of the top local students away from such schools as Beijing University, Qinghua University, or the University of Science and Technology, considered the country's top schools. For secondary school administrators and students, such links removed some examination pressure, although the students still had to meet a minimum standard to be accepted at the linked university.

If one purpose of sharpening the top of the pyramid had been to convince less well endowed secondary schools to cease attempting to compete with the best keypoints, the actual result was often just the opposite. Ordinary schools, as well as less favoured keypoints, such as those at county level, stepped up their competitive efforts. With local schools unable to meet their 'quota' of university enrollees likely to be chosen for transformation into vocational or agricultural secondary schools, it seemed rational for school administrators to violate provincial or national guidelines if such violations might lead to a higher promotion rate. Thus, constant exhortations from higher levels that secondary schools should be concerned with educating <u>all</u> their students, not just promising ones, often fell on deaf ears. Students not considered 'university timber' quickly became demoralised by the lack of attention. Even in some keypoint schools, as many as half the graduating lower secondary class was unable to continue into their school's upper section. Such rejects were hungrily absorbed by schools of lesser rank. Lesser keypoint and ordinary schools were running faster and faster and falling further and further behind. By late 1982 prominent intellectuals like Fei Xiaotong were calling for the abolition of keypoint primary and secondary schools.[34] In March 1983, an article in the authoritative People's Daily complained that the keypoints had outlived their usefulness. As the author put it, "the keypoints are too key, the ordinary schools are too weak. The ordinary schools cannot learn from the experience of the keypoints so the keypoints are isolated.... Under these conditions, even if these schools have a very high promotion rate, it has lost its significance."[35] The debate over the value of the keypoint system is likely to persist. Officials at the Ministry of Education have staunchly defended it, while articles in the press claim that "the fact that their proportion of graduates entering universities reaches 90% and more proves [the keypoints'] worth."[36]

How successful have the keypoints been in producing university students? What specific advantages are they given over their competitors? Since these are sensitive issues, national statistics are not readily available. The first question is further complicated because available aggregate statistics tend to obscure the great variance between the best provincial and municipal keypoints (over 90% promotion rate) and the poorest county-run keypoints. In addition, just as keypoints are clearly distinguishable from one another, so are universities. Many of China's 715 universities are of questionable quality, including several hundred two- and three-year schools offering specialised (zhuanke) rather than regular (benke) courses. Ideally, one would like to obtain data that disaggregates the 94 key universities, or the 26 universities earmarked for priority investment through World Bank Funds, from lesser institutions. Data that differentiates keypoint secondary school by level of administration would also be helpful. With these caveats in mind, some limited data has appeared. In Sichuan province, in 1981, only 22% of the upper secondary graduates were in keypoint schools, but they made up 70% of the province's university recruits.[37] In Guangdong province in 1980, 50.89% of the students in the 16 provincially-run keypoints who took the university entrance exams 'passed' (not everyone who meets the passing standard makes it to university, however).[38] In Liaoning province, the keypoint promotion rate between 1979-1981 was about 33.3%; the rate for all upper secondary schools in the province was 1.22%.[39] In Inner Mongolia the best keypoints had a promotion rate of 60-70%.[40] A visiting scholar was told by two key universities in 1980 that 60-70% of their freshman classes came from key schools.[41]

The keypoint schools have been given a number of benefits denied ordinary schools. In terms of funding, key schools have larger budgets than ordinary schools, with the main difference lying in increased allocations for building construction and equipment. One key school in north China reported an allocation of 50,000 yuan in 1978 and 30,000 yuan in 1979 for the purchase of new equipment. Ordinary schools in the same city were granted only about 5,000 yuan each annually for this same budgetary item. The total budget reported for the school in 1979 was as follows:[42]

<u>Total: 189,000 yuan</u>

Wages:	95,000	yuan
Student Aid:	2,000	yuan
Maintenance of Equipment, Plant, etc.:	31,000	yuan
Staff Welfare:	5,000	yuan
Equipment:	30,000	yuan
Miscellaneous:	26,000	yuan

The key schools have also been given extra equipment such as television sets, tape recorders, and video-recording equipment outside their allocated expenditures. After the nation's best keypoints were singled out for priority investment in autumn 1980, various provinces began to list specific requirements for running keypoints well. For example, at a meeting of the principals of the 16 provincially-run keypoint secondary schools in Guangdong, the deputy head of the provincial education bureau spelled out some of the benefits to be accorded to these schools. Among others, they included the allocation of the most qualified teachers (upper secondary teachers should be graduates from four year tertiary normal schools; lower secondary teachers should be graduates from specialised two and three year normal colleges); first priority in the allocation and improvement of a wide range of equipment and facilities, such as student dormitories, language laboratories, athletic fields, libraries, faculty housing, and clinics; priority in the addition of an extra year of schooling for upper secondary students (from a two to a three year programme); limitations on the number of classrooms (24) in a school and students per classroom (48 in lower secondary and 46 in upper secondary) for municipal and district keypoints (provincial keypoints were even more restrictive and had been regulated earlier); recruitment throughout a county, district, municipality, or province, depending on the level of administration of the keypoint; the right to increase administrative, teaching or labouring personnel (provincial keypoints could increase their staff by 10%); the employment of three vice-principals; the allocation of 15 yuan per student for educational administrative expenses, a subsidy of 7.5 yuan per year for each lower secondary student and 15 yuan per year for each upper secondary student.[43]

RURAL SECONDARY SCHOOLING

In the preceding section we discussed various inequalities that have followed in the wake of the renewed stress on quality. With rural education the inequalities vis-a-vis urban education have been continuous. While education has not been a high priority budget item in China - of the 151 states in the world, China's per-capita expenses for education ranks third from the last - most of the available funds have been invested in the urban, regular school system.[44] As one source points out, it costs 6,900 yuan to educate the average urban child, usually from kindergarten through at least lower secondary school, and an additional 6,000-7,000 yuan to put him or her through a regular tertiary education programme. By contrast, the average expenditure for the entire education of a rural child, usually including up to five years of primary schooling and, for a far smaller number, three years of lower secondary, is about 1,600 yuan. The difference can be traced to poorer salaries, facilities, and educational materials in the countryside, in addition to the low educational attainments of rural youths.[45]

Rural education is expected to serve the needs of the rural economy, with organisation, staffing, curriculum and funding in the main to be provided locally. Educational efforts in each area are therefore part of a local integrated system, with rural schools much more dependent on local agricultural bureaux, production brigades, youth and women's organisations, and so forth, than on outside educational authorities.[46] The great variation one finds in rural education stems from the rather limited direction and control provided by the central authorities.[47] In rural communes and brigades in which education is accorded low priority, little investment has been provided.

At the secondary level, rural education seems to exhibit many of the familiar problems of urban education, often in exacerbated form. For example, common problems in the urban schools have included the low quality of the majority of students in the ordinary schools, the increasing difficulty of moving from lower to upper secondary, the concentration on those students with the potential to pass the university entrance examinations, and the unpopularity of vocational schooling. These are also problems in the countryside.

In the rural areas, the problems start at the primary level. While 90% of those eligible by age are on the rolls, only 60% attend regularly and just 30% are up to standard.[48] Of those who do graduate, only about 60% can be promoted to lower secondary, with fewer than 20% of lower secondary graduates entering upper secondary.[49] For all schools - urban and rural - according to 1980 figures, 75.5% of primary school graduates entered lower secondary and 45% of lower secondary graduates entered upper secondary or secondary specialist schools.[50] To take one example, Jiangsu province began to adjust its lower secondary/upper secondary ratio in 1979. Upper secondary schools in the province recruited only 270,000 lower secondary graduates that year - 25% of the graduating class - after recruiting 500,000 in 1976. They planned to recruit 250,000 per year through the early 1980s, to accommodate 60-70% of urban lower secondary graduates but only 20-30% of rural lower secondary graduates.[51] Other provinces have comparable situations. In Guangdong, only about 30% of lower secondary graduates can enter upper secondary; in the city of Guangzhou the promotion rate has been 70-75%.[52]

An explanation of the problems of rural secondary education often starts with an analysis of peasant attitudes. Reading through a wide variety of articles and investigation reports in the Chinese press, one theme repeatedly suggests itself: rural education is supported locally if it will lead to an 'escape from the countryside' (tiaochu nongmen). As one report described it, students in rural secondary schools tend to be divided into those with good academic achievement, who study eagerly and "make every effort to be noticed," and those with poor academic achievement who "make use of the opportunity to screw around for two years" until it is time to return to their families and take part in labour.[53] It is not merely the individual student and his parents who lay stress on escaping from the countryside by gaining entrance to university. Local cadres and educational officials from county level on down support these aspirations in their attempts to maintain high promotion rates to upper secondary and university.[54] Among those who see secondary education as terminal, drop-out rates are high. In Shaanxi province, the drop-out rate in the countryside in lower secondary is 15%, rising to more than 30% in some districts.[55] There are a variety of reasons why students withdraw from school, including inability to afford tuition, the assignment of non-agricultural jobs on the basis of family connections rather than educational attainments, the poor quality of schools and teachers, the production responsibility system (which puts a premium on extra labour power), and the attitude that educating girls is unnecessary.[56]

Even those who make it to agricultural colleges often find a return to the countryside unrewarding. Because of low pay and poor working conditions, 500,000 of the 860,000 agro-technicians trained since 1949 have left the villages to work in the urban areas. In the past few years, half the graduates never returned to their home villages. For every 10,000 peasants, there are less than four qualified agricultural experts.[57] Currently, concerted efforts are being made to reverse this outflow. University enrollment regulations for 1983 stipulate that colleges of agriculture, forestry, medicine and teaching - which traditionally have trouble recruiting students - will lower the admission standard for applicants in rural areas who agree to return upon graduation.[58]

Educational development in the rural areas will continue to vary greatly depending on local conditions. A recent 'Notice on Some Problems in the Strengthening and Reform of Rural Schooling' reiterated that under the Party's 'walking on two legs' strategy, each locality must solve its own funding problems.[59] Thus, front page coverage in China Youth Daily was accorded to a brigade in Zhejiang province that offered any child of a brigade member who made it to university a 1,000 yuan scholarship. Those going to upper secondary were given 50 yuan a year; lower secondary students got 20 yuan a year. Another brigade has stipulated that no children under 15 are allowed to work in the labour force; they must attend school, with education fees from primary school to upper secondary to come from the brigade's public welfare funds.[60] Such investment in 'science and culture' is not common.

One complicating factor affecting educational reform in the countryside is the basic contradiction that apparently exists between state policy and local attitudes. The thrust of current policy is the shutting down or transformation of upper secondary schools into agricultural secondary schools. But county educational bureaux, arguing that the peasants regard such schools as inferior, have resisted this transformation. Reports from China indicate that recruitment to such schools is difficult, with most of the students enrolled only because they failed the qualifying exam for 'regular' schools. For example, only 40 of Yunnan province's 129 counties had set up agricultural secondary schools through 1980.[61]

Acknowledging the unpopularity of these schools, several tentative reforms have been introduced. In Jiangsu province, the system of student recruitment and allocation has been altered for autumn 1983. Formerly, students for agricultural secondary schools were recruited together with university students, with the low scorers on this unified examination becoming entrants to the agricultural schools. Generally, these students had little knowledge of agricultural production techniques and even less interest. No longer tied to the university exam, the new plan emphasises the recruitment of educated youths with at least two years of practical experience in agricultural production and others already serving in a technical capacity. Graduates will be expected to work in their home counties.[62] In Liaoning province, a small number of schools in the countryside are experimenting with a four year lower secondary programme, which offers enough academic coursework to prepare students for the upper secondary entrance examination, at the same time increasing the time spent on technical and vocational education.[63]

Finally, the blame for the lack of development of agricultural secondary schools is being laid at the feet of leading cadres in the countryside. A revealing investigation report from Zhejiang province published in People's Daily claimed that cadres and educational officials had long argued that it was foolish to expand agricultural schools in the countryside since the masses would not support such terminal schooling. They wanted schooling which offered their children the possibility of a university education and a future in urban China. The investigation concluded that such desires were in fact only held by the cadres and educators themselves. Ordinary peasants saw no realistic possibility that their children could get to university and welcomed agricultural secondary schools. By pointing to the discrepancy between the will of the officials (guan yi) and the will of the masses (min yi), pressure has been put on cadres at the county level and below to take the lead in implementing the national policy of educational transformation.[64]

CONCLUSION AND FUTURE DIRECTIONS

Our discussion of Chinese secondary education has stressed four basic characteristics: (1) The transitional nature of the current system; (2) its hierarchical structure; (3) the trend back to the diversity of the 1960s; and (4) the value many attach to the mobility function, leading to university entrance, over other functions. For the immediate future, these characteristics should continue to dominate.

Hierarchy and diversity are likely to figure prominently over the next several years. The high priority accorded to developing outstanding university students, leading to greater concentration of resources in a smaller number of keypoint secondary schools, has already turned the best keypoints into university preparatory schools, sending virtually entire graduating classes on to higher education. The gap between these schools and other keypoints, not to mention ordinary schools, should continue to widen. At the same time, the transformation of China's unbalanced secondary school structure - with over 95% of all students in regular, academic track classrooms - has become a high priority. The focus of current policy is at the upper secondary level. Options similar to those of the 1960s are being reintroduced for lower secondary graduates, although most of the options being offered are for the unpopular vocational and agricultural secondary schools. Following a recent government circular, secondary school transformation, with its concomitant elimination of opportunities for regular upper secondary schooling, is being stepped up. By 1987, upper secondary vocational school students are expected to account for over 40% of the total upper secondary enrollment. By 1990, the number of students in vocational and technical schools in the countryside is expected to equal or slightly surpass those in regular upper secondary schools.[65] It may be difficult, however, to convince the localities to meet this latter target. Because of financial difficulties and a lack of opportunities for graduates, there were 830 fewer agricultural secondary schools in 1981 than there had been in 1980, while the number of students in such schools declined by 16.3% over this same period. This trend, however, was reversed in 1982.[66]

What is the likely secondary school structure after transformation? One recent proposal from Shanghai suggests seven kinds of schools, most of which are already in place:[67]

1. <u>Lower secondary schools</u> *(chuji zhongxue)*: These schools would provide basic knowledge in a three year programme. In the rural areas, depending on need and finances, vocational courses could be an important part of the programme.

2. <u>Complete secondary schools</u> *(wanquan zhongxue)*: These schools would be the best in the country, containing lower and upper secondary sections of three years each, with the best lower secondary graduates moving on to the upper secondary section. As cuts in academic track upper secondary enrollment continue - by 1985 the number of students entering regular upper secondary schools is projected to be about 2.8 million, one million less than in 1980 - these schools, as the major route to university, will become increasingly competitive. Keypoint schools and, perhaps, a small number of the best ordinary schools will be in this category. For graduates of these schools unable to continue on to university, further vocational training in a tutorial school (see below) for one or two years prior to job assignment will be available.

3. <u>Comprehensive upper secondary</u> *(zonghe gaozhong)*: These schools will include both regular and vocational school classrooms, each with a three year programme. Students will choose which track to enter, with adjustments possible after the first year. Those on the regular track can take the university entrance exam; those on the vocational track will receive a certificate upon graduation. Most of the current ordinary schools should fill this category.

4. <u>Secondary specialist schools</u> *(zhongdeng zhuanye xuexiao)*: These schools, as before, will train middle-level professional personnel, in a four to five year programme. Since 1977, they have been recruiting a majority of their students from upper secondary graduates. Gradually, they have been returning to the pre-Cultural Revolution practice of recruiting lower secondary graduates. The schools should remain popular with students although, because they are expensive to establish and operate, expansion will be minimal. In 1980 secondary specialist schools recruited 467,600 students. The current plan calls for 500,000

recruits in 1985.

5. Workers' training schools *(jigong xuexiao)*: These schools will train workers in fields requiring relatively high or difficult technical skills, in a three year programme. Those who perform well in these schools can transfer to secondary specialist schools for one additional year, after which they will be qualified as assistant technicians. At present, because of low quality, the offering of unpopular specialties, and problematic job prospects upon graduation, these schools have had trouble recruiting students. In 1983, these schools recruited 280,000 students. In future, they are likely to take on the task of training in-service workers and job-awaiting youths.

6. Vocational schools *(zhiye xuexiao)*: These schools will train labourers with relatively simple skills in a two year programme. The greatest expansion during the Sixth Five Year Plan (1981-1985) will occur in vocational (and agricultural) secondary schools. By 1985, 1.4 million students are expected to enter these schools, compared to the 240,000 entrants of 1980. Compared with 1980, the number of students enrolled in vocational secondary schools will have increased 6.5 times in 1985, and the number of students enrolled in agricultural secondary schools, 7.1 times in 1985.

7. Tutorial schools *(buxi xuexiao)*: These will be 'adjustment' *(tiaojie)* schools, recruiting students of lower secondary level or above for a variable programme of one to four years. Academic and vocational courses will be offered, with flexible schedules for those needing day classes, evening classes, or Sunday classes. Some youths unable to attend the schools listed in categories two through six above will be accommodated here.

Successful implementation of the above proposal - which represents current thinking in large cities like Shanghai - should alleviate some of the problems associated with the unbalanced secondary school structure. By tracking students earlier, however, the hierarchical nature of secondary schooling will be reinforced. Entrance to a complete secondary school or, for some students, a specialist school, will remain the top choice; entrance to a vocational (agricultural) secondary or workers' training school will remain at the bottom. In part because such distinctions are widespread throughout Chinese society, the less popular forms of schooling will not be made dead ends; 'escape routes' are being built in for talented students. The possibility of students in workers' training schools moving on to specialist schools has already been mentioned. In addition, the above proposal allows outstanding graduates of vocational and workers' training schools to enter tutorial schools and later sit for the

Secondary Schooling

university entrance examinations.

With the installation of a meritocratic educational system designed to produce efficiently the talent required for the Four Modernisations, the secondary schools - in meeting their mobility function - are likely to face increasing difficulty in their socialisation function. The combined effect of a large population increase, an expansion of basic level schooling, and the virtual disappearance of the Maoist vision has been to raise the hopes and limit the opportunities of Chinese youths. At the same time, ideo-political appeals, seven years after the repudiation of the Cultural Revolution, still encounter a skeptical, even cynical audience. In an increasingly technological future, it will not be easy to convince those unable to climb the educational ladder that they are nonetheless essential to the modernisation process; that, to use a 1965 slogan, 'all work is for the revolution.' In the final analysis, the Chinese may discover, as Mao warned, that the pursuit of 'modernisation' has heavy social costs.

Chapter Five

HIGHER EDUCATION: THE TENSION BETWEEN QUALITY AND EQUALITY

Jürgen Henze

INTRODUCTION: THE CULTURAL HERITAGE

The choice of the two keywords 'quality' and 'equality' as essential elements for a descriptive-analytical study of Chinese higher education has by no means been made accidentally. Rather it should highlight our opinion that the history of higher education in the People's Republic of China has been largely determined by dissent between political elites favouring 'quality' education in order to achieve a maximum socio-economic efficiency, based on Soviet or Western social and economic indicators, and those who were more in favour of the 'equality' of distribution, either in terms of material goods or services. As the analysis will reveal, it is necessary to differentiate between genuine Chinese concepts and interpretations of 'quality' and 'equality' and those related categories which were quite often used by foreign 'China-watchers' who evaluted Chinese policies and structures from a point of view which originated from classical European philosophical traditions and was ill suited to the Chinese case. The roots of Chinese concepts of 'quality' and 'equality' in education - and their continuing influence on contemporary Chinese views of how to organise education in accordance with a projected modernisation of society - are closely related to the history of China's civil service examination system and can be traced back for more than 2,000 years to the first time in Chinese history when candidates for official positions were recruited by special examinations.[1] Along with this came the establishment of Confucian philosophy as the state doctrine, which was supported by a growing availability of printed materials. "Beginning with the Sung period the examinations became the major road to power and wealth, contrary to the old practice whereby a strong economic position had entitled one to special political priviliges."[2]

To succeed in these examinations the candidate had to study the classical canons of Confucian philosophy. This philosophy interpreted learning first of all as a tool to develop in an individual such "moral qualities as human-heartedness, righteousness, uprightness, and conscientiousness,"[3] and laid stress on "a scholar's belle-lettristic cultivation" instead of "a vocational, technical, 'useful' knowledge".[4] The Confucian school interpreted society as functionally divided with "a specific number of role positions, a hierarchical relationship between these positions, and a code of conduct governing this relationship in the interest of certain social values or virtues."[5] On the basis of a "natural-equality doctrine" equality of opportunity was assured to everyone in theory at least, and learning became the means to reach a specific social position by acquiring not only pure "knowledge" but a frame of reference for individual "action".[6] Until the abolition of the civil service examination system in 1905, power and wealth could be achieved by participation in these competitive examination, which provided the main road of upward mobility. This caused an extraordinary appreciation of book-learning throughout ancient China from as early as the Song dynasty.

The Emperor Zhen Zong wrote a poem which described this system with great vividness:

> To enrich your family, no need to buy good land:
> Books hold a thousand measures of grain.
> For an easy life, no need to build a mansion:
> In books are found houses of gold.
> Going out, be not vexed at absence of followers:
> In books, carriages and horses form a crowd.
> Marrying, be not vexed by lack of a good go-between:
> In books there are girls with faces of jade.
> A boy who wants to become a somebody
> Devotes himself to the classics, faces the window,
> and reads.[7]

If a boy finally became a 'somebody' and called himself one of the 'literati' (ru) or a 'scholar' (shi) he was "capable of engaging in only two kinds of activity: that of holding governmental office and that of teaching."[8] It is precisely this constellation of possibilities for a professional career that was attacked by so many of the Cultural Revolution critics discussing educational developments between 1949 and 1966. Still today this aspect of China's cultural heritage strongly influences debates over the orientation of higher education.[9]

HIGHER EDUCATION BETWEEN 1949 AND 1965

When the Chinese Communists came to power in 1949 they quickly tried to transform the educational heritage left by the Nationalist Government and the period of the anti-Japanese war. In view of the "anticipation of economic development and the conscious planning for industrialisation"[10], the reorganisation of higher education institutions and readjustment of university departments received top priority on the agenda of education policy. Based on the experience of the Soviet Union since 1928 and on the growing influence of Soviet financial and personnel assistance, a system of higher education emerged which was "characterised by the coexistence of general universities, polytechnical institutes, and technical institutes on the same level without distinction in status."[11] As indicated in Table 5.1, the number of universities in the field of science and engineering increased from 28 in 1949 (13.6% of the total number of institutes of higher education) to 43 in 1952 (21.4% of the total) and throughout the period of the First Five Year Plan (1953-1957) ranged between 21.7% and 19.2% of the total number, followed by teacher training, medical and agricultural institutions. This

Table 5.1

DISTRIBUTION OF INSTITUTIONS OF HIGHER EDUCATION
BY SPECIALISATION (1949 - 1965)

	1949	%	1952	%	1953	%	1957	%	1962	%	1965	%
TOTAL	205	100	201	100	181	100	229	100	610	100	434	100
Comprehensive Universities	49	23.9	22	10.9	14	7.7	17	7.4	31	5.1	29	6.7
Science and Engineering	28	13.6	43	21.4	38	21.0	44	19.2	206	33.8	127	29.3
Agriculture	18	8.8	25	12.4	26	14.4	28	12.2	69	11.3	45	10.4
Forestry	-	-	3	1.5	3	1.7	3	1.3	9	1.5	8	1.8
Medicine	22	10.7	31	15.4	29	16.0	37	16.2	118	19.3	92	21.2
Teacher Training	12	5.8	33	16.4	33	18.2	58	25.3	110	18.0	59	13.6
Language and Literature	11	5.4	8	4.0	8	4.4	8	3.5	6	1.0	16	3.7
Finance and Economics	11	5.4	12	6.0	6	3.3	5	2.2	17	2.8	18	4.1
Politics and Law	7	3.4	3	1.5	4	2.2	5	2.2	3	0.5	6	1.4
Physical Education	2	1.0	2	1.0	4	2.2	6	2.6	11	1.8	10	2.3
Fine Arts	18	8.8	15	7.5	15	8.3	17	7.4	28	4.6	22	5.1
Other	27	13.2	4	2.0	1	0.6	1	0.4	2	0.3	2	0.5

Source: Zhongguo Gaodeng Xuexiao Jianjie, Beijing: Jiaoyu Kexue Chubanshe, 1982, p.2

quantitative development seemed to be in line with policy statements of the Education Minister Ma Xulun who had explained in 1956 that

> educational construction should be designed to complement construction; the focal point of economic construction lies in industrial construction; and the focal point of industrial construction lies in heavy industries.[12]

As it turned out, however, the number of graduates in natural and engineering sciences fell far short of economic need. This had been caused mainly by inadequate educational and manpower planning and problems in the utilisation of specialised manpower.[13] Tables 5.2, 5.3 and 5.4 give precise details on enrollments, entrants and graduates by field of specialisation over the period from 1949 to 1965. Changes in emphasis on specific fields can be traced by examining these tables.

Up to the end of the First Five-Year Plan 'quality' in higher education was for the most part equated with high growth rates in the natural and engineering sciences (number of institutions, students, teachers, and research projects), with copying Soviet teaching materials and curricula and adapting Soviet administrative structures to the higher education and research system. Newly admitted students were enrolled on the basis of their results in centrally organised college entrance examinations from 1952 and the 'class line' was of minor importance only. For Mao Zedong, universities and colleges had become 'ivory towers' with intellectuals who did their research and teaching for personal interest instead of society's well-being and with students who were absorbed in book-learning, and had work-loads so heavy that their health was seriously affected.

So far as the issue of 'equality' is concerned, public discussion was centered on the equality of access to higher education. It emphasised two main aspects: Regional inequalities in the supply of higher education institutions and the preferential treatment of population groups according to their 'class origin', professional or ethnic status and sex. Changes in regional distribution are illustrated by Tables 5.5 and 5.6.

The Great Leap Forward of 1957 was Mao's attempt to change these developments. Education was to be combined with productive labour, administration was decentralised and students were selected not only on the basis of their examination results but on preferential treatment according to the class line. However he did not succeed in a long lasting revolution in education and from 1961 those political factions favouring traditional academic standards got the upper hand in organising teaching and research and, most importantly, the enrollment system in favour of 'academic achievement' at the expense of 'political commitment'. This development is typical of the Chinese policy fluctuation which has been described in terms of Chinese political historiography as 'the two-line struggle'.[14]

Table 5.2

ENROLLMENT AT INSTITUTIONS OF HIGHER EDUCATION BY FIELD OF SPECIALISATION (1949 - 1965)

	1949	%	1952	%	1957	%	1965	%
TOTAL	116500	100	191100	100	441200	100	674400	100
Engineering	30300	26.0	66600	34.8	163000	37.0	295300	43.8
Agriculture	9800	8.4	13300	6.9	33800	7.7	53500	7.9
Forestry	500	0.5	2200	1.1	6100	1.4	9800	1.5
Medicine	15200	13.1	24700	13.0	49100	11.1	82900	12.3
Teacher Training	12100	10.3	31500	16.5	114800	26.0	94300	14.0
Social Sciences	11800	10.2	13500	7.1	19600	4.4	46000	6.8
Natural Sciences	7000	6.0	9600	5.0	28700	6.5	62200	9.2
Finance and Economics	19400	16.6	22000	11.5	12100	2.7	18100	2.7
Politics and Law	7300	6.3	3800	2.0	8200	1.9	4100	0.6
Physical Education	300	0.2	300	0.2	3300	0.7	4000	0.6
Fine Arts	2800	2.4	3600	1.9	2500	0.6	4200	0.6

Source: Zhongguo Gaodeng Xuexiao Jianjie, p.6

Higher Education

Table 5.3: ENTRANTS INTO INSTITUTIONS OF HIGHER EDUCATION, BY FIELD OF SPECIALISATION (1949-65)

	1949-1952		1953-1957		1958-1962		1963-1965	
TOTAL	219,500	100%	561,800	100%	1,138,700	100%	444,100	100%
Engineering	81,000	36.9	203,300	36.2	430,400	37.8	182,700	41.1
Agriculture	14,400	6.6	38,100	6.8	103,000	9.0	39,600	8.9
Forestry	2,700	1.2	7,400	1.3	18,400	1.6	7,200	1.6
Medicine	23,300	10.6	52,300	9.3	125,400	11.0	49,300	11.1
Teacher Training	31,800	14.5	156,400	27.8	283,100	24.9	70,300	15.8
Social Sciences	17,400	7.9	29,300	5.2	41,300	3.6	33,800	7.6
Natural Sciences	15,100	6.9	34,800	6.2	93,000	8.2	36,800	8.3
Finance and Economics	26,500	12.1	20,800	3.7	17,600	1.6	15,000	3.4
Politics and Law	3,900	1.8	10,000	1.8	5,900	0.5	3,500	0.8
Physical Education	400	0.2	5,800	1.1	10,600	0.9	3,300	0.8
Fine Arts	3,000	1.4	3,600	0.6	10,000	0.9	2,600	0.6

Table 5.4: GRADUATES OF INSTITUTIONS OF HIGHER EDUCATION, BY FIELD OF SPECIALISATION (1949-65)

	1949-1952		1953-1957		1958-1962		1963-1965	
TOTAL	89,700	100%	269,800	100%	606,900	100%	588,800	100%
Engineering	24,100	26.9	88,000	32.7	180,900	29.8	237,600	40.4
Agriculture	7,100	7.9	15,400	5.7	52,300	8.6	50,400	8.6
Forestry	1,100	1.2	2,900	1.1	7,400	1.2	10,500	1.6
Medicine	7,700	8.6	25,900	9.6	60,100	9.9	72,900	12.4
Teacher Training	6,800	7.6	65,500	24.4	207,300	34.2	112,400	19.1
Social Sciences	8,700	9.7	19,000	7.1	28,100	4.6	26,800	4.6
Natural Sciences	6,700	7.4	12,100	4.5	36,800	6.1	56,800	9.7
Finance and Economics	17,400	19.4	29,400	10.9	16,000	2.6	8,500	1.4
Politics and Law	8,400	9.4	4,600	1.7	7,800	1.3	2,300	0.4
Physical Education	300	0.3	2,400	0.9	6,200	1.0	5,200	0.9
Fine Arts	1,400	1.6	3,800	1.4	4,000	0.7	5,400	0.9

Source: Zhongguo Gaodeng Xuexiao Jianjie, p.7

Higher Education

Table 5.5

REGIONAL DISTRIBUTION OF INSTITUTIONS OF HIGHER EDUCATION
1949 - 1980

Region	1949	%	1952	%	1957	%	1965	%	1976	%	1978	%	1980	%
Beijing	15	7.3	25	12.4	31	13.5	53	12.2	24	6.1	36	6.0	50	7.4
Tianjin	8	3.9	7	3.5	6	2.6	13	3.0	10	2.6	11	1.8	17	2.5
Hebei	3	1.5	4	2.0	4	1.7	12	2.8	22	5.6	29	4.8	27	4.0
Shanxi	1	0.5	3	1.5	4	1.7	11	2.5	11	2.8	16	2.7	16	2.4
Nei Monggol			3	1.5	4	1.7	8	1.8	7	1.8	8	1.3	14	2.1
Liaoning	8	3.9	17	8.5	14	6.1	26	6.0	24	6.1	34	5.7	36	5.3
Jilin	6	2.9	7	3.5	7	3.1	17	3.9	12	3.1	26	4.3	25	3.7
Heilongjiang	6	2.9	9	4.5	7	3.1	19	4.4	19	4.8	24	4.0	28	4.1
Shanghai	37	18.0	17	8.5	18	7.9	24	5.5	16	4.1	26	4.3	32	4.7
Jiangsu	15	7.3	17	8.5	15	6.6	30	6.9	25	6.4	35	5.9	42	6.2
Zhejiang	5	2.4	5	2.5	8	3.5	13	3.0	11	2.8	19	3.2	22	3.3
Anhui	2	1.0	3	1.5	5	2.2	12	2.8	12	3.1	20	3.3	22	3.3
Fujian	8	3.9	5	2.5	4	1.7	10	2.3	7	1.8	15	2.5	16	2.4
Jiangxi	5	2.4	4	2.0	4	1.7	12	2.8	10	2.6	17	2.8	17	2.5
Shandong	7	3.4	7	3.5	7	3.1	16	3.7	19	4.8	31	5.2	34	5.0
Henan	2	1.0	4	2.0	7	3.1	12	2.8	12	3.1	22	3.7	25	3.7
Hubei	10	4.9	10	5.0	18	7.9	23	5.3	22	5.6	34	5.7	36	5.3
Hunan	2	1.0	4	2.0	6	2.6	12	2.8	16	4.1	22	3.7	22	3.3
Guangdong	12	5.9	11	5.5	7	3.1	21	4.8	20	5.1	29	4.8	30	4.4
Guangxi	3	1.5	4	2.0	3	1.3	10	2.3	9	2.3	16	2.7	18	2.7
Sichuan	36	17.6	19	9.5	21	9.2	30	6.9	26	6.6	40	6.7	43	6.4
Guizhou	3	1.5	3	1.5	3	1.3	6	1.4	8	2.0	14	2.3	15	2.2
Yunnan	3	1.5	2	1.0	4	1.7	6	1.4	9	2.3	15	2.5	17	2.5
Xizang	-		-		-		-		3	0.8	4	0.7	4	0.6
Shaanxi	3	1.5	6	3.0	12	5.2	21	4.8	16	4.1	24	4.0	33	4.9
Gansu	4	2.0	4	2.0	4	1.7	7	1.6	8	2.0	11	1.8	12	1.8
Qinghai	-		-		1	0.4	2	0.5	4	1.0	6	1.0	6	0.9
Ningxia	-		-		-		1	0.2	3	0.8	4	0.7	4	0.6
Xinjiang	1	0.5	1	0.5	5	2.2	7	1.6	7	1.8	10	1.7	12	1.8
TOTAL	205	100	201	100	229	100	434	100	392	100	598	100	675	100

Source for Tables 5.5 and 5.6: *Zhongguo Gaodeng Xuexiao Jianjie*, pp.1, 5.

Higher Education

Table 5.6

REGIONAL DISTRIBUTION OF STUDENTS AT INSTITUTIONS OF HIGHER EDUCATION (1949 - 1980) (thousands)

Region	1949	%	1952	%	1957	%	1965	%	1976	%	1978	%	1980	%
Beijing	14.7	12.6	30.6	16.0	79.7	18.1	108.7	16.1	45.7	8.1	64.5	7.5	83.0	7.3
Tianjin	4.2	3.6	7.5	3.9	15.5	3.5	22.4	3.3	18.9	3.3	29.4	3.4	29.9	2.6
Hebei	1.1	0.9	2.6	1.4	6.6	1.5	22.7	3.4	19.9	3.5	30.1	3.5	41.5	3.6
Shanxi	0.9	0.8	2.1	1.1	7.3	1.7	14.1	2.1	12.7	2.2	20.6	2.4	33.1	2.9
Nei Monggol	-	-	0.6	0.3	2.9	0.7	8.6	1.3	6.0	1.1	9.9	1.2	17.4	1.5
Liaoning	6.5	5.6	16.3	8.5	25.9	5.9	37.1	5.5	40.4	7.2	53.0	6.2	63.3	5.5
Jilin	4.2	3.6	9.0	4.7	18.2	4.1	26.0	3.9	24.5	4.3	31.6	3.7	38.0	3.3
Heilongjiang	5.9	5.1	9.3	4.9	17.8	4.0	32.9	4.9	23.5	4.2	34.6	4.0	43.6	3.8
Shanghai	20.9	17.9	21.3	11.1	38.7	8.8	52.0	7.7	33.6	6.0	50.0	5.8	73.4	6.4
Jiangsu	7.2	6.2	11.3	5.9	29.3	6.6	40.7	6.0	37.4	6.6	60.5	7.1	82.5	7.2
Zhejiang	3.4	2.9	4.5	2.4	12.3	2.8	16.6	2.5	10.5	1.9	24.2	2.8	37.6	3.3
Anhui	1.1	0.9	2.5	1.3	8.6	1.9	18.2	2.7	18.3	3.2	29.6	3.5	37.6	3.3
Fujian	3.9	3.3	4.7	2.5	7.5	1.7	15.2	2.3	11.4	2.0	31.1	3.6	38.6	3.4

Higher Education

Province														
Jiangxi	2.1	1.8	3.0	1.6	4.3	1.0	11.8	1.7	12.0	2.1	21.8	2.5	35.6	3.1
Shandong	3.9	3.3	6.8	3.6	12.6	2.9	22.2	3.3	21.3	3.8	38.4	4.5	51.4	4.5
Henan	0.7	0.6	2.1	1.1	9.6	2.2	14.0	2.1	20.1	3.6	27.3	3.2	45.0	3.9
Hubei	4.3	3.7	8.9	4.7	29.3	6.6	35.6	5.3	30.7	5.4	49.5	5.8	65.3	5.7
Hunan	2.7	2.3	6.1	3.2	13.6	3.1	20.7	3.1	25.5	4.5	36.1	4.2	52.0	4.5
Guangdong	5.8	5.0	9.9	5.2	14.6	3.3	28.8	4.3	24.0	4.3	36.0	4.2	44.1	3.9
Guangxi	2.0	1.7	2.4	1.3	3.9	0.9	7.8	1.2	14.7	2.6	21.1	2.5	25.5	2.2
Sichuan	14.0	12.0	14.9	7.8	35.5	8.0	45.7	6.8	43.4	7.7	57.2	6.7	74.7	6.5
Guizhou	1.0	0.9	3.3	1.7	3.5	0.8	6.8	1.0	8.3	1.5	13.9	1.6	17.1	1.5
Yunnan	1.7	1.5	1.4	0.7	7.0	1.6	9.4	1.4	11.0	1.9	15.9	1.9	18.1	1.6
Xizang	–	–	–	–	–	–	0.4	0.05	2.5	0.4	2.1	0.2	1.5	0.2
Shaanxi	2.3	2.0	6.3	3.3	25.0	5.7	35.7	5.3	25.7	4.6	37.1	4.3	53.2	4.7
Gansu	1.6	1.4	2.8	1.5	7.3	1.7	11.5	1.7	11.5	2.0	14.1	1.6	18.1	1.6
Qinghai	–	–	–	–	0.2	0.04	0.6	0.09	2.5	0.4	3.5	0.4	4.2	0.5
Ningxia	–	–	–	–	–	–	1.0	0.1	2.1	0.4	2.9	0.3	4.2	0.4
Xinjiang	0.4	0.3	0.9	0.5	4.5	1.0	7.2	1.1	6.6	1.2	10.3	1.2	14.2	1.2
TOTAL	116.5	100	191.1	100	441.2	100	674.4	100	564.7	100	856.3	100	1143.7	100

THE IMPACT OF THE CULTURAL REVOLUTION ON HIGHER EDUCATION

Radical Destruction and the Search for New Models

At the beginning of the Cultural Revolution the Central Committee of the Chinese Communist Party and the State Council passed the decision on the 'Reform of Entrance Examinations and Enrollment in Higher Educational Institutions' which clearly stated:

> Meanwhile though it has been constantly improved since Liberation, the method of examination and enrollment for the higher educational institutions, has failed - in the main - to free itself from the set pattern of the bourgeois system of examination; and such a method is harmful to the implementation of the guiding policy on education formulated by the Central Committee of the Party and Chairman Mao... This system of examination must be completely reformed.[15]

Whereas the original intention was to postpone the 1966 enrollment of new students for higher education institutions for half a year only, in reality academic training was completely paralysed until 1970. Signs of planned reactivation appeared in the form of a published and widely discussed series of articles in the People's Daily dealing with the question 'How to Run Socialist Universities'.[16] As it turned out this question was not easily answered. Throughout 1969 contributors to the series emphasised various models of how to reorganise higher education institutions and looking back it is possible to extract at least three alternative versions of a model university, either in the field of science and engineering or arts.

The first to appear was the model of the early days of the anti-Japanese Military war, called 'Kangda', the 'Chinese People's Anti-Japanese Military and Political College'. According to an article in a Shanghai newspaper this was

> an educational institution of the newest type, the most revolutionary and the most progressive in fully implementing the educational ideology of Chairman Mao, and a sample of proletarian educational enterprise... The educational policy of Kangda which Chairman Mao personally formulated was: a firm and correct political orientation, a working style of hard work and simple living, and creative and flexible strategy and tactics. The fashion of Kangda was unity,

alertness, earnestness and liveliness. Kangda's centre of education was political education, the transformation of the non-proletarian thoughts of students to make them gradually establish a proletarian world outlook. Kangda's educational principle was to learn less but the essentials, and for theoretical study to be linked with practice. Kangda's method of teaching was the combination of instructiveness, research and practice and the combination of education and labour in production.[17]

Obviously this 'model' was closely related to Mao Zedong's 'May 7' directive of 1966, in which he had stated concerning students:

While their main task is study, they should, in addition to their studies, learn other things, that is, industrial work, farming and military affairs. They should also criticise the bourgeoisie. The school term should be shortened, education should be revolutionised, and the domination of our schools by bourgeois intellectuals should not be allowed to continue.[18]

Relevant sources give evidence for the assumption, that it was not Mao himself who favoured Kangda as a general 'model' for higher education. Rather it seems probable that the well known experience of Kangda and Mao's personal affiliation with it during its earlier years were used by the more radical political factions in their struggle against conservatives.[19] The decline of its importance in public discussions over time seems to be closely correlated with the diminishing influence of the radical Cultural Revolution left during the same period.

Against this background, Mao himself voted for maintaining universities in a more classical sense when he issued his famous 'July 21' directive in 1968 and took the initiative in creating a second model:

It is still necessary to have universities; here I refer mainly to colleges of science and engineering. However, it is essential to shorten the length of schooling, revolutionise education, put proletarian politics in command and take the road of the Shanghai Machine Tools Plant in training technicians from among the workers. Students should be selected from among workers and peasants with practical experience, and they should return to production after a few years' study.[20]

In contrast to Kangda with its clearly dominating politico-ideological mission, this 'workers university' was originally only a part of the adult education system with no importance for regular full-time universities and colleges because of the strongly technical orientation of its curriculum. According to the investigation report which was published in connection with Mao Zedong's directive in July 1968 this special university was of twofold importance. First, besides its mission to transmit mainly technical knowledge according to the plant's production needs, the university's leadership comprised technicians of worker origin instead of so-called "reactionary bourgeois technical 'authorities' who formerly controlled the leadership in technical matters". It now laid stress on the workers, and students' revolutionary consciousness, so combining technical and politico-ideological education. Secondly, the curriculum favoured the part-time study of workers and thus enabled them to combine study and work.

With these two characteristics, this type of university, in the radicals' view, came closest to the famous requirement for every form of education, which Mao Zedong had laid down in 1957: "our educational policy must enable everyone who receives an education to develop morally, intellectually and physically and become a worker with both socialist consciousness and culture."[21] However it had little importance in the process of reactivating full-time higher education institutions in 1970. Its main influence can be seen in the fact that a small number of universities and colleges enrolled workers in so-called 'experimental classes' in 1968-69. These were held on the basis of part-time study and obviously followed the road of the Shanghai Machine Tools Plant and its 'workers university'.

The last logical step further in the direction of modelling a new higher education system could be identified in July 1970 when the 'Qinghua University Workers and People's Liberation Army Mao Zedong Thought Propaganda Team' published a report which, according to Yao Wenyuan, "quite fully summarises their experiences in carrying out Chairman Mao's thought on proletarian educational revolution."[22] In contrast to the somewhat limited value of the 'July 21 Workers University' this report of Qinghua University for the first time spelled out how the reopening of universities and colleges and the admission of new students should be organised:

> Those admitted to science and engineering universities should be selected by and large from among the workers and peasants (with special attention given to enrolling intellectual youths who have settled in the countryside or who have returned to their home villages), Liberation Army men, and young cadres, all of

whom are active elements who have emerged in the course of the Three Great Revolutionary Movements and who, in general, have had three or more years of practical experience, are about nineteen years old, and have a cultural level corresponding to junior or senior middle school training. Older workers and poor and lower-middle peasants who have rich practical experience can enter school regardless of their age or cultural level."[23]

The Emergence of a Cultural Revolution System of Higher Education [24]

When in July 1970 a small number of universities and colleges were reactivated[25] to accept the first batch of students since 1965, a new higher education system could be identified. As part of the overall 'revolution in education' (jiaoyu geming), it looked completely different from the structure in 1965. From a systematic point of view this 'revolutionised' system could be described as follows.

Probably not more than 80-90 universities and colleges reopened in 1970 and accepted new students and so - according to our definition - became reactivated. In contrast to this estimate which is based on the analysis of provincial broadcasts, recently published statistics of the Chinese Ministry of Education revealed that in 1971 there were 328 higher education institutions with an enrollment of 83,000 and a batch of probably 42,000 new entrants. Obviously only a fraction of those institutions in existence were actually involved in admitting new students. Up to now we do not know the distribution of students by fields of specialisation. We have only been able to collect facts on the distribution of higher education institutions. As Table 5.7 shows, the majority of institutions were in the fields of science and engineering (35.1% of the total in 1971), medicine (23.8% of the total in 1971), and teacher training (13.4% of the total in 1971), a distribution which was not changed over time. The most striking difference to the situation in 1965 was that institutions in the field of finance and economics only made up 0.6% of the total in 1971 (4.1% in 1965) and up to 1976 only increased to 1.8%. The situation in politics and law was even worse, where no enrollment was reported up to 1976 (1.4% in 1965). It is of special interest to note that China's institutions in the field of agriculture made up only 9.5 to 9.9% between 1971 and 1976. Yet China is a developing country with a rural population of at least 80%.

The management of the new system was characterised by the fact that there was no central leading organ responsible for higher education. With the abolition of the Ministries of Education and Higher Education in the wake of the Cultural

Higher Education

Table 5.7: DISTRIBUTION OF INSTITUTIONS OF HIGHER EDUCATION BY SPECIALISATION (1971-1976)

	1971		1972		1973		1974		1975		1976	
TOTAL	328	100	331	100	345	100	378	100	387	100	392	100
Comprehensive universities	27	8.2	27	8.2	28	8.1	29	7.7	29	7.5	29	7.4
Science and Engineering	115	35.1	116	35.0	118	34.2	120	31.7	123	31.8	126	32.1
Agriculture	31	9.5	32	9.7	34	9.9	37	9.8	38	9.8	38	9.7
Forestry	3	0.9	3	0.9	3	0.9	4	1.1	5	1.3	5	1.3
Medicine	78	23.8	78	23.6	78	22.6	85	22.5	88	22.7	89	22.7
Teacher Training	44	13.4	44	13.3	45	13.0	57	15.1	58	15.0	58	14.8
Language and Literature	7	2.1	8	2.4	10	2.9	10	2.6	10	2.6	10	2.6
Finance and Economics	2	0.6	2	0.6	4	1.2	6	1.6	6	1.6	7	1.8
Politics and Law	--	--	--	--	--	--	--	--	--	--	--	--
Physical Education	5	1.5	5	1.5	6	1.7	7	1.9	7	1.8	7	1.8
Fine Arts	12	3.7	12	3.6	13	3.8	14	3.7	14	3.6	14	3.6
Other	4	1.2	4	1.2	6	1.7	9	2.4	9	2.3	9	2.3

Source: Zhongguo Gaodeng Xuexiao Jianjie, p.2

Revolution, no specialised national agency could be identified in 1970 which was to coordinate the process of reactivating higher education institutions. Until the formation of the 9th Central Committee of the Chinese Communist Party in April 1969 the 'Cultural Revolution Small Group' ('Zhongyang Wenhua Geming Xiaozu') was responsible for educational affairs as well as many other areas.[26] After its disappearance these functions were taken over by the newly elected Central Committee until the 'Science and Education Group' ('Guowuyuan Kejiaozu') under the State Council was set up in 1971. It was the predecessor of the Ministry of Education, which was reactivated finally in 1975.[27] Throughout the country 'revolutionary committees' became leading administrative organs and their regional subcommittees on culture, science and education replaced those special bureaux for education (or science and culture) which were in charge of educational administration before the Cultural Revolution. Intra-university adminstration followed this revolutionised structure with the 'Communist Party University Committee' on top of the administrative hierarchy and the 'University Revolutionary Committee' in each institution replacing the former 'University Council', as well as revolutionary committees at lower echelons within the university administrative structure.[28]

In contrast to regulations before the Cultural Revolution, 'access' to higher education was transformed in accordance with central documents issued between 1966 and 1969. The 'admission' process was organised along lines of the experience of Qinghua University in Beijing, which had been publicised in July, 1970. Until 1976 the 'recruitment base'[29] mainly comprised graduates of lower or upper secondary schools (or those with an equivalent educational level) who had at least two years of work experience in the fields of industry, agriculture or military service and who were between 20 and 25 years old, unmarried and healthy. Special arrangements were made for experienced workers and peasants in terms of age and educational level or qualification.[30]

In the wake of twists and turns in domestic policy, these qualifications were often called in question by those political factions in the Chinese leadership normally associated with Zhou Enlai and Deng Xiaoping between 1970 and 1976. When a national conference on education work was held in 1971 this group stressed the value of re-introducing an entrance examination to make sure that the great disparity in candidate qualification could be diminished. Beginning in 1972 several provinces started 'cultural tests' on an experimental base. A special conference on enrollment in 1973 laid down guidelines for nationwide regionally administered tests and up to 1976 periodic changes and great regional differences in organising these simple tests occurred.

Finally, we may ask whether the Cultural Revolution indeed had redistributive, egalitarian consequences for higher education, as parts of the Chinese leadership and lots of foreign observers so often claimed at least until 1976. The general problem is that we hardly possess any reasonable indicator to measure 'equality' in the Chinese case. But what we can do as a first approximation is to look at the regional distribution of higher education institutions and at the quantitative dimension of what we called the 'recruitment base' in order to give a very rough estimate of the transition rate to higher education. First, as Table 5.8 indicates, the regional distribution of higher eduction institutions was affected mainly in the areas of Beijing, which is the only region where the regional share in the total national student enrollment dropped to one half of its value before the Cultural Revolution, Ningxia, which is the most positively affected region with the regional share in the total national student enrollment increasing by 400% of its 1965 value, Qinghai which reported a 200% increase, and in similar but somewhat lower percentages the provinces of Hebei, Guizhou and Yunnan. A noteworthy decrease was reported from Shanghai, Fujian and Jilin. So, besides an increase in regions where a high population of rusticated youth, sent to the countryside from major East Coast cities, made up the 'recruitment base', no substantial change regarding the enrollment of students took place. Only in Beijing and Shanghai can a substantial decrease be noted. From an overall point of view, one can hardly describe these developments as successful 'redistribution'.

The second possible indicator, the proportion of supply and demand in access to higher education can roughly be calculated on the basis of the following assumptions. Given the estimated numbers of graduates of upper secondary schools and the total number of graduates of regular secondary schools, the recruitment base can be estimated as the total number of graduates of secondary schools between 1966 and 1968 for entrants into higher education institutions in 1970; the total number of graduates between 1966 and 1969 for entrants in 1971; those of 1967 to 1970 for entrants in 1972; those of the 1968 to 1971 for entrants in 1973 and in a similar way for entrants until 1976. The explanation for this calculation is simple. The guidelines for higher education enrollment laid down that only those persons who had at least two to three years of working experience and an educational level equivalent to that of graduates of upper or lower secondary school could apply for entrance. So a candidate entering in 1970 could be a student who had graduated in 1968 or earlier. We have drawn the line with 1966, because the candidate then should be around twenty years old in line with the requirement concerning age. The pity is that we do not know the proportion of entrants who were graduates from upper or lower secondary schools. The recruitment base may therefore be a mixture of both populations and the transition rate of these groups may be calculated roughly as ranging between 0.28% and 0.74% (1970-76) so far as

Higher Education

Table 5.8

THE IMPACT OF THE CULTURAL REVOLUTION ON THE REGIONAL DISTRIBUTION OF INSTITUTIONS OF HIGHER EDUCATION AND STUDENTS: Proportional Change of the Regional Share in Relation to the National Total.

Region	Regional Share in the National Total of Higher Education Institutions (1965) / Regional Share in the National Total (1976)	Regional Share in the National Total of Students (1965) / Regional Share in the National Total (1976)
Beijing	0.5	0.5
Tianjin	1.0	0.9
Hebei	1.0	2.0
Shanxi	1.0	1.1
Nei Monggol	0.8	1.0
Liaoning	1.3	1.0
Jilin	1.1	0.8
Heilongjiang	0.9	1.1
Shanghai	0.8	0.7
Jiangsu	1.1	0.9
Zhejiang	0.8	0.9
Anhui	1.2	1.1
Fujian	0.9	0.8
Jiangxi	1.2	0.9
Shandong	1.2	1.3
Henan	1.7	1.1
Hubei	1.0	1.1
Hunan	1.5	1.5
Guangdong	1.0	1.1
Guangxi	2.2	1.0
Sichuan	1.1	0.95
Guizhou	1.5	1.4
Yunnan	1.4	1.6
Xizang	-	-
Shaanxi	0.9	0.9
Gansu	1.2	1.3
Qinghai	4.4	2.0
Ningxia	4.0	4.0
Xinjiang	1.1	1.1

the population of upper and lower secondary schools graduates is concerned and as ranging between 1.4% and 3.0% in the case of upper secondary school graduates only. In reality the actual rate of transition is probably a mixture of these figures, at an average of around 0.5% to 1.0%. It should be noted however that this kind of 'transition rate' is absolutely not comparable to related terms used in the international comparison of education systems because of its 'mixed character'. It is only of use to compare changes in Chinese higher education over time! Table 5.9 gives the figures from which these transition rates are calculated.

Another way of constructing an indicator for access to higher education may be the calculation of the relevant age groups' percentage share in students. Due to the fact that throughout the 1970's no one single age group but several age groups made up the recruitment base it is extremely difficult to calculate, but we will use the following method for a very rough estimate. Given the regulations that normally candidates for admission had to be between 20 and 25 years of age we may take the birth rate from 1949 to 1954 and 1950 to 1955 to estimate the age group of 20 to 25 year-olds in 1974 and 1975 as examples. According to actual statistics in 1974 there should have been around 127,000,000 persons between 20 and 25 years of age in contrast to a total student population of 430,000. This means that approximately 0.3% of the 20 to 25 age

Table 5.9

ESTIMATED GRADUATES OF UPPER AND LOWER SECONDARY SCHOOLS AND ENTRANTS INTO UNIVERSITIES AND COLLEGES (1966-1976)

Year	Graduates of Upper & Lower Secondary schools	Graduates of Upper Secondary Schools	Entrants into Universities or Colleges
1966	3,100,000	625,000	--
1967	3,100,000	673,000	--
1968	3,500,000	835,000	--
1969	5,100,000	1,213,000	--
1970	6,600,000	1,849,000	42,000
1971	7,800,000	2,502,000	42,000
1972	9,000,000	2,866,000	134,000
1973	8,600,000	2,757,000	153,000
1974	9,100,000	2,920,000	167,000
1975	11,200,000	3,573,000	166,000
1976	15,000,000	4,470,000	217,000

Source: Information will be supplied by the author on request.

group was enrolled at higher education institutions. Assuming that the majority of these students are formed by three age groups only, we could estimate that 0.7% of this group was enrolled. In 1975 the same method of calculating would reveal that 0.4% of the 20 to 25 age group and 0.8% of a three year age group was enrolled. This very restricted access to higher education can be demonstrated, also, by taking into account the percentage share of students at higher education institutions in the total number of students. Between 1970 and 1976 this figure climbed up from 0.04% in 1970 to 0.12% in 1972, 0.24% in 1974 and 0.27% in 1976.[31]

Facing the posssibilities of finding access into higher education demonstrated by these statistics, the majority of Chinese youth became extremely pessimistic. As a result the lower echelons of the education system were characterised by a growing absence of motivation in students.[32] We now know that high rates of educational wastage, mainly in terms of drop-outs, followed in the course of this development.

DEVELOPMENTS IN HIGHER EDUCATION SINCE 1977

Policy Guidelines

One of the first blueprints for a new education and science policy that still had to be fixed in detail became public in December 1977, when Fang Yi, a member of the Politbureau of the Chinese Communist Party and Vice-President of the Academy of Sciences at the time, delivered his 'Report on the State of Science'.[33] According to this document, besides readjustments in administration, planning, institutional cooperation, and financing, the coming education and science policy should encompass

- programmes "to teach children and young people the most up-to-date science and technology"[34],

- "studiously learning advanced foreign science and technology and actively strengthening international science exchanges under the premise of independence and self-reliance"[35] to "master the world's most advanced scientific and technological achievements as soon as possible to serve as a new starting point for our advance."[36]

According to Fang Yi, these programmes were necessary to "rapidly develop the national economy on a new technological basis, greatly increase labour productivity, and equip our national defence with the most up-to-date technology... to catch up with and surpass the most advanced world levels in major fields of science and technology by the end of the present century."[37]

In March 1978 Deng Xiaoping for the first time went beyond these statements in public, when he tried to legitimise the new efficiency-oriented policy on the ground of a Marxist theory of science and education. He pointed out that "science and technology are productive forces" in contrast to the dominant interpretation up to 1976 that science and education are simply parts of the superstructure.[38] Closely related to this reevaluation was the question of how to assess the intellectuals' role in society and contribution to development under the 'four modernisations'. According to Deng's interpretation, the business of science and education is clearly part of the social division of labour where manual workers and intellectuals no longer form a unity of contradictions, as in Mao Zedong's thinking, but instead represent two social groups of equal value. According to the new guidelines, the value of intellectuals should be estimated in terms of their direct participation in scientific work and not their participation in political meetings. Parts of the Chinese leadership have challenged Deng's evaluation of science and education, but up to the present it still represents the nut-shell of present official policy. So far we have evidence that the most important structural changes in higher education which have been shaped by this policy up to the middle of 1983 are as follows:

- The restitution of college entrance examinations;
- Institutional diversification and expansion in higher education;
- The reform of the curriculum;
- Intra-university administrative reforms;
- A new concept of higher education planning.

The Restitution and Development of College Entrance Examinations (1977 - 1983)

One of the first and most important measures in reorganising the education system after the fall of the 'Gang of Four' was the radical transformation of access to higher education[39], an area of education policy which has always been the most sensitive in twists and turns of Chinese domestic politics. In the wake of the campaign to criticise the 'Gang of Four' between fall 1976 and summer 1977 numerous articles appeared in the Chinese media calling for the restitution of pre-Cultural Revolution entrance examinations. Arguments were based on concepts of 'quality' and 'efficiency' now favoured by the 'dominant leadership subgroup' who were described as 'efficiency maximisers' by one scholar.[40] As became evident in subsequent years, these concepts and their implementation were dominantly influenced by Deng Xiaoping. His interpretation of quality and efficiency in education and science was by no means elaborated by theoretical academic analysis but was simply based on indicators used in Western industrialised countries such as the number of higher institutions, students, teachers and researchers as well as research projects. Quality, then, would have to be evaluated in comparison with related topics in industrialised countries. This concept was the logical outcome of a newly favoured ideal of modernisation, which became possible due to changed power constellations, and it quickly became evident that in this context a reform of higher education would shake the education system as a whole.

From the comparative educationists' point of view, this should not be a surprising development. Since the beginning of the 1960's 'access to higher education' has been interpreted as a process which, in all analysed cultures, follows a three stage development where the students' transition from secondary to higher education institutions is only the last part of a selection process which already starts at the beginning of the primary level of education:

1. In the first stage it (the education system) establishes a basic group of primary school students who enter subsequent programmes preparing for higher education. These students, bound together by a common objective, may be termed the 'admissions group'.

2. In its second stage the process reduces the size of the admissions group through actions which take place during secondary education...

3. It its third stage the process makes a terminal adjustment in the size of the group in accordance with the requirements and capacity of specific programmes of higher education.[41]

The following part of our analysis can only deal with developments in the third stage of the admission process and the readers' attention can only be drawn to a number of relevant publications elsewhere covering problems concerning stage one and two.[42]

The new post-Cultural Revolution enrollment system was first outlined in public during a national work conference on enrollment in October, 1977. According to guidelines laid down, students to be enrolled should include

> workers, peasants, educated young people who have settled in the countryside or returned to their home villages (including those who have been retained in town for policy reasons and have not been given a work assignment), rehabilitated armymen, cadres and graduating high school students. They must be around 20

years old but not more than 25, and must be unmarried. Their qualifications: They must have untarnished political backgrounds, support the Chinese Communist Party, have an ardent love for socialism and labour, observe revolutionary discipline, and be resolved to study for the revolution. They must have a scholastic attainment equivalent to that of a secondary school graduate (students still in secondary school with especially outstanding achievements may file applications by themselves for enrollment with their schools' recommendation), and be physically fit. In addition, the maximum age may be extended to 30 for those who have achievements in study or who possess special skills and in these cases marital status may be waived...'[43]

Candidates for admission had to participate in a standard entrance examination which was to be organised and held by the county or district. These tests were to be prepared by the province, municipality or autonomous region. Depending on his or her future specialisation the candidate had to take an examination in politics, language, mathematics, history and geography for liberal arts or in politics, language, mathematics, physics and chemistry for natural sciences. Those who wanted to take up studies in foreign languages were to succeed in a special foreign language examination which was to be organised by the county. It is noteworthy that applicants for liberal arts and sciences were not asked to participate in any foreign language examinations, a situation which was changed beginning in 1978. Looking at these new regulations we can identify three main differences to those regulations which governed higher education entrance until 1976.

First, although the majority of applicants had working experience of at least two years, this was no longer formally required as it had been up to 1976. The recruitment base was now widened, comprising all those who already had working experience, those who would graduate from upper secondary schools (not lower secondary schools as before 1977) and those who were still attending secondary classes but had outstanding results and "abilities equivalent to those of an upper secondary graduate."[44] Second, for the first time since 1965, all candidates had to succeed in a regionally standardised entrance examination with clearly defined tests in selected specialities and the marks received became the main criterion for access into higher education institutions. Third, in contrast to decentralised enrollment procedures up to 1976, now as a first stage of centralisation, enrollment quotas were controlled generally by provinces, municipalities and autonomous regions, not by the basic levels.[45]

In the consciousness of the majority of Chinese youths, this new recruitment system quickly became the one and last chance of their life to enter higher education institutions and thereby to climb up the ladder of social status. At least 10 million people applied for participation in the regional entrance examinations and after a first stage of screening, 5,700,000 were accepted to take part in examinations. In cities and towns all secondary schools which were able to provide special services to bright candidates organised special classes for reviewing secondary school curricula related to required examination subjects.[46] In the countryside those who benefitted from living in an area where personnel and material conditions permitted the arrangement of special services to review curricula tried to catch up with the required knowledge. But in the end only 278,000 new entrants were admitted to universities and colleges in spring 1978. As a result of these regionally administered examinations a great variety in quality was observed all over China and criticised by leading officials. High ranking cadres tried to push the children of relatives into universities and colleges by using 'the back door'. In response new regulations were fixed in 1978 with entrance examinations to be organised centrally by the Ministry of Education and standardised for the whole nation. A major change occured in the requirements for candidates in liberal arts and natural science. From 1978 onwards they had to participate in a foreign language test, too. In the first year the results of this test were for reference only, but in subsequent years the results were taken into consideration at an increasing percentage. In 1979 they were counted at 10% of the maximum theoretical result, in 1980 this percentage was raised to 30%, in 1981 to 50%, in 1982 to 70% and finally, in 1983 to 100%.[47] Besides minor changes regarding the recruitment base, up to 1983 the most important changes in the regulations formulated each year were as follows:[48]

- In 1980 for the first time the organisation of pre-tests by provinces, municipalities and autonomous regions to select possible condidates for the national entrance examinations.
- In 1981 the addition of the subject of biology as a required test for science applicants;
- The experimental recruitment of cadres with a working experience of at least two years for selected departments of a small number of universities;
- The experimental participation of students in practical work and military exercises in selected key point universities administered by the Ministry of Education;
- The preferential treatment of those candidates who undertook in advance to work in less developed regions after graduation, as well as the preferential treatment of candidates of minority origin;

Higher Education

- The possibility of signing contracts between higher education institutions and production units for training students.

Table 5.10 gives transition rates to higher education from 1976 to 1983, against the background of the pre-Cultural Revolution situation. Table 5.11 gives undergraduate enrollments by subject specialisation from 1980 to 1982.

Table 5.10
GRADUATES OF UPPER SECONDARY SCHOOLS AND ENTRANTS INTO HIGHER EDUCATION INSTITUTIONS (1950-1983) [49]

Year	Graduates at Upper Secondary Schools (A)	Entrants into Higher Education Institutions (B)	Transition rate (B)/(A)
			%
1950	62,000	58,000	93.54
1951	59,000	52,000	88.13
1952	36,000	79,000	219.44
1953	56,000	82,000	146.43
1954	68,000	92,000	135.29
1955	99,000	98,000	98.99
1956	154,000	185,000	120.13
1957	187,000	106,000	56.68
1958	197,000	266,000	135.03
1959	299,000	274,000	91.64
1960	288,000	323,000	112.15
1961	379,000	109,000	28.76
1962	441,000	107,000	24.26
1963	433,000	133,000	30.72
1964	367,000	147,000	40.05
1965	360,000	164,000	45.56
1976	4,470,000	217,000	4.85
1977	5,172,000	273,000	5.28
1978	5,858,000	402,000	6.86
1979	6,827,000	275,000	4.03
1980	6,699,000	281,000	4.19
1981	4,861,000	278,800	5.73
1982	3,106,600	315,000	10.14
1983	2,700,000	387,000	14.33

Higher Education

Table 5.11: ENTRANTS AND ENROLLED STUDENTS AT INSTITUTIONS OF HIGHER EDUCATION, BY FIELD OF SPECIALISATION (1980-1982)

	Entrants 1980	%	Enrollment	%	Entrants 1981	%	Enrollment	%	Entrants 1982	%	Enrollment	%
TOTAL	281,200	100	1,143,700	100	278,777	100	1,279,472	100	315,135	100	1,153,954	100
Engineering	92,200	32.8	382,000	33.4	91,261	32.7	461,265	36.0	102,825	32.6	398,214	34.5
Agriculture	16,300	5.8	71,600	6.3	16,170	5.8	78,837	6.2	18,313	5.8	64,327	5.6
Forestry	2,800	1.0	11,800	1.1	2,728	1.0	13,618	1.1	3,201	1.0	11,472	1.0
Medicine	31,300	11.1	139,600	12.2	29,241	10.5	158,986	12.4	29,486	9.4	164,038	14.2
Teacher Training	89,000	31.7	338,300	29.6	88,207	31.6	321,444	25.1	97,177	30.8	289,448	25.1
Social Sciences	13,200	4.7	58,700	5.1	12,763	4.6	69,076	5.4	16,048	5.1	59,663	5.2
Natural Sciences	18,600	6.6	83,700	7.3	18,914	6.8	99,840	7.8	20,573	6.5	81,132	7.0
Finance and Economics	11,600	4.1	36,600	3.2	12,405	4.5	47,895	3.7	18,274	5.8	55,980	4.8
Politics and Law	2,900	1.0	6,100	0.5	3,751	1.3	9,944	0.8	4,982	1.6	14,635	1.3
Physical Education	2,100	0.8	9,400	0.8	1,889	0.7	11,241	0.9	2,646	0.9	9,505	0.8
Fine Arts	1,200	0.4	5,900	0.5	1,448	0.5	7,326	0.6	1,610	0.5	5,540	0.5

Table 5.12: NUMBER OF ENROLLED AND GRADUATED RESEARCH STUDENTS (1949 - 1983)

	1949-52	1952-57	1958-63	1963-65	1966-69	1978-80	TOTAL 1949-80	1981	1982	1983
Enrolled	4,174	8,362	7,380	3,477	—	22,434	45,827	11,500	9,472	15,134
Graduates	1,059	7,639	3,627	4,072	4,546	625	21,568	—	—	—

Sources: Zhongguo Baike Nianjian, 1981; Statistical Yearbook of China, 1983; Zhongguo Gaodeng Xuexiao Jianjie, p.4

Higher Education

Along with this newly organised and enlarged enrollment of undergraduates since 1977/78, a growing number of graduate students, called 'research students' (*yanjiusheng*), have been accepted at universities, colleges and research institutes.[50] After preparation made in these institutions in the fall of 1977, the number of research students admitted to 208 higher education institutions and 162 research institutes was reported to be 10,708 in 1978.[51] Of them, about 77% were admitted to universities and colleges, about 13% to institutes under the Academy of Sciences, about 4% to institutes under the Academy of Social Sciences and about 7% to research institutes administered by ministries and commissions under the State Council. In 1979 another 8,231 research students were admitted and by 1983 an intake of 15,134 was achieved.[52] Tables 5.12 and 5.13 give the enrollment of research students by specialisation over the period from 1949 to 1980, as well as composite figures for 1981 to 1983.

Table 5.13

NUMBER OF RESEARCH STUDENTS BY FIELD OF SPECIALISATION
(1949-1980)

	1949	1952	1957	1965	1978	1980
TOTAL	629	2,763	3,178	4,546	10,934	21,604
Engineering	94	508	628	1,808	4,011	7,206
Agriculture	21	90	223	395	331	724
Medicine	83	--	239	248	1,474	3,651
Teacher Training	78	115	724	--	693	1,704
Social Sciences	119	878	686	306	1,358	2,628
Natural Sciences	87	57	419	1,740	2,774	4,705
Finance and Economics	121	908	112	14	49	451
Politics and Law	26	168	5	10	--	171
Physical Education	--	10	139	18	62	200
Fine Arts	--	29	3	7	182	164

Source: *Zhongguo Gaodeng Xuexiao Jianjie*, p.4.

The recruitment of graduate students was organised in close relation to that of undergraduates. Since the beginning candidates have had to pass a special examination, which is jointly organised by the Ministry of Education, which sets questions in foreign languages and politics, and local research units. The number of examination subjects has changed but, in general, candidates have had to work on politics, foreign language, and four to five speciality subjects (three up to 1980). From 1983 "in addition to the five or six tests in political theory, foreign languages, basic courses and the basics in a specialised field, a comprehensive test will be given to applicants covering certain academic fields and specialities. The comprehensive test will include basic knowledge, theories and skills. It will be aimed at testing the students' ability to use the knowledge they acquire in analysing and solving problems as well as their intelligence, creativeness, and speed in reacting."[53] Table 5.13 reveals that the majority of research students in 1980 were in the fields of engineering (33%), natural sciences (22%), medicine (17%), social sciences (12%) and teacher training (8%). This distribution differs somewhat from the situation in 1965 with engineering (40%), natural sciences (38%), agriculture (9%), and medicine (5%).[54]

In line with the newly organised recruitment system for undergraduates and research students we have to mention a third item in the overall reform of higher education to ensure improved quality in the output of graduates: The restitution of the system of academic degrees which was put into effect in 1981. According to the new guidelines, higher education graduates may receive a bachelor's, master's or doctor's degree in accordance with their study programmes. These degrees are conferred by about 458 universities and colleges which were selected by the State Council's Academic Degrees Committee. By early 1983 "nearly 15,000 students had received masters' degrees and more than 320,000 bachelors' degree."[55] So far as the doctorate is concerned only 18 degrees were conferred during the same period.[56]

Institutional Diversification and Expansion in Higher Education

Looking at the quantitative development of China's higher education system one must admit that the Chinese government has been quite successful in reoganising the structure of higher education in accordance with the anticipated needs of the 'four modernisations'. From 1976 until 1982 the number of universities and colleges increased by 182% from 392 to 715, and the number of full-time students by 204% from 564,700 to 1,153,954.[57] The distribution of institutions by specialisation in some specialities changed drastically: Between 1971 and 1976 about 7.4% to 8.2% of the total number of institutions were comprehensive universities. In 1982 this dropped to 4.5% and probably will remain at that level in the near future. Institutions in science and engineering in 1982 made up 28.8% of the total, a slight decrease compared with 32.1% in 1976. Major changes mainly occured in finance and economics where the percentage share went from 1.8% in 1976 to 5% in 1982; in teacher training from 14.8% in 1976 to 27.2% in 1982; and in medicine, where a decline from 22.7% in 1976 to

15.7% in 1982 can be observed. (See Tables 5.7 and 5.14)

So far as regional distribution is concerned, it is interesting to note that the present percentage share of provinces, municipalities and autonomous regions comes close to the distribution given in 1965. Beijing has still not reached its original share of 16% in the national total enrollment, but has already reached 8.2% (8.1% in 1976, see Table 5.6) The majority of those regions where the percentage share declined during the Cultural Revolution managed to return to their original level. In contrast, regions which increased their share during the Cultural Revolution had come back down by 1982. Qinghai, with an enrollment of 0.5% of the national total in 1965 and 1% in 1976 is now down to 0.4% again. Ningxia moved from 0.2% in 1965 to 0.8% in 1976 and is now at 0.4%. The most striking example, Xizang (Tibet), 0.8% in 1976, was down to 0.1% by 1982. We do not know the reason why this development took place but it fits with our earlier assumption, that the student population in these regions was dominated by rusticated youths. It seems a logical development that the regional share should decline along with new policies which no longer encourage the transfer of secondary school graduates to these regions.[58]

Finally, who is responsible for administering this 1982 total of 715 institutions of higher education? Although we do not have detailed statistics for 1981 and 1982 we may use those for 1979 and 1980 to give a rough characterisation of the present situation. The majority of universities and colleges are administered by regional bureaux of education and higher education under the supervision of the central Ministry of Education. In 1979 a total of 392 institutions were administered in that way and in addition 35 colleges and universities were controlled directly by the Ministry of Education. The remaining fraction of 206 institutions came under the jurisdiction of Ministries/Commissions of Industry, Agriculture, Forestry, Commerce and Finance etc. In 1980 these institutions made up 226 or 33% of the total number of universities and colleges, whereas the rest were controlled and financed by the Ministry of Education and regional subordinated bureaux. Table 5.15 gives precise details on the administrative control of the 633 higher institutions in existence in 1980.

As a new trend in Chinese higher education a number of private universities and colleges have been opened or reactivated.[59] At first glance the existence of private schools *(sili xuexiao)* and universities or colleges *(sili daxue, xueyuan)* may appear as a paradox in a socialist country. But in China private schools as well as private universities and colleges have a long standing tradition and made up 29% of the total number of universities and colleges in 1950 before they disappeared during the first half of the 1950's.[60] In the case of private schools, especially private schools for trade, commerce, and finance this form of schooling still was

Table 5.14

DISTRIBUTION OF INSTITUTIONS OF HIGHER EDUCATION BY SPECIALISATION (1978-1982)

	1978	%	1979	%	1980	%	1981	%	1982	%
TOTAL	598	100	633	100	675	100	704	100	715	100
Comprehensive Universities	32	5.4	33	5.2	32	4.7	32	4.5	32	4.5
Science and Engineering	184	30.8	191	30.2	203	30.1	207	29.4	206	28.8
Agriculture	50	8.4	52	8.2	56	8.3	55	7.8	56	7.8
Forestry	8	1.3	9	1.4	10	1.5	10	1.4	10	1.4
Medicine	98	16.4	107	16.9	109	16.2	112	15.9	112	15.7
Teacher Training	157	26.3	161	25.4	172	25.5	186	26.4	194	27.2
Language and Literature	10	1.7	10	1.6	10	1.5	10	1.4	10	1.4
Finance and Economics	21	3.5	22	3.5	30	4.4	36	5.1	36	5.0
Politics and Law	2	0.3	6	0.9	7	1.0	7	1.0	9	1.3
Physical Education	8	1.3	11	1.7	11	1.6	12	1.7	13	1.8
Fine Arts	19	3.2	22	3.5	26	3.9	27	3.8	27	3.8
Institutes for Nationalities	--	--	--	--	9	1.3	--	--	10	1.4
Other	9	1.5	9	1.5	--	--	10	1.4	--	--

Source: Zhongguo Baike Nianjian, 1981; Statistical Yearbook of China 1981, 1983.

Higher Education

Table 5.15

HIGHER EDUCATION INSTITUTIONS, BY ADMINISTRATIVE RESPONSIBILITY (1979)

Ministry	Number of Institutions		
	Central	Provincial	TOTAL
Education	35	392	427
Machine Building	29		29
Agriculture, Forestry, etc.	26		26
Railways, Communications, etc.	19		19
Metallurgical Industry, etc.	22		22
Water Conservancy, Power	7		7
Public Health	16		16
Light Industry, Textile Ind.	13		13
Construction	9		9
Coal, Oil	18		18
Finance, Commerce	16		16
Culture, Sports	15		15
Others	16		16
Total	241	392	633

Source: World Bank, China: Socialist Economic Development, Vol.III: The Social Sectors: Population, Health, Nutrition, and Education, Washington, D.C., 1983, p.161.

in existence until the outbreak of the Cultural Revolution in 1966. The reactivation of private schools as well as universities and colleges can be dated back to around 1979 and was first centered on the secondary level. This reactivation clearly was in line with an ongoing debate over how to compensate for problems which arose out of a lack of job vacancies for graduates from secondary schools. A growing number of secondary school graduates were not able to enter universities and colleges due to failure in the national entrance examinations and there was no place for them in specialised secondary or technical schools either. These schools seemed to be one method of absorbing this student population. Up to the present a great variety of private schools have developed all over China. Curricula for the most part cover such areas as book-keeping, tailoring, typing, repairs, fine arts, music and foreign languages.[61] In addition to secondary school graduates, including jobless or job-awaiting young people, "workers, government functionaries, soldiers, retired workers, housewives and peasants"[62] make up the student body of private schools. Candidates for recruitment are selected according to their education records or by organising special entrance examinations. In accordance with central and regional documents these private schools can be run by "retired engineers, technicians, doctors, teachers, experts, professors, artists and other personnel with a certain degree of specialised knowledge or particular skills who are enthusiastic to promote the cause of socialist education."[63] As a rule, "people who are working at present are not permitted to operate private schools."[64]

In contrast to state-run or collectively-run schools, private educational institutions charge a considerable annual tuition fee, set up their own curricula, organise their own entrance and final examinations and have to be self-financed. As examples we may cite the experiences of the 'Beijing Language Self-Education University' (BLSEU), the 'Xinghua College' in Beijing, the 'Tianjin Union Spare-Time University' and, as semi-private institutions, the 'University of Shantou' in South China's Guangdong province, as well as the 'Central Socialist Academy' run by the National Committee of the Chinese People's Political Consultative Conference. The BLSEU "was set up in March (1982) by fifteen 1962 graduates of the Beijing Teachers College"[65]. The university produced its own "three-million-charater text-book" which is mailed to students in "36 monthly installments, for a tuition fee of 30 yuan".[66] Students do not have examinations and after graduation have to look for jobs by themselves. They normally attend three-hour classes three times a week and besides the text-book fee have to pay 24 yuan every six months for coaching. If the students attend special lecture series another 6 yuan is charged. Even higher tuition fees of about 250 yuan per year are charged at the Xinghua College, Beijing. Its specialities are machinery-electricity and civil engineering, and courses last for four years.[67] The Tianjin Union Spare-Time University, "a private undertaking sponsored by the alumni of five noted universities of the country, including Beijing, Qinghua, Zhejiang and the former Yenching and Southwestern universities"[68] was opened in Tianjin in August 1983. The university offers 13 specialities and more than 1000 students have been selected by entrance examination.

In contrast to these private universities, two other universities which might be described as semi-private have been set up recently in Beijing and in Shantou. The Central Socialist Academy, run by the National Committee of the Chinese People's Political Consultative Conference, originally opened in Beijing in October 1956 and had been closed down at the beginning of the Cultural Revolution. The curriculum covers "the basic theory of Marxism and theory and policies on the United Front"[69] and courses last for one year. The University of Shantou was built with the donation of a Hong Kong Chinese near Xiamen University and it is the second university in China built through donations by 'patriotic overseas compatriots'.[70] The university will consist of "departments of Chinese language, law, economics, foreign languages, history, mathematics, physics, chemistry, biology, fine arts, civil engineering and electronics".[71]

In addition to these private universities and colleges in recent times a new type of public higher education institution has emerged, the 'short-term vocational university' (*duanqi zhiye daxue*). In contrast to regular universities and colleges administered by organs of the State Council (ministries or commissions) and regional governments these colleges are different in at least seven aspects:

- the students accepted have to pay tuition, at an average 20-25 yuan per semester;
- after graduation students are not assigned to jobs according to unified state plans;
- students have to pay their own transportation and medical expenses;
- the colleges do not provide dormitories and students have to be commuters;
- the faculty is mostly drawn from other existing higher education institutions in the same city, and the physical facilities of these institutions are utilised as efficiently as possible;
- curricula are adapted to regional needs and courses last two to three years;
- after graduation all graduates of locally run higher education institutions receive the same wages as graduates from regular (four to five year) institutions in comparable specialities, in theory at least.[72]

Official statistics in 1983 revealed that the total enrollment at these institutions in 1982 was 20,460, the number of entrants 3,315 and the number of graduates 2,430. At present these are very modest numbers only, but one has to expect growth in these figures during the coming years because this form of higher education institution is well suited to China's limited financial resources and should produce many medium-level qualified personnel needed by the national economy.[73]

Finally, this discussion of institutional diversification would be incomplete if we did not mention a special type of higher education institution, which is clearly aimed at increasing the quality of students' output, teaching work and research: the keypoint, or 'priority higher education institutions' (*zhongdian gaodeng yuanxiao*). In 1981/1982 a total of 96 such priority universities and colleges with approximately 10% of the total national student population was distributed all over China.[74] Priority universities and colleges are characterised by a number of distinctive features. First, within the scope of central or regional education and science budgets these institutions receive a higher proportional share in financial allocations. Second, they have a more differentiated administrative structure. Third, they are likely to have a more advanced teaching and research staff. Fourth, the students they select normally have received more points in their enrollment examination than their counterparts at non-priority schools. Fifth, they are equipped with far more and better scientific instruments and instruction media. Sixth, they are more likely to have an international academic reputation and in some cases publish their own research journals.[75]

The Reform of the Curriculum

Parallel to quantitative changes in China's higher education system, a number of measures have been taken to improve the quality of teaching and research at universities and colleges. The length of study increased from an average of 3 years between 1970 and 1976 to 4 years in 1977, and in special cases 5 to 6 years in 1983. The majority of undergraduates (benke xuesheng) will study their speciality for about 4 to 5 years at regular universities and colleges while another group will study for 2 to 3 years (zhuanke xuesheng) at colleges which have been termed as specialised or vocational colleges, or, with reference to the American pattern, as junior colleges (gaodeng zhuanke xuexiao).[76] Table 5.16 gives comparative figures for enrollment at these two distinct levels within higher education. It should be noted that only graduates of regular 4 to 5 year universities and colleges will qualify to apply for higher degree programmes.

According to the international classification of educational systems, this form of college should be termed a 'higher technical college'.[77] At the present stage of development these mainly comprise institutions in the fields of engineering, finance, trade, commerce, and teacher training. According to Table 5.17, undergraduates in the fields of engineering and teacher training made up the main proportion with 78% and it can be assumed that in the medium range future the percentage of students in engineering may be increased, partially at the expense of teacher training.[78]

If one follows what has been written in general as well as in academic journals, a whole series of problems in the higher education curriculum are being discussed. As seen from the students' and teachers' point of view, "in recent years some youths, when they register to take examinations for entry into a school of higher learning, tend to show an unwillingness to choose certain subjects which are regarded as 'having forlorn prospects'. Such subjects include geology, metallurgy, petroleum, coal, chemical engineering, water conservancy, teacher training and other specialities."[79] General complaints are also made about the teaching style in higher

Higher Education

Table 5.16: ENROLLMENT AT REGULAR AND SPECIALISED INSTITUTIONS OF HIGHER EDUCATION (1949-82)

Type of Institution	Enrollment								
	1949	1952	1957	1965	1976	1978	1980	1981	1982
Regular universities/Colleges (4-5 yrs of study)	93,900	131,300	393,300	644,000	—	458,500	861,900	1,060,645	928,901
Higher Technical Colleges (2-3 yrs of study)	22,600	59,800	47,900	30,400	564,700	397,800	281,800	218,827	225,053
TOTAL	116,500	191,100	441,200	674,400	564,700	856,300	1,143,700	1,279,472	1,153,954

Type of Institution	Enrollment (in %)								
	1949	1952	1957	1965	1976	1978	1980	1981	1982
Regular Universities/Colleges (4-5 yrs of study)	80.6	68.7	89.2	95.5	—	53.5	75.4	82.9	80.5
Higher Technical Colleges (2-3 yrs of study)	19.4	31.3	10.8	4.5	100	46.5	24.6	17.1	19.5
TOTAL	100	100	100	100	100	100	100	100	100

Source: Zhongguo Gaodeng Xuexiao Jianjie, p.4;
Education in China: The Past Five Years, Ministry of Education, 1982.

Table 5.17

ENROLLMENT AT REGULAR AND SPECIALISED INSTITUTIONS OF HIGHER EDUCATION, BY FIELD OF SPECIALISATION (1982)

Field of Specialisation	Regular Universities and Colleges (4-5 years of study)		Higher Technical Colleges (2-3 yrs. of study)	
		%		%
TOTAL	928,901	100	225,053	100
Engineering	362,763	39.1	35,451	15.8
Agriculture	54,764	5.9	9,563	4.2
Forestry	11,020	1.2	452	0.2
Medicine/Pharmacy	114,267	15.5	19,771	8.8
Teacher Training	149,532	16.1	139,916	62.2
Social Sciences	55,649	6.0	4,014	1.8
Natural Sciences	79,140	8.5	1,992	0.9
Finance & Economics	45,341	4.9	10,639	4.7
Politics and Law	12,561	1.3	2,073	0.9
Physical Education	8,875	1.0	630	0.3
Fine Arts	4,988	0.5	552	0.2

Source: Education in China: The Past Five Years, 1983.

education. The method of instruction has been described as "dull, dry, and stereotyped"[80] and as a process in which "the teacher copies the content of the textbook on the blackboard and the students recopy it into their notebook. With this repeated copying of the contents of the book, the teacher is writing until he is soaked with sweat, the students are copying to exhaustion, and their desire to seek knowledge is abating considerably."[81] Alternatives, however, are not easy to arrange. The curriculum design at universities and colleges for the most part clearly favours class room organised, teacher-centred instruction and reinforces the problem.

At a number of universities and colleges the credit system (xuefenzhi) has been introduced and students may have a choice between compulsory and optional courses within their speciality. However, at most institutions up to now the bulk of instruction is fixed. About 20-25% of the total instruction is spent on courses in the history of the Chinese Communist Party, political economy, philosophy, foreign languages and sports. The rest is fixed on studies in the core subjects of the selected speciality, and at a maximum, only 7-10% of the total instruction may be given in the form of optional courses.[82]

Noted scientists are concerned about this situation. In their view "for many years our teaching method has been 'spoonfeeding'[83] and "teaching over-emphasises the transmission of knowledge and fails to cultivate the ability to do independent work."[84] The absence of this ability seems to be the most serious weakness many teachers and administrators see in contemporary students. A study prepared by the Hubei Provincial Education Bureau in 1982 evaluates the capabilities of students in the River Control Department of the Wuhan Hydraulic and Electric Engineering Institute in the following way:

> They are strong in acquiring knowledge but weak in creative research; Strong in their grasp of book knowledge but weak in resolving concrete problems; Strong in abstract thought but weak in comprehensive applications; Strong in mathematical reasoning but weak in means of expression. Generally speaking, the students have good intellectual qualities, they are young and have quick, lively minds. But there also is a tendency to value theory and slight practice, which influences their ability to apply theory and knowledge in reaching independent solutions to real problems.[85]

This evaluation can be taken as a general one and one may ask how it will be possible to change this situation. Although lots of foreign teaching materials have been translated, adapted to Chinese needs and introduced into higher education, the prevailing structure, modelled on the basis of Soviet interaction and the experience the First Five-Year Plan, probably will prevent China's universities and colleges from being rapidly transformed. This problem was neatly captured by Suzanne Pepper in the provocative question, "Can American branches be grafted onto a Soviet tree planted in a Chinese garden?"[86] Finally from society's point of view, particularly with regard to the national economy, the present structure of the higher education curriculum is characterised by an extremely unbalanced distribution of the supply and demand of graduates in various specialities and by the fact, that "a large number of institutes and universities specialise in only one particular field of science and their great weakness is their narrow scope".[87]

Intra-university Administrative Reforms

Although Chinese newspapers and academic journals have published lots of articles on general reforms in higher education administration and management in recent years, the foreign observer is far from being able to draw a comprehensive picture of the ongoing debate on that issue.[88] The following introduction to recent developments in administrative reforms can not be any more than a first step in the direction of empirical analysis. In our view, the following three issues constitute the core of reforms and reform debates:

- Attempts to separate Party and administrative work;
- Measures to increase the effectiveness of training and allocation of teachers and scientists;
- Attempts to increase the administrative-academic autonomy of higher education institutions.

Attempts to separate Party and administrative work are part of an overall reform of universities and colleges which aims to break the Party committees' monopoly over decision-making. Based on regulations revived from the 1960's,[89] the new model of university administration favours a 'university affairs committee', or 'university council' (xiao-wu weiyuanhui), as the supreme decision-making body of the university administration. Its members are to be elected rather than appointed, as earlier. Similar organs will be organised at the department level and the department chairman is "responsible for teaching, scientific research, and administrative work"[90] while the Party committee "will retain a watchdog function to guarantee that party policies are being implemented correctly."[91] Figure 5.1 presents the administrative pattern now in use at Shanghai's Jiaotong University, which is regarded as a model of administrative reform.

Measures to increase the effectiveness of the training and allocation of teachers and scientists seem to be highly necessary due to an extremely unbalanced distribution of teaching and research staff at universities and colleges. So far as available statistics give evidence, higher education teaching staff, comprising full and associate professors (jiaoshou, fujiaoshou), lecturers (jiangshi), teachers (jiaoyuan) and assistants (zhujiao), on a national level were distributed as follows in 1980: lecturers - 111,700 or 45.2%, teachers - 52,600 or 21.3%, assistants - 66,000 or 26.7%, associate professors - 13,000 or 5.3% and full professors - 3,600 or 1.5%, forming a total teaching staff of 246,900 persons and a teacher-student ratio of 1:4.5.[92]

In contrast to these nationwide statistics, figures for various universities and colleges draw quite different pictures with a wide range of possibilities. For example we may cite the prestigious Beijing University as an extremely well equipped university with full professors making up 5%, associate professors 15%, lecturers 56%, assistants 26%, and teachers 3% of the total teaching staff. The Beijing Institute of Technology appears even more advanced with a teaching staff composed of 3% full and 15% associate professors, 64% lecturers, 17% teachers and less than 1% assistants.[93] The

Figure 5.1: ORGANISATIONAL CHART OF SHANGHAI JIAOTONG UNIVERSITY

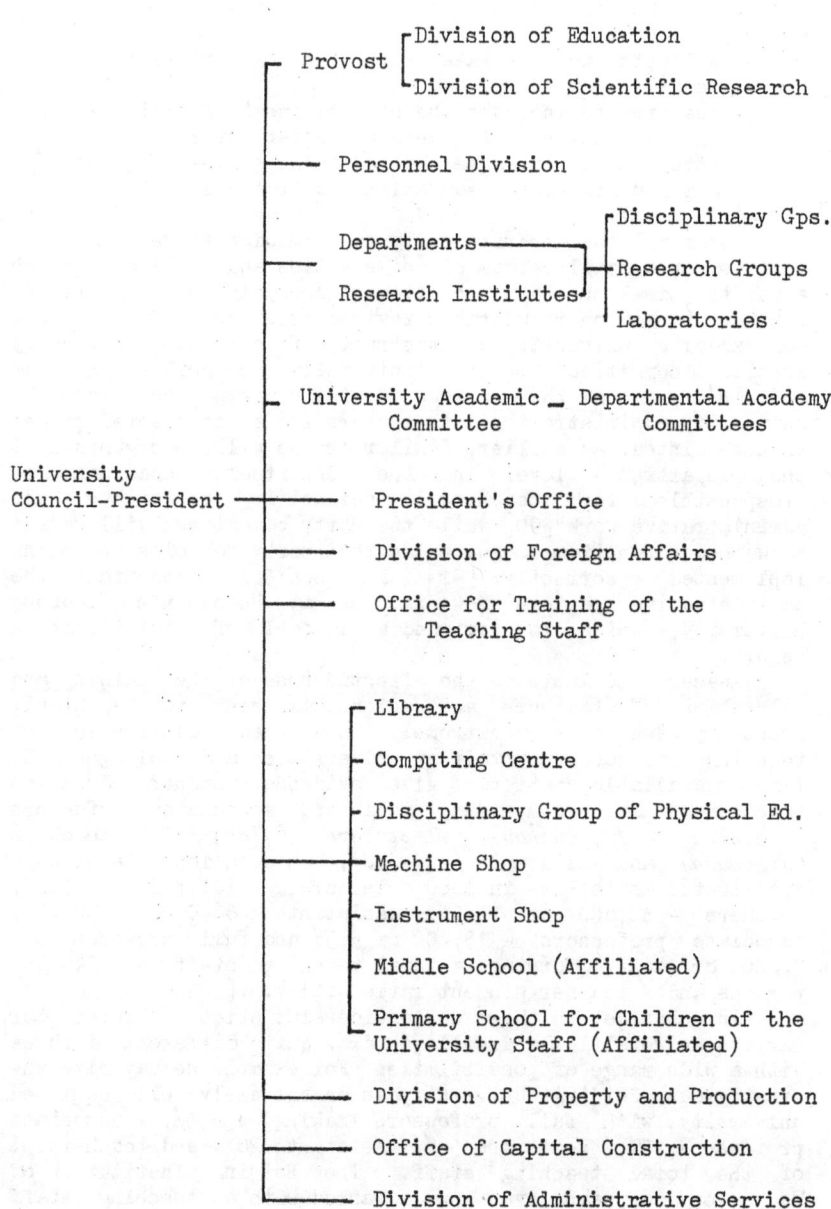

Source: Jiaotong University Introductory Handbook.

other extreme situation may be seen in the example of the Beijing College of Chemical Engineering, where full (0.5%) and associate professors make up 4.1% of the teaching staff only, and lecturers form 69.5%, assistants 22.4% and teachers 4%.[94] Taking these figures into account the total population of teaching personnel looks like an onion with a large quantity of lecturers in the middle, a small proportion of assistants and teachers at the bottom and only a minor fraction of full and associate professors on top. In addition the majority of professors seem to be over age. At Beijing University, for example, "the average age of professors is close to 70, associate professors 53.5, lecturers 46.6, and teaching assistants 34.4. Those who are 51 years of age and over make up 24.8% of the teaching staff".[95] What complicates the situation is that due to the principle of 'seniority' most of those on top of the academic career structure were trained during the 1950's and 1960's or even earlier, and may have an outdated knowledge of their speciality.

Moreover due to the distribution of academic teaching, administration and research, the total number of teaching staff is far from being the exact figure for those persons actually doing teaching work. Only a part have a regular teaching load - between 6 and 12 hours per week in general - while about 20-40% are engaged in other work.[96] Still another part of the teaching staff has been characterised as "members of the faculty who are (a) unqualified to teach (especially the young faculty trained during the Cultural Revolution); (b) unable to teach (usually because they are too old); and (c) unwilling to teach (because they only do research)".[97] If these groups "are subtracted from the total, there are not enough faculty members left to teach effectively. The result is a high ratio of students to teachers, which overburdens the faculty and leaves them little time to keep up in their own fields."[98] In light of this situation, it is easy to understand why the Chinese government is trying at present to increase the number of scientists doing teaching work, even though statistics suggest a good teacher-student ratio. Foreign observers often describe this in their trip reports, overlooking what is going on 'behind' the scenes.

In response to these aspects of mis-management, leading organs have already formulated guidelines for promoting bright candidates to higher positions in the universities' administrative hierarchy. "According to preliminary statistics through the end of 1981, over 145,000 teachers throughout the nation were promoted to lecturers or above, approximately equivalent to 3.9 times the number of lecturers and above prior to the 'Cultural Revolution'. Among them, over 2,700 were made professors, over 21,000 associate professors, and over 121,000 lecturers... According to the statistics on this period, the higher schools throughout the nation promoted 550 assistants to associate professors by grade skipping and 196 lecturers to professors... Today, compared with 1977, among the total number of teachers throughout the nation, the number of professors has risen from 1.2% to around 2%, that of associate professors from 2.9% to around 8% and that of lecturers from 14.8% to around 49%".[99] It can be expected that during the next years the potential of well qualified staff, by 'ideological-political' and 'professional' criteria,[100] may well be increased. What probably will remain uncertain is the extent to which a change of positions, and thereby of social status and power, will really take place in the administration of universities and colleges.

Attempts to increase the administrative-academic autonomy of higher education institutions at present mainly focus on issues of finance, teaching and research, and enrollment. The demand for more autonomy by Chinese universities and colleges appears strange to a foreign observer because these institutions already look like a mother who looks after everything. As Liu Da, president of Beijing's Qinghua University, pointed out, his "energy has not been spent in directly organising teaching and scientific research in the university, but has been spent in dealing with administrative affairs relating to the housing, clothing, food, transportation, childbirth, retirement, sickness and death problems of the teachers, staff, workers and students in the university... It is not society which manages the universities but rather the universities which manage society."[101] In this context Suzanne Pepper correctly pointed out, "that the terms autonomy and decentralisation, although often used interchangeably, are not necessarily synonymous in Chinese practice. Thus in education, the increased autonomy of individual institutions has typically been accompanied by increased centralisation within the system as a whole. The educational establishment retreats into its own sphere and reasserts control over itself, cutting off outside political and nonacademic interference."[102]

Under the aspect of finance, universities mainly demand more autonomy in decision-making over such issues as how to spend revenues generated by a surplus in the state budgetary allocation, by transferring knowledge or lending scientific instruments to other units, by signing contracts with production units or other scientific institutions.[103] Teaching and research issues for the most part center around the upgrading of teaching staff, either by on- or off-the-job training and especially by sending teachers and researchers abroad, either as visiting scholars or as research students, and the question of how to recruit persons for leading administrative positions inside the universities - by appointment or election. Finally, enrollment issues mostly centre on the question of how to evaluate and assess candidates' examination results and secondary school records and how to capture a reasonable quota of good quality future students in the course of the national enrollment plan.[104]

Higher Education Planning

The planning of higher education in China since the First Five-Year Plan (1953-57) has always been an important part of national economic planning and so an area of planning where education and cadre formation overlapped. Sources reveal that in the late 1950's planning was organised by means of 'planning tables' based on the 'balance method'.[105] In this context higher education was part of "cultural, educational, and health services planning tables" as well as of "cadre planning tables"[106]. Throughout the years after 1957 we have no details on how higher education was planned but especially in the period of the Cultural Revolution there appears to have been no planning process except discussion, not least because of the paralysed state statistical system. In 1982 for the first time a new Five-Year Plan was published, the Sixth Five-Year Plan of Economic and Social development' (1981-1985). It was apparently modelled on the basis of the same planning techniques used during the First Five-Year Plan. In this new plan, the following projections were laid down for higher education: The number of entrants in 1985 should be around 400,000, the number of enrolled undergraduate students around 1,300,000 the number of newly enrolled research students around 20,000 and the total number of enrolled research students around 50,000.[107] Between 1981 and 1985 around 1,500,000 undergraduates and 45,000 research students would graduate from universities and colleges and around 15,000 students and scientists would be sent abroad for further study and research. During the same period about 11,000 students and scholars would return from abroad.

In addition to this plan, a special plan for the development of higher education was discussed and approved in 1983. According to this plan, the number of undergraduates will increase at an average annual rate of 121,000 and will reach 1,760,000 by 1987, a 53% increase over the 1,153,000 who were enrolled in 1982."[108] The total annual number of entrants will reach to 550,000 in 1987 "a 75% increase over the 1982 figure of 315,000".[109] In contrast to earlier projections these figures look quite reasonable and it should be no problem for the Chinese leadership to reach these goals.

The problems will not be quantitative provision, rather the main issue will be on how to reach adequate quality in terms of national manpower needs. As early as 1978 the first news about problems in graduates' job assignments were reported and during the last two to three years the demands for reform have become more strident.[110] In addition, centrally and regionally organised research revealed a strong imbalance between the population of graduates at universities and colleges and the population of skilled manpower needed in production and service units in order to foster national economic growth. As an example we give reference to information which was released by Shanghai authorities to the World Bank delegation and is presented in Table 5.18. As can easily be seen, the greatest imbalance in supply and demand was in the fields of computers and automatic control, where only 8% of the need could be met.[111] On a national level, the 280,000 graduates of 1983 are faced with 570,000 vacant jobs, a 49% degree of satisfaction of needs only.[112]

The situation appears even worse if one has a look at supply and demand in specific economic sectors and regions. The reason for this imbalance is a general weakness in educational and labour planning. Leading authorities recently pointed out that "the present enrollment plan does not proceed entirely from national requirements and is often determined according to the existing conditions of vaious schools. This has brought about the following situation: some specialities enroll too

Table 5.18

REQUIREMENT AND SUPPLY OF NEW SCIENTIFIC AND TECHNICAL MANPOWER IN SHANGHAI, 1979

Field	Requirement	Supply	Supply as % of requirements
Automatic Control	251	20	8.0
Electronic computers	176	15	8.5
Industrial & Civil Engineering	480	47	9.8
Hydraulic Drive	97	10	10.3
Radio Communication	115	12	10.4
Industrial Automation(electric)	250	30	12.0
Architecture	107	13	12.1
Programme Design	241	31	12.9
Radio Technology	104	14	13.5
Boilers	162	23	14.2
Industrial Automatic Dials	123	20	16.3
Computing Mathematics	90	15	16.7
Chemistry	585	104	17.8
Motors	168	34	20.2
Machining Methods & Equipment	111	24	21.6
Physics	552	124	22.5
Chemical Engineering	89	21	23.6
Biology	319	80	25.1
Total	4,020	637	16.0

Source: World Bank, 1983, p.140.

many students who can not be assigned to jobs after graduation, while other specialities have too few students."[113] This seems to be a general picture. The main defects in administrative prerequisites for producing a skilled labour force have been identified as follows:

1. There is a lack of planning for long-range personnel training.
2. Annual student recruitment plans lack over-all balance with regard to the classification of specialities.
3. The structure of specialities is not rational and some specialities are too finely divided.
4. The employing units do not have definite job requirements.
5. Errors are common in making assignments.[114]

Table 5.19 indicates the distribution of graduates by specialialisation from 1977 to 1982.

The last point of the above list brings us to the next most important problem in the process of an optimal allocation of manpower. In the final stage of manpower planning and policy implementation, that is the placement of graduates, there is considerable mis-management relative to region and speciality. The imbalance between economic demand and higher education is exacerbated by failure to assign appropriate work posts. "According to incomplete statistics, of the 600,000 graduates who graduated in 1981 and 1982, more than 20,000 do not have jobs suited to their special training."[115] In a number of cases it has been reported that graduates have been assigned to jobs which have absolutely nothing in common with their speciality, a situation which has been caused by "a too rigid allotment by our planning departments. The placement of all students from institutions of higher learning graduating in various specialised fields is carried out in a unified centralised operation by the State Planning Commission, and down at the level of departmental commissions again in a unified centralised operation by the personnel departments... We must realise that this system of placement may leave some departments without the needed personnel."[116] The aspect of regional distribution of graduates is especially problematic because "a relatively large number of college graduates are assigned to large cities, the interior, large units, and state-operated enterprises, where they become 'superfluous' personnel, but small cities, outlying districts, small units, and collectives, which already had shortages, have been assigned a small number of college graduates, which has made the phenomenon of a shortage of qualified personnel even more serious."[117]

By mid-1983 the situation must have become very serious, especially in the case of regional distribution. Measures were taken by the Ministry of Education to transfer a number of

Higher Education

Table 5.19: GRADUATES OF INSTITUTIONS OF HIGHER EDUCATION, BY FIELD OF SPECIALISATION (1977-82)

	1977	%	1978	%	1979	%	1980	%	1981	%	1982	%
Engineering	73,562	37.8	56,512	34.3	21,362	25.1	44,000	30.0	12,199	8.7	172,136	37.7
Agriculture	12,706	6.5	13,929	8.5	9,748	11.5	4,200	2.9	7,902	5.6	32,562	7.1
Forestry	2,119	1.1	2,605	1.6	1,281	1.5	1,200	0.8	933	0.7	5,488	1.2
Medicine	34,860	17.9	27,459	16.7	13,483	15.8	*17,700	12.1	9,512	6.8	25,963	5.7
Teacher Training	37,038	19.1	35,430	21.5	24,331	28.6	61,800	42.2	103,422	74.1	129,463	28.3
Social Sciences	13,992	7.2	11,808	7.2	5,421	6.4	6,400	4.4	1,210	0.9	27,449	6.0
Natural Sciences	11,693	6.0	12,743	7.7	5,682	6.7	8,500	5.8	1,989	1.4	40,747	8.9
Finance and Economics	4,589	2.4	1,627	1.0	1,904	2.2	1,200	0.8	2,079	1.5	13,143	2.9
Politics and Law	294	0.2	99	0.06	-	-	100	0.07	-	-	1,238	0.3
Physical Education	2,135	1.1	1,256	0.8	1,498	1.8	1,000	0.7	73	0.05	5,647	1.2
Fine Arts	1,438	0.7	1,113	0.7	375	0.4	500	0.3	321	0.2	3,308	0.7
TOTAL	194,426	100	164,581	100	85,085	100	146,600	100	139,640	100	457,244	100

Source: World Bank, 1983; Zhongguo Baike Nianjian 1981; Statistical Yearbook of China 1981, 1983.
* It is unknown whether the figure includes graduates of pharmacy, or not.

graduates to backward regions but the population of graduates rebelled. Quite a number of cases were reported where graduates objected to state job assignments, if they had to leave for frontier and less developed regions.[118] Finally in June 1983 the Ministry published an open letter to parents of graduating college students entitled 'Let your children go wherever the motherland needs them most to put their abilities to good use'.[119] It said parents should let their children "face the world, brave the storms and boldly allow them to go to places where they can temper themselves, grow and accomplish something. It is no way of really loving our children to keep them at our side and arrange a comfortable living environment and easy work for them."[120] As often heard, some leading cadres had used their position to push their own children - or those of relatives - into jobs in their home area, a situation which will hardly be changed quickly during the coming years. In response to these imbalances, the Ministry of Education decided to organise a special Commission for Higher Education Planning and changed regulations governing enrollment into higher education institutions. Candidates willing to take up jobs in less developed regions after graduation will now receive preferential treatment. However, in light of traditional bias against the countryside and poor living conditions, we may expect that these problems will not be solved within the period of the next two Five-Year Plans.[121]

Finally, we must turn to the problem of the economics of higher education for a brief review, since the financing of higher education is one of the most important issues under debate in education circles at present. The majority of the Chinese political leadership seem to have accepted the view that education, and especially higher education, must be viewed as a productive force, instead of taking the view that it only belongs to the superstructure of society. Great efforts have been made to increase the share of higher education in the state budget for education. Investments in higher education as part of the total capital investment in school buildings (excepting specialised secondary schools) made up 30.1% in 1977, 51.7% in 1978 and increased to 61.5% in 1979, 64.1% in 1980, reaching a maximum with 65.6% in 1981 and coming down to 60.4% in 1982.[122] As Table 5.20 points out, 30.5% of the total expenditures in formal and nonformal education were made on higher education in 1979, and nearly the same (33.6) on primary education. Table 5.21 indicates the importance placed on higher education by the present leadership in the funding of its recurrent expenses relative to other levels of education. In light of the experiences of other Less Developed Countries (LDCs), this seems to be a quite high proportion for higher education in relation to primary education expenditures.

So far as international experience may give a frame of reference, the similar proportion of nearly one third for higher and primary education indicated in Table 5.22 is not the

Table 5.20

EXPENDITURES IN FORMAL AND NONFORMAL EDUCATION OF ALL TYPES, BY SOURCE, 1979
(billion yuan)

	Total Expenditure		Ministry of Education		Expenditure by provinces, counties, brigades enterprises, etc.		Private Expenditure (fees, books, etc.)
Primary education	4.4	33.6%	2.5	29.8%	1.2	32.5%	0.7
Secondary education	4.7	35.9%	3.4	40.4%	1.1	29.7%	0.2
Tertiary education	4.0	30.5%	2.5	29.8%	1.4	37.8%	0.1
Total	13.1	100%	8.4	100%	3.7	100%	1.0
Of which:							
Capital expenditure	1.4		0.7		0.7		—
Recurrent expenditure	11.7		7.7		3.0		1.3

Source: World Bank, 1983, p.181.

Higher Education

Table 5.21

GROWTH OF RECURRENT EXPENDITURE, BY TYPE, 1977-1980

	1977	1978	1979	1980
		(billion yuan)		
Higher Education	0.78	1.14	1.61	n.a.
Primary Teacher Training	0.15	0.20	0.24	n.a.
Secondary Schools	1.74	2.17	2.40	n.a.
Primary Schools	1.57	1.77	1.95	n.a.
Special allowance	0.73	0.81	0.84	n.a.
Teacher upgrading	--	--	0.07	n.a.
Nonformal education	0.07	0.07	0.08	n.a.
Miscellaneous	0.26	0.40	0.51	n.a.
Total	5.30	6.56	7.70	8.80

Source: World Bank, 1983, p.185.

Table 5.22

PERCENTAGE DISTRIBUTION OF EDUCATIONAL EXPENDITURES, BY LEVEL OF EDUCATION

	China*	Other LDCs**	OECD countries**
		(percentages)	
Primary Education	34	45	37
Secondary Education	36	32	39
Tertiary Education	30	23	24

* Data for 1979.
** Data for 1975.

Source: World Bank, 1983, p.184.

Higher Education

optimum distribution of finance. Table 5.23 shows the vast gap between unit costs at primary and tertiary levels in China. According to World Bank studies, the experiences of developing countries "leave no doubt that top priority should be given to primary education as a form of human resource investment".[123] Psacharopoulos calculated the social rate of return as 27% for primary education, 16% for secondary education and only 13% for higher education, based on an analysis of 22 African, Asian and Latin American countries.[124] On the other hand one has to admit that the Chinese government is clearly on the right track in increasing education and particularly higher education budgets, partially at the expenses of other productive branches of the economy.[125] The problem for the Chinese at present surely is that they have to catch up by increasing science and education budgets in order to compensate for the under-estimation of education during the Cultural Revolution. In earlier sections of this chapter, it has been shown how higher education suffered more severe disruption than other levels of education in that period. It may be predicted that the proportion of expenditure on higher education will be lowered in the coming years in order to increase primary and secondary education budgets. At present overall educational expenditures still lag behind the international standard for developing education. With around 3% of the Gross National Product spent on education, 2.1% if we take central government expenditure only, China now stands where the average developing country stood at the beginning of the 1960's. See Figure 5.2.

Table 5.23

UNIT COSTS OF EDUCATION AT DIFFERENT LEVELS,
AS A PERCENTAGE OF GNP/CAPITA

	China	Other LDCs	OECD countries
		(percentages)	
Primary Education	8	15	16
Secondary Education	19	52	21
Tertiary Education	442	362	55

Source: World Bank, 1983, p.183.

Higher Education

Figure 5.2

PUBLIC EXPENDITURE ON EDUCATION AS A PERCENTAGE OF G.N.P.

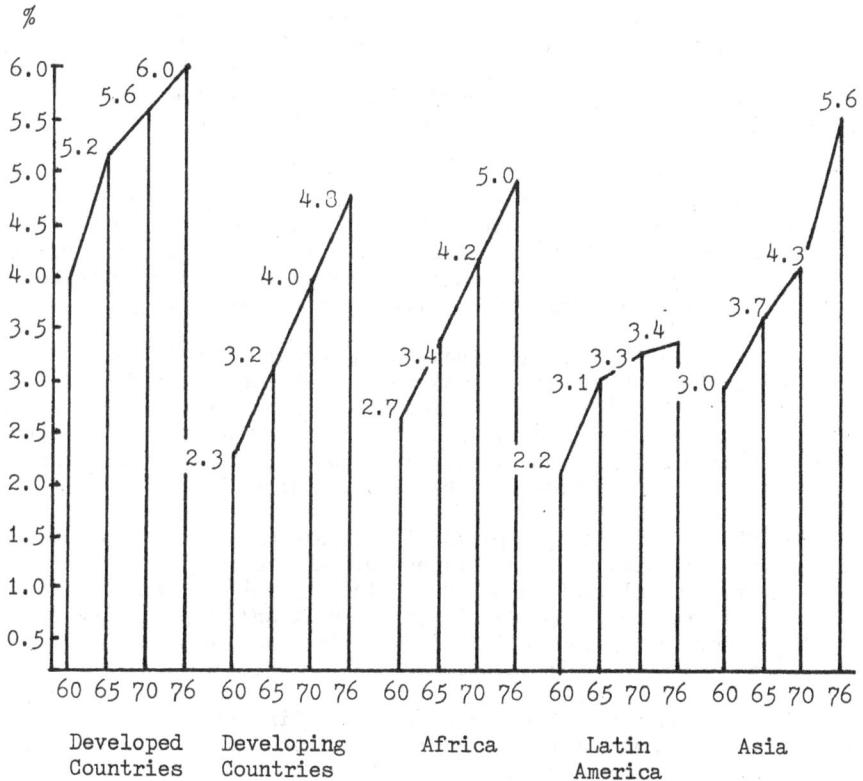

Source: G. Carceles, 'Development of Education in the World: A Summary Statistical Review', in International Review of Education, Vol. XXV, 1979, p.164. (Permission to copy this figure has been granted by the publisher).

QUALITY AND EQUALITY IN HIGHER EDUCATION: A RETROSPECTIVE VIEW

Throughout the 1970's an internationally growing stream of literature on Chinese economic, social and educational development appeared which generated three 'myths' of Chinese reality: The myth of the transferability of Chinese revolutionary experience to other developing countries, the myth of democratic and egalitarian structures in Chinese society, and the myth of an appropriate implementation of the unity of mental and manual labour.[126] China was identified as a new model for the process of societal development and the following educational points were emphasised:

1) The apparent "increase of educational opportunity for children from culturally deprived families, by a changed admissions, examinations and promotion system; the decentralisation of schools and greater stress on rural schools; the diversification of types of schools, with such new types as 'half-work, half-study schools'."[127]

2) "Integrating intellectuals with worker-peasants and thus closing the gap between intellectual and manual labour"[128] by politico-ideological education, the transfer of secondary graduates to the countryside, sending teachers to do manual work and incorporating a much higher proportion of practice into school curricula.

3) "Raising the participation level, status and self-esteem of worker-peasants"[129] by establishing special 'revolutionary' administrative organs as leading units in schools and universities, by linking up schools and universities with other production units and accepting non-academic teachers at educational institutions.

4) "Eliminating standard-of-living differentials between cities and rural areas"[130] by transferring schools and universities to the countryside, and

5) "Eliminating Western, Soviet and 'bourgeois-revisionist' influence in the schools by downgrading the role of teachers and school administrators..., scrapping all former textbooks... (and) politicising the curriculum".[131]

Clearly, the extent to which these principles were implemented, the more rigorous the better, formed one definition of educational quality, but it was only one among several competing definitions put forward by different political groups. It is essential to note that this definition was the <u>prevailing</u> standard for evaluating education policy and educational structures until 1976, and it was the definition of that group which the Chinese later termed 'the Gang of Four and their followers' and which was internationally been termed as the radicals or 'Cultural Revolution left'.[132] The mistake of quite a number of scholars attracted by the Chinese experience was that they took this definition at face value, at the same time overlooking many constraints that were kept out of the political arena of discussion in China. They accepted this definition as their own and assessed Chinese education on the basis of an internal Chinese interpretation instead of making their own independent assessment. As it turned out later, this definition could only guide education so long as the ideal of modernisation was not related to Western economic theories, something difficult to maintain with China's growing international interaction, which started in 1971/1972 and led to increasing economic contacts up to 1976. As soon as the general orientation of how to modernise the country was changed, this definition would become useless, and that's just what happened after 1976. Information which has been published since then reveals that the 'quality' of education until 1976 was actually very poor by international standards. We will try to assess the situation in retrospective, taking into account that figures now given for the period of the Cultural Revolution might be biased, as would be politically expedient, to legitimate the new policy.

First, a central question may be the quality of output in higher education, that is the quality of graduates between 1966 and 1976. As we noted earlier, Chinese universities were not reactivated before 1970 and due to the reduction in yearly admissions we calculated the loss of graduates at about 2.4 to 3.3 millions. (See note 112) So far as quality is concerned we have great difficulty in generating an ideal indicator for Chinese reality. As a rough estimate we may use an idea of Crombag which defines "quality of graduates as the average amount of subject matter and the depth in which it is mastered by the graduates."[133] According to this approximation "the quality of graduates can be expressed in terms of the following components:

(a) the number of standardised pages of subject matter to be studied;
(b) the number of different tasks the students can perform successfully;
(c) the length of learning experiences, which cannot be broken down into a set of separable learning tasks."[134]

Although this method of assessing educational quality looks rather oversimplified, we have to admit that even for this type of evaluation we do not have enough facts on Chinese higher education reality due to regional variations. What can be said is if these were turned into questions, the Cultural Revolution answer on all three points must be "very small". In contrast, todays' situation would yield as answers a high work load for

Higher Education

students, a greater number of different tasks to be performed and an increased length of learning. Present day higher education clearly favours the cognitive over affective and psycho-motor teaching aims, while until 1976 the focus of instruction was upon affective and psycho-motor domains.[135]

So far as the issue of 'equality' is concerned, until 1976 the prevailing interpretation was given in the light of what has been listed under point 1 of what constituted the definition of quality of education: "the increase of educational opportunity for children from culturally deprived families." For our evaluation we will make use of a concept of educational equality which has been elaborated by Farrell in a recently published study on comparative education. From his point of view "several facets of equality can be usefully distinguished":

1. Equality of <u>access</u> - the probabilities of children from different social groupings getting into the school system.
2. Equality of <u>survival</u> - the probabilities of children from various social groupings staying in the school system to some defined level, usually the end of a complete cycle (primary, secondary, higher).
3. Equality of <u>output</u> - the probabilities that children from various social groupings will learn the same things to the same level at a defined point in the school system.
4. Equality of <u>outcome</u> - the probabilities that children from various social groupings will live relatively similar lives subsequent to and as a result of schooling (have equal incomes, have jobs of roughly the same status, have equal access to the sources of political power).[136]

An evaluation of these facets of equality depending on the candidates origin can only be done under the aspects of sex, class origin and ethnic origin in the Chinese case, because no more data are available. Even for these aspects, statistics are often no more than rough estimates.

Access to higher education related to sex was reported officially to be around 20-30%, depending on the specialisation of higher institutions. In reality we do not have representative statistics for the distribution of female students at higher education institutions during the Cultural Revolution or for their proportion in yearly admission. The situation changed after the new leadership came to power, and figures for 1979 onwards were reported. These are given in Table 5.24. In 1980, 23.4% of all students were females, and 25.1% of the teaching staff at universities and colleges was female. In 1981 respective figures were 24.4% and 25.6% and in

1982 the proportion went up to 26.2% for students and 25.8% for teachers.[137]

Class origin as a criterion for preferential treatment has gone out of use since 1978.[138] Until 1976 statistics spoke of 'worker-peasant-soldier-students' relating to the kind of job the candidates had had before applying for admission to a university or college, and not relating to the position of the head of the family (whether the head was a worker, peasant, soldier, or cadre). This means these statistics are incompatible with present day statistics, and those for the pre-Cultural Revolution period. As reported in 1982, the percentage of new students out of families of workers and poor and lower-middle peasants in 1979 made up 54.31%, in 1980 55.58%, and in 1981, 56.90%.[139] It becomes clear that the children of staff members, intellectuals and cadres form the bulk of potential candidates for higher education, a situation similar to that of the 1960's.

Access to education for candidates of minorities origin is easier to assess, especially in the light of new publications. According to the results of China's 1982 population census the population of minority nationalities was 67,233,254, or 6.7% of the total population[140] and occupied 50-60% of China's land area mostly frontier regions and regions rich in raw materials. In the wake of the present policy of the 'four modernisations', the Chinese government has taken a more favourable view towards the development of minority social, cultural, and educational affairs. This is the realisation, by no means new, that "without a large number of cadres of minority nationalities who uphold the socialist road and the party's leadership and possess professional knowledge and ability - in particular, experienced scientific, technical and management personnel - it will be impossible to eliminate the de facto inequality among nationalities and to fundamentally solve the nationality problem in China" and "the most far-sighted approach to helping minority nationalities is to begin with good education for training and bringing up experienced people."[141]

Up to mid-1983 the Chinese media reported a great variety of measures on a national and regional scale to solve these problems. So far as an evaluation is already possible, developments may be summarised in the following six points: [142]

- A higher proportion of the State budget expenditures has been offered as financial aid to regional governments' culture, science, and education budgets (especially Xizang, Xinjiang and Nei Monggol);

- At regular and specialised universities and colleges preparatory classes and regular courses have been established for students of minorities origin;

- The required national entrance examinations' minimum

Higher Education

Table 5.24

PROFILE OF HIGHER EDUCATION ENTRANCE EXAMINATION CANDIDATES (1977 - 1983)

Examination Candidates	1977	1978	1979	1980	1981	1982	1983
TOTAL	5,700,000	6,000,000	4,684,000	3,300,000	2,589,000	1,860,000	1,670,000
			%	%	%		
Male			77.49	65.1	66.3		
Female			22.51	34.9	33.7		
Rusticated Youths				17.2	17.8		
Workers, Cadres, Demobilised Soldiers				3.4	2.4		
Graduates of Urban Secondary Schools				20.3	24.9		
Graduates of Rural Secondary Schools				50.1	44.4		
Minority Nationalities			3.63	5.2	5.38		
Overseas Chinese (incl. Hong Kong, Macao, Taiwan)				0.05	0.07		

Fields of Applications			
Institutions of Social Sciences and Teacher Training	37.0	33.2	26.4
Institutions of Engineering, Agriculture and Medicine	63.0	66.8	70.9
Institutions of Fine Arts and Physical Education			2.5

Source: Xinhua News Agency, (London), 13 May, 1978; Beijing Review, No.31, 1978, p.4; Zhongguo Baike Nianjian 1980, p.538; Guangming Ribao, 4 August, 1981. In addition figures for 1982 disclosed that of the 305,000 admitted students 21.40% were graduates of urban secondary schools of 1982, 18.76% were graduates from county towns (1982), 15.63% were graduates from rural areas (1982) and 20.93% were rusticated youths. The remaining 23.28% consisted of workers, cadres, transferred and demobilised soldiers, and others. See Wen Hui Bao, 3.November, 1982, p.1; Rosen, Stanley, 'Secondary and Higher Education in the People's Republic of China', Paper prepared for the conference on 'The Relation between Secondary Education and Higher Education: An International View', University of California, Los Angeles, 25-28 July, 1983. For 1983, recently published data show that of the total of 1,670,000 candidates 850,000 (50.9%) were graduates of upper secondary schools of 1983, 770,000 (46.1%) were graduates of upper secondary schools of earlier years, 30,000 (1.8%) were currently employed and the rest made up 20,000 or 1.2%. See: Zhongguo Jiaoyu Bao, 7 August, 1983. According to the same source, in 18 provinces, municipalities and autonomous regions pre-tests had been organized to select 1,220,000 successful candidates (out of 2,790,000) for participating in the national entrance examination. At least 387,000 students were admitted. See: Xinhua News Agency, (London), 2 September, 1983.

standard has been lowered for applicants of minorities origin in order to increase their percentage in total entrants and enrollments;

- Special teaching materials and preparatory literature for higher education entrance examinations have been published;

- Correspondence education is offered at a small number of universities and colleges; and

- A comparatively small number of graduates from institutions of higher education and scientists have been tranferred to minorities regions for periods between several weeks and several years.

So far as our discussion of the tension between quality and equality is concerned, the point of major interest seems to be how students of minority origin were able to enter institutions of higher education. As statistics for the period 1950 to 1981 reveal, minority students never exceeded 4.2% of the total enrollment, except in 1976, and so lagged behind the minorities' share in the total population, which ranged between 6 and 6.7% during the same period, Table 5.25 gives these national figures and percentages. Only very recently have statistics become available to document the regional distribution of minorities at institutions of higher education. These are given in Table 5.26. So far as scattered information gives evidence, only in the case of Nei Monggol has the percentage of newly admitted students and the total enrollment of students of minority origin exceeded the regional percentage of population of minority origin. In 1979 minorities made up 15.5% of Nei Monggol's total population. As early as 1979 the percentage of newly admitted students of minorities origin came up to 26.5% and the percentage of totally enrolled students of minorities origin was 24.9% in 1979 and 27.5% in 1981. Xinjiang may be cited as an example where the distribution of minorities at institutions of higher education closely follows the regional percentage of population of minority origin. In 1981, 52.5% of newly admitted students were of minority origin and in 1979, 45% (1981: 56.4%) of the total enrollment of students was of minority origin.

In contrast to these quite balanced distributions, in the cases of Guizhou and Xizang a highly unbalanced structure emerged. Between 1977 and 1980, the percentage of newly admitted students of minority origin in Guizhou increased from 7.2% to 9%, whereas the regional percentage of population of minority origin stood at approximately 51%. Even more unbalanced was the situation in Xizang in 1981, when only 50.3% of newly admitted students of minority origin were reported in contrast to the 95.2% minority share in the total population.

Higher Education

Table 5.25:

STUDENTS AND TEACHERS OF MINORITY ORIGIN AT INSTITUTIONS OF HIGHER EDUCATION (1949-1981)

Enrollment	1950	1953	1957	1965	1976	1978	1980	1981
TOTAL	138,700	216,400	444,400	674,400	564,700	856,300	1,143,700	1,279,472
Minorities	1,300	5,500	16,100	21,900	36,600	36,000	42,900	51,200
Minorities as a percentage of total enrollment	0.9%	2.6%	3.6%	3.2%	6.5%	4.2%	3.8%	4.0%
Teachers								
TOTAL	17,300	33,600	70,000	138,100	167,400	206,300	246,900	249,876
Minorities	—	600	1,900	3,300	3,000	5,900	7,800	8,400
Minorities as a percentage of total staff	—	1.9%	2.8%	2.4%	1.8%	2.9%	3.2%	3.4%

Source: Zhongguo Gaodeng Xuexiao Jianjie, p.9; Zhongguo Tongji Nianjian 1981, p.26.

Higher Education

Table 5.26: REGIONAL DISTRIBUTION OF MINORITIES AT INSTITUTIONS OF HIGHER EDUCATION

Region	Newly Admitted Students of Minority Origin as a Percentage of Total	Total Enrollment of Students of Minority Origin as a Percentage of Total Enrollment	Percentage of Population of Minority Origin (1982)
	%	%	%
Guizhou	7.2 (1977) 8.2 (1978) 7.8 (1979) 9.0 (1980)		51.0
Nei Monggol	26.5 (1979)	24.9 (1979) 27.5 (1981)	15.5
Ningxia	18.5 (1981)		31.9
Sichuan	3.1 (1981)		3.7
Xinjiang	52.5 (1981)	45.0 (1979) 56.4 (1981)	59.6
Xizang	50.3 (1981)		95.2
National	5.1 (1977) 4.2 (1978) 3.6 (1979) 4.3 5.2 (1980)* 4.8 5.4 (1981)**		6.7

* For 1980 two different figures were reported: 5.2% according to Guangming Ribao, 4 August, 1981, 4.28% in Zhongguo Baike Nianjian 1982, p.573.
** For 1981. Figures of 5.38% and 4.77% were disclosed in the same sources.

On a national scale figures disclose that in the case of entrants the percentage of minorities dropped immediately after 1976 to the lowest point in 1979 when only 3.6% were of minority origin. This resulted in strong pressure on the Chinese leadership. Signs of a response can be seen at the beginning of 1980 with the '1980 Regulations on Enrollment in Institutes of Higher Education' which laid down the following stipulations:

1) For schools and departments in the autonomous regions that teach in local national languages, the autonomous regions themselves will set examination questions, and administer the examinations and enrollment.

2) Some of the nation's key schools of higher learning will give special classes to minority nationality students this year; minimum acceptance scores will be lowered as appropriate for them; and enrollment will mainly be for examination candidates from border, mountainous and pastoral regions where minority nationalities live together.

3) Students who graduate from minority nationality secondary schools that teach in their own national languages and who take examinations to enroll in schools that teach in Chinese, can translate answers in their own languages to examination questions given in the subjects of politics, history, geography, mathematics, physics and chemistry. In the past two years, examination questions on language for schools that teach in Chinese were also translated and answered in national languages but due to some problems, beginning with 1980 examination questions on language will not be translated any more, they must be answered in Chinese ... and its standard will be lower than those of Han students.

4) Minority nationality students who live scattered in cities, when all conditions are equal, will be given priority over Han students in enrollment.[143]

As statistics indicate, these new guidelines for enrollment in higher education institutions have led to modest success in increasing the proportion of entrants and enrolled students from minority origin and up to 1983 the preferential treatment of candidates of minority origin was given high priority. In addition to the minority colleges (*minzu xueyuan*), which were established in the early 1950's and in 1981 comprised 10 institutions with an enrollment of probably 11,000 students, 126 graduate students and 2,345 entrants (1980: 9 colleges, 500 graduate students, 1,200 entrants and a total of 5,900 enrolled students),[144] altogether 10 national keypoint institutions of higher education, directly administered by the Ministry of Education, enrolled 446 students in preparatory courses between 1980 and 1981, and in 1982, 360 from 15 provinces.[145] In addition a number of non-key universities and colleges in the provinces of Sichuan, Hunan, Yunnan, Ningxia, Gansu, and Heilongjiang admitted between 400-500 students of minority origin in each.[146]

The notion of a tension between 'quality' and 'equality' in higher education which was the guiding theme for this chapter appears in retrospect to be less applicable to the Chinese situation than conventional wisdom would suggest. First, it has been demonstrated how definitions of quality changed over the three decades of the post-Liberation period, with a Soviet-oriented definition in the fifties, replaced by a radical revolutionary definition in the Cultural Revolution decade, then a concern for quality in relation to the achievements of the western industrialised world and Japan in the post 1976 period. In the Cultural Revolution period equality was not seen as antithetical to quality rather as the primary characteristic of a 'quality' higher education from a politico-ideological points of view. What remains in serious question, however, is whether Cultural Revolution provision, especially in the area of higher education, can be evaluated in terms of the classical western concepts ranging from equality of opportunity to equality of outcome. The quantitative evidence presented in this chapter suggests rather that politically defined 'quality' resulted in an 'equality' that was expressed more in revolutionary rhetoric than in the concrete provision of higher education on a more equal basis in terms of class, sex or ethnic origin.

In looking at the present situation, western notions of equality in education remain inappropriate for a country of over one billion people, whose leaders are still struggling to ensure that basic human needs are met. The term 'equity', as defined by Mary Warnock, might be more appropriate to the Chinese case: "We hold that everyone should have an equal right to two different things; to a certain amount of education and the chance or opportunity to get more than this if they want it."[147] For the first time in post-Liberation Chinese history, the constitution of 1982 expressed the obligation of the state to provide a substantial amount of education for the whole population, and the right and duty of all citizens to take advantage of this provision.[148] In a reconsideration of the concept of equality of educational opportunity, Coleman makes the point that the notion itself leads to a mistaken focus of attention on inequalitites within the education system rather than within society. What is of primary importance is the provision made by society, formally or informally, for access to a lifelong education that enables people to improve their social and economic conditions of life.[149] Chapter Seven of this book shows how far the Chinese have gone already through the development of informal adult education institutions which complement the expanding yet still limited provision for higher education in the formal sector. As for the formal sector, it appears that the service of economic modernisation and concepts of 'quality' associated with that task will remain fundamental to higher education policy for some time to come, a course which does not differ greatly from the Eastern European pattern.[150]

Chapter Six

TEACHER EDUCATION IN THE EIGHTIES

Billie L. C. Lo

INTRODUCTION

Deng Xiaoping's speech at the National Education conference held in April, 1978, marked a new direction in educational policies during the period of the Four Modernisations.[1] In the speech, Deng called upon educators to devote their efforts to four main areas: 1) raising the quality of education; 2) restoring order and discipline in schools; 3) reforming education to meet the needs of national economic development; 4) raising the quality and status of teachers. What runs through the whole speech is the theme that educational policies must be changed to bring up more and better qualified people to meet the demands of the Four Modernisations. Clearly the education of teachers is of crucial importance, since, in Deng's own words, "teachers hold the key to the success of a school in training qualified personnel for the proletariat; namely, workers with both socialist consciousness and culture who are developed morally, intellectually and physically." At the same time many other aspects of Chinese education have been affected by this shift in policy which emphasises quality. Examinations have been re-introduced; higher and secondary education have been reorganised; keypoint schools have been reinstated and new curricula proposed. Every measure has been geared towards raising the quality of education in terms of academic achievement.

Will the teaching profession be able to cope with these increased demands and altered functions? If the re-structured educational system aims at raising the students' educational level, then teacher training must first be re-structured to reflect this aim; and if the system aims at reproducing in students the dominant values of the present government, then this function must first be clearly observable in the training of teachers. The importance of teacher education to the development of the Chinese educational system as a whole cannot be under-estimated.

The implications of these policy changes in two major

areas may be regarded as relevant to the study of teacher training. Firstly, the emphasis on 'quality' in education in terms of academic achievement means that teachers have to be equipped with adequate knowledge in the subjects they teach. Now that aspirations among students have been raised, they expect more from their teachers. A 'good' teacher is now thought to be one who possesses valuable knowledge which is the key to attaining higher levels of education or ultimately a worthwhile vocation. Secondly, to meet the needs of the Four Modernisations, educational institutions, especially those at the secondary level, are being reorganised[2] to offer more varied forms of education in different fields, as chapter four has demonstrated. Correspondingly, teachers for these new and different forms of education have to be trained. Thus, teachers or potential teachers not only need to raise the level of their own knowledge, they also need to orientate themselves to different and more appropriate types of knowledge. Moreover, the rapid expansion of educational opportunities for school-age children makes it imperative to expand teacher training facilities at a comparable rate.

We need to ask then, if teacher education itself has been reformed to match the reorganised educational structure. What kind of new provisions, if any, have the authorities made to equip the teaching force to meet the new challenges? To answer these questions, one must look beyond the teacher training institutions themselves and analyse the general educational system to which teacher education is most closely linked. The wider socio-economic factors which affect its existence have to be considered also.

The approach to the study of teacher education in this chapter assumes that teacher education has to be viewed in relation not only to the internal structure of the educational system, but also to the external social and economic structure.[3] Hence, social factors such as those that affect the perceptions of teaching have to be considered. In the given economic structure, teaching should also be viewed as one occupation in a general manpower utilisation pattern. Recruitment into the occupation, level of training necessary for the occupation and career opportunities open to the person upon receiving this training are all factors which have to be considered.

Four facets of teacher education will be considered in relation to the above-mentioned social and economic factors:

1) The perceptions of teaching. This refers to the authorities' perception of what an ideal teacher should be, and the role and skills expected of him. These perceptions determine the kind of training the authorities want to provide to teachers and prospective teachers.

2) Teacher socialisation. This refers to the processes by

which prospective teachers are orientated to their expected roles. Teacher training strives to offer prospective teachers the experiences, concepts and values underlying these role-perceptions. External social and economic factors may combine to either enhance or act against the institutional process of orientating prospective teachers towards their roles.

3) Content or curriculum of teacher-training programmes. These are the means by which perceptions of teaching are conveyed while professional skills are developed for those in training. Ideally, the curriculum will try to develop all qualities expected by the authorities of a teacher; in practice, training provisions are often made only for skills deemed most necessary by the authorities.

4) Structure and organisation of teacher education and its relationship to other forms and levels of education. These set the conditions under which teacher education operates.

PERCEPTIONS OF AN IDEAL TEACHER

The desirable qualities of an ideal teacher in ancient China included many of the traits and qualities which are still being advocated in China today. These qualities can be listed under three main categories: 1) competence in subject matter, 2) teaching ability and 3) moral character. Confucius, the greatest teacher in the Chinese history of education, had established a reputation as a good teacher by the age of twenty because of his good moral standing and his profound knowledge. His ability to teach students according to their needs and abilities has often been upheld by Chinese educators as a requisite to be acquired by all later teachers.[4] Mencius, another great teacher in Chinese history, also saw the importance of using different methods in approaching different students.[5]

These qualities have remained goals for the ideal teacher even after the establishment of the Communist regime in 1949. In addition to these traditional qualities, one more category has been added to the ideal communist teacher: that is, his standing as a communist in the new society, an attribute measured by his dedication to communist ideology and willingness to serve the people in spite of hardships.

Changes in educational policies after the fall of the Gang of Four mean that what is required of the teacher has changed. The requisites of a 'good' teacher have become so different that they deserve some detailed treatment. These requisites can be observed in different articles in newspapers and journals;[6] but have been most systematically summarised into four categories in a section of the 'Temporary Regulations for Full-Time Secondary Schools'.[7]

1) The ability to teach academic subjects well:
Very clearly stated is the demand that "a teacher must teach his subject well". He has to "equip students with advanced scientific knowledge". To do this, a teacher has to take a most active role in preparing lessons, marking exercises and assisting students. It is specially emphasised that teachers should be allowed more freedom to do their job than they enjoyed in the past.

2) Love for Students:
Teachers should be responsible for the all-round development of students, understand their problems in daily life and in their studies. They should guide the students with patience and approach them with appropriate methods. "A teacher's love for his students is the prerequisite for teaching them well".

3) Willingness to be an exemplar:
A teacher must set an example of morality because what he does or says will eventually affect the students. Schools are urged to set strict standards on teachers' "moral and cultural training, life style, behaviour, and learning aptitude". To establish the exemplar-teacher, school authorities are reminded that they should never criticise the teachers in front of the students.

4) Professional competence:
This refers to competence in applying pedagogical principles to teaching. Teachers are urged to "master the tools of pedagogy, psychology and physiology". A good teacher should constantly improve himself in the mastery of the subject matter and in pedagogical practice.

The 'ideal' teacher in the post-Gang of Four period is one that is quite different from the 'ideal' teacher in any period of the regime. For one thing, his dedication to the communist ideology is not emphasised as much as before. There is a return to stressing the traditional requisites (i.e. competence in his subject, his teaching ability and his moral character). The reason for this change would make an interesting thesis for another paper, but for the purpose of this study, it suffices to point out that much more is now demanded from teachers. They not only have to know their subjects well, but also have to apply pedagogical principles to teach the subjects well. More is demanded from them in terms of their moral standing. Although the emphasis now is not so much on their ideological commitment as Marxists, they still have to "work hard without thought of personal profit or fame", given inadequate educational funds and facilities.

TEACHER SOCIALISATION

Once the roles expected of a teacher in a particular society are identified, it is then possible to determine how successfully teachers are socialised into these roles. Teacher training is given the responsibility of offering potential teachers the experiences, concepts and values underlying their prescribed roles. However, even before the institutional process of socialisation begins, a prospective teacher often enters a teacher training institution with certain preconceived ideas of what a teacher is. There are many social and economic factors that combine to form the social image of a teacher which affects a prospective teacher's acceptance of the roles. As a matter of fact, what is perceived from outside the teacher training institutions may have more impact on prospective teachers than what is being advocated inside. If the image of teachers is favourable and they command respect and acquire rewards commensurate with their responsibilities, then the process of communicating social and professional role expectations to potential teachers is relatively easy; if not, the process of conveying these role expectations becomes a constant struggle with forces outside.

China has, unfortunately, developed a rather unfavourable social image for her teachers. As early as the beginning of the regime, complaints and dissatisfaction about the hard life teachers experienced were expressed.[8] In spite of the severe shortage of teachers, few people were willing to join the profession;[9] and those who could find other jobs left the profession for a better life. However, those few who remained teachers were respected for the sacrifices they made and the hardships they suffered in order to educate the next generation.[10]

A more severe blow to the image of teachers came with the Great Proletarian Cultural Revolution when teachers' traditional status and role were severely criticised. Teachers were attacked, both physically and verbally. They were told to learn from workers, peasants and students in order to reform themselves.

Thus, communist teachers who had already been given insufficient material rewards were later deprived of the respect traditionally due to them. "It is unfortunate to become a teacher" was the popular feeling among teachers.[11] This difficult situation, in which teachers received neither respect nor enough income for a living, persisted throughout the period of the Gang of Four (1966-1976).

The situation has improved for teachers since the fall of the Gang of Four. the present government has made great efforts to give teachers a more favourable public image. Teachers are now given the glorious titles of 'People's Soul Engineers', 'People's Heroes' and 'Gardeners'[12] There is now a call for "respect for teachers and concern for teachers".[13]

However, history has made its impact on the teaching profession and the harm done cannot be remedied in a short time. "Many people are still afraid; they are reluctant to study in teacher training institutions and become teachers. Some still look down upon the teaching profession".[14] Social attitudes towards teachers have not improved significantly despite the government's call for respect for teachers. This is illustrated by the ill treatment that a group of primary school teachers received in a guest house in Dalian in August 1981. These teachers had come from all parts of China to participate in a national conference on the teaching of the national language in primary schools. They arrived at the Dalian Guest House to find that the beds which they had booked were taken by others. When they asked for water, they were refused and they were not allowed to use the lifts. Their humiliation stood out in stark contrast to the reception given to the participants of the national dance contest on the next day. This latter group came to the same guest house and were given rooms with clean beds and excellent service.[15] The Dalian incident is not an uncommon one. Disrespect for teachers, especially primary school teachers, is still very strong in many places.[16]

Negative social attitudes towards the teaching profession are also expressed in many other forms. Some parents who were once teachers themselves strongly oppose their children's becoming teachers because of the suffering they themselves experienced.[17] Teachers are discriminated against when they apply to join the Communist Party.[18] Verbal insults and even physical assaults are not uncommon treatment for teachers.[19] The Committee of the National Educational Workers' Trade Union recently listed twelve ways in which teachers' basic rights have been totally ignored.[20]

A low financial return to the teaching profession is another persistent problem. Most teachers, especially primary and secondary school teachers, receive salaries much lower than those of workers who have the same qualifications and number of years of working experience.[21] Salaries of even 'backbone' teachers who have taught for twenty years are still lower than those of workers who have just started working.[22] Even teachers with responsible positions in universities receive only 50 to 70 Chinese yuan a month.[23] Average monthly salaries of teachers have actually decreased, both in relative and in absolute terms. In 1956, a qualified primary school teacher could earn 70-75 yuan; [24] in 1980, a primary school teacher with ten to twenty years of teaching experience earns 40-50 yuan.[25]

In a developing country like China with limited skilled manpower resources, people with a relatively good education are much needed in many sectors of the economy. The Four Modernisations are now opening up more alternative occupations where both the financial returns and the prestige are higher. This tends to discourage teachers with good educational standing from staying within the profession. Fortunately, the policy that a change of occupation has to be approved by the authorities (except for rural teachers who can return to farming if they choose to)[26] has prevented an even more severe loss of teachers to other professions. However, with different sectors competing for qualified people, the teaching profession still loses many experienced personnel.[27] In the rural areas, many rural teachers simply return to farming because the new economic policies of share-cropping and of allowing private plots have made farming a more remunerative profession, if not a more respectable one.

The authorities are not unaware of the problems caused by teachers' low income and efforts have been made to raise it. In November 1981, there was a large-scale wage reform which raised the salaries of 12 million middle and primary school teachers by an average of 10 percent. However, only government teachers benefited from this salary readjustment. The majority of teachers who are rural commune teachers received an increase of only 50 yuan in their annual government subsidy.[28]

Unfortunately, even this system of granting subsidies to rural commune teachers is abused by local cadres. Subsidies for teachers are often used for more 'needy' purposes. There have also been cases in which local cadres have demanded a 'service charge' per teacher for every issuing of a subsidy.[29] So far, the most effective policies of improving teachers' livelihood are those advocated and implemented by concerned local cadres themselves.[30]

In addition to the social discrimination described above, recruitment to teacher education shows other biases. Available opinion and literature suggest that the quality of students in teacher-training institutions limits the achievement of the aims of teacher training.[31] As far as recruiting students is concerned, institutes of other forms of higher education and upper secondary schools are given priority in recruiting the best students.[32] All secondary teacher-training schools and most higher teacher-training institutes,[33] recruit students from among those who have failed to enter upper secondary schools or other institutes of higher learning.[34] This is true even with teacher-training institutes in big cities like Beijing and Shanghai.[35] Many of those recruited into teacher education have a strong sense of failure. Society looks at them as 'university failures'. For these student-teachers, teaching is not their desired goal. Many are looking for ways to 'escape' teaching. Thus, attempting to convey to them the role-expectations of a teacher and to orientate them towards these roles are futile efforts from the start.

Not only do recruitment policies make it difficult to develop in student-teachers a devotion to the profession, but the low standards of recruitment also make it difficult for teacher training institutions to turn out competent teachers. A considerable number of graduates assigned to teach in secondary schools have not attained an academic standard equal to that of upper secondary school graduates.[36] In one commune, 28 teacher training school graduates were rejected by the Commune Education Bureau because of poor standards.[37]

Under such conditions, training prospective teachers to fulfil the role-expectations outlined above is a very difficult if not impossible task. The social image of a teacher, his material returns, and the quality of students in teacher training in comparison to those of students in other forms of higher learning are all factors acting against the successful process of teacher socialisation before it has even begun.

To remedy the situation, the authorities have resorted to persuasion to improve negative social attitudes and to induce teachers to fulfil their roles. Appeals are made to their patriotic fervour, calling on them to dedicate themselves to the "glorious task of bringing up a new generation of revolutionary workers".[38] Titles of 'Special-Grade Teacher' and 'Model Educational Worker' are awarded to outstanding teachers; medals, certificate, and material awards are also given.[39]

The process of teacher socialisation in training institutions closely follows the government policy. Persuasion is the main strategy adopted, and efforts are made to convince students that teaching is a glorious profession. Occasions like convocations and opening ceremonies, are often used for this purpose. The following example is illustrative:

> In the beginning of a new term, we hold a big welcome ceremony to welcome them (the new student-teachers). Young Pioneers will present them flowers. When they graduate, the president will congratulate them and encourage them, enhancing their feeling of pride and glory in becoming people's teachers... On these occasions, we invite leading cadres and older teachers to talk about the five traditions of teacher training. 'Special-Grade Teachers' and alumni are also invited to talk about their personal experiences and feelings. Evening programmes of orientation include performances with 'Praise the Gardeners' as the main theme. We also show meaningful movies like 'The Rural Teacher'. All these are done to instil in new students a sense of glory in becoming a teacher.[40]

At other times, student committees hold discussions on themes like 'The Glory of being a People's Teacher' and 'A Respectful Profession'.[41] 'Special-Grade Teachers' and 'Model Teachers' are also invited to training institutes to talk about their teaching experiences and to boost the morale of the

Teacher Education

student-teachers.[42] Some training institutes have affiliated primary and secondary schools. They help student-teachers develop a love for children by organising 'friendship parties' in which student-teachers can have more contact with children.[43]

The very fact that the authorities and teacher-training institutions are constantly combating the idea that 'teaching is useless' shows that this problem is a very real one. The effects of these institutional efforts remain small as long as the conditions and atmosphere in wider Chinese society are not conducive to the development of a more positive attitude towards the profession. Right now, the low social status and meagre material rewards for teachers are hardly commensurate with their duties and obligations.

CURRICULUM

The curriculum of teacher-education is the precise means by which the kinds and quality of behaviour expected of teachers are developed. A close examination of the actual teacher-education curriculum gives some idea as to the kind of behaviour and professional skills most likely to be developed in prospective teachers. The term 'actual curriculum' is used because what the authorities decide on as the essential components of a teacher-education programme are very often not included. Due to different kinds of social and economic constraints, the actual curriculum is often very different from the projected one. Its provisions are more likely to relate to the kinds of behaviour and professional skills which are actually valued by the authorities than those made explicit in government plans and directives.

In China, those skills and attitudes seen by the authorities as being essential to the development of teacher education fall within four categories:[44]

1) Political and professional dedication. Teacher education should raise the students' political consciousness, and help them to realise the 'glory' of being People's Teachers, as well as the responsibility

2) A sound and rich knowledge in the subjects they teach. Teacher-training programmes should help students to raise their level of knowledge in specialised subjects.

3) A good understanding of pedagogical principles and the ability to apply them in teaching. Teacher education should familiarise students with the principles of education, child psychology and the psychology of adolescents. It should also help students develop morally, intellectually and physically through teaching and guidance.

4) The ability to analyse and discuss educational problems. Teacher-training institutions should make efforts to develop research abilities in teachers and students.

These skills and attitudes to be developed by teacher education are in accordance with the role-expectations outlined above. Pronouncements on the goals of teacher-training find their expression in an 'ideal' teacher-training curriculum:

> The curriculum of teacher-training institutions has four parts: 1) Political theories and other fundamental courses 2) Pedagogical studies (including pedagogy, psychology, teaching methods etc.) 3) Courses in specialised subjects areas and 4) teaching practice.[45]

Not all four parts of the 'ideal curriculum' are given equal emphasis. Among courses of the four categories, courses in specialised subject areas are stressed most. The official training programmes for secondary teacher-training schools in Tables 6.1 and 6.2 show this quite clearly.

The same is true with higher teacher-training institutes for which there is no standardised official training programme. Each higher teacher-training institute plans its own training programmes with the 'ideal curriculum' as the general guide. Information obtained about the Physics Department in Beijing Teacher Training University shows the proportion of different courses in its four-year training programme to be as follows:[46]

Total Number of Class Hours	3500 (approximately)
Class Hours for Courses in Specialsed Fields	2000 (approx.)
Class Hours for Foreign Language and Foundation Courses	1000 (approx.)
Class Hours for Courses in Pedagogy	36
Class Hours for Courses in Psychology	36
Class Hours for Teaching Methods	72

In actual implementation, the emphasis given to specialised subject areas is even greater than what is revealed from the official training programmes. Most resources have been channelled towards courses in specialised subject areas. Other courses are either not offered or are offered in a perfunctory manner.

There is little in the available literature to suggest that regular courses of political studies, in the form of Marxism, Leninism and Mao Zedong Thought, are offered in many teacher-training institutions. Political consciousness is now

Teacher Education

Table 6.1: SECONDARY TEACHER-TRAINING SCHOOL TENTATIVE FOUR-YEAR TRAINING PROGRAMME FOR PRIMARY SCHOOL TEACHERS

Subjects	First Year	Second Year	Third Year	Fourth Year	Total No. of Class Hours	Total No. of Class Hours as a % of 4-yr Curriculum
Politics	2	2	2	1	239	6.20
National Language						
-Reading & Writing	5	5	4	4	818	21.22
-Basic Grammar	2	2	2			
-Nat. Lang. Teaching in Primary				2	62	1.61
Mathematics						
-Maths	4	4	4	4	416	10.79
-Maths Teaching in Primary				4	124	3.22
Physics		3	3		328	8.51
Chemistry	4	3			246	6.38
Biology	4				144	3.74
History	3			3	201	5.21
Geography					102	2.65
(Foreign Languages)*	(3)	(3)	(3)	(3)	(405)	
Psychology		3			102	2.65
Pedagogy			2	2	130	3.37
Physical Educ. & Teaching Methods	2	2	3	3	335	8.69
Music & Music Teaching	2	2	2		0	
Art & Art Teaching	2	2	2	2	270	7.00
Science Teaching in Primary Sch*				(2)	(62)	7.00
Total No. of Class Hours/week	30	30	27	27	3,855	100
Total No. of School Weeks/Year	36	34	34	31		
Teaching Practice (in weeks)		2	2	2		
Productive Labour (in weeks)	2	2	2	6		

* These courses are offered only in schools which have the necessary resources.

Teacher Education

Table 6.2: SECONDARY TEACHER-TRAINING SCHOOL TENTATIVE THREE-YEAR TRAINING PROGRAMME FOR KINDERGARTEN TEACHERS

Subjects	First Year	Second Year	Third Year	Total No. of Class Hours	Total No. of Class Hours as a % of 3-yr Curriculum
Politics	2	2	1	171	5.46
National Language	6	6	4	544	17.38
Nat. Lang. Teaching in Kindergartens			2	62	1.98
Maths	4	4		280	8.94
Maths Teaching in Kindergartens			1	31	0.99
Physics		3	3	195	6.23
Chemistry		2	2	130	4.15
Biology	2	2		140	4.47
History	3			108	3.45
Geography			3	93	2.97
Child Psychology		3		102	3.26
Child Pedagogy			4	124	3.96
Child Care				108	3.45
Physical Educ. & Teaching Methods	3	2	3	233	7.44
Music & Music Teaching	2	4	4	404	12.90
Art & Art Teaching	4	2	3	269	8.59
Dancing	3	1	1	137	4.38
Total No. of Class Hours/week	31	31	31	3,131	100
Total No. of School Weeks/Year	36	34	31		
Teaching Practice (in weeks)		2	6		
Productive Labour (in weeks)	2	2			

Source: Tables 6.1 & 6.2 are translated from an official document 'Secondary Teacher-Training School Tentative Training Programmes', issued in Oct., 1980. I am grateful to Mr.Peter Mauger for supplying this document.

basically interpreted as the willingness to become a good People's Teacher.[47] Provisions for the development of this attitude are mostly the informal processes described above rather than regular training courses.

As for pedagogical studies, great debates are still going on among Chinese educators as to whether or not pedagogical courses should be included in the teacher-training curriculum. In most teacher-training institutions, pedagogical courses are still not offered. The following quotations are revealing:

> Even now, (pedagogical courses) are still not restored in many training institutions. Even when they are restored in some institutions, they are offered in a very disorganised manner... compressing a systematic field of study to a few talks or seminars.[48]
> Some faculties use pedagogical courses as 'fill-in the-gap' courses. When fewer courses in specialised subject areas can be offered, pedagogical courses are called upon to fill up the time table.[49]

In extreme cases, teachers and students of teacher-training institutions have made joint-petitions for the abolition of pedagogical courses.[50]

Teaching practice is in more or less the same situation. Different excuses are made to cut down teaching practice.[51] Even when teaching practice is organised, preparations are poor, primary and secondary schools do not co-operate, and standards of performances are not set.[52] In theory, each student-teacher is assigned four to five different lessons. In actual practice, many of them exchange lessons so that one student-teacher only writes one or two lesson plans.[53]

In a speech given to a national conference on teacher education in June, 1980, the Vice-Minister of Education, Gao Yi, called for the restoration of pedagogical courses and teaching practice.[54] He made a special appeal to the six keypoint higher teacher-training institutes to establish courses in pedagogical science.[55] If these courses are not offered even in the keypoint institutes, Beijing Teacher Training University and Shanghai Teacher Training University quoted, the chance that they are offered in other teacher-training institutions is small.

The heavy emphasis on courses in specialised subject areas can be explained by a) the requirements of the Four Modernisations and b) the need to raise the low academic standards of those under training.

Education in the period of the Four Modernisations is given the important task of producing socialist workers with high scientific and cultural levels of attainment. The need for qualified people in different sectors of the country is great, and the urgent task is to quickly turn out specialists in different fields. To meet this need, examinations are designed to screen students according to their performance in different subjects. In so doing, it is hoped that the right kind of students will be picked for the right fields. Schools, gearing their curriculum and teaching towards entrance examinations, also place heavy stress on achievement in academic subjects. The teachers they require, then, are naturally teachers who have good standards in the subjects they teach. For teacher-training institutions, therefore, the pressure to develop in their students competence in specialised subjects is far greater than the pressure to develop other qualities. The best qualification that teacher-training can provide to its students is still the mastery of subject-matter. At present, the main subjects taught in primary and secondary schools and therefore required for teachers to master are: politics, mathematics, Chinese, English, geography, history, elementary natural science, physics, chemistry and biology.[56]

The lower quality of those recruited into regular teacher education has already been mentioned. Knowing that their students have a low standard of achievement in academic subjects, teacher-trainers feel the need to devote more efforts to courses concerned with subject matter. The emphasis on subject matter is even more explicit in non-formal in-service teacher-training programmes. Most of these training programmes have been set up for the sole purpose of improving teachers' standards in their subject areas.[57] The principle of "learn what you teach, make up for what you are inadequate in" is applied in almost all non-formal teacher-training programmes.[58]

A look at the standard of primary and secondary school teachers makes obvious the reason for this emphasis on subject matter in in-service training. A survey made by the Ministry of Education revealed that 60% of the nation's secondary and primary school teachers need refresher courses.[59] The statistics in Table 6.3 show that there is a need to increase the percentages of qualified teachers in the three levels of schooling (primary, lower secondary and upper secondary).

The principle of self-reliance is stressed in many non-formal in-service training programmes.[60] More experienced teachers of the area in which the programmes are organised are requested to teach these programmes. These teachers also help to construct 'self-study' materials for less competent teachers so that they can improve their standards on their own. Appeal is made to older and more experienced teachers to "transmit knowledge to, help, and lead"[61] younger teachers. These in-service training programmes are carried out in many different forms varying in level and length of training. The most common ones are: training courses in various subjects, discussion groups for lesson preparation, seminars, correspondence courses and TV broadcast courses.[62]

Teacher Education

Table 6.3

PERCENTAGES OF QUALIFIED TEACHERS*
IN PRIMARY AND SECONDARY SCHOOLS

Year	% of Qualified Primary School Teachers	% of Qualified Lower Secondary School Teachers	% of Qualified Upper Secondary School Teachers
1965[1]	47.4	71.9	70.3
1973[1]	28.0	-	-
1977[1]	-	14.3	33.2
1970[2]	47.0	10.6	50.8
1980[3]	47.0 approx.	10.0 approx.	50.0 approx.

Notes: - Statistics not available
* Qualified primary school teachers are defined by the Chinese officials as teachers with secondary normal education or above; qualifed lower-secondary school teachers are graduates from specialised higher institutes and qualified upper-secondary school teachers are graduates from academic higher institutes. See <u>Banhao Shifan Jiaoyu, Fazhan Jiaoyu Kexue</u>, p.32.

Sources: 1. <u>Banhao Shifan Jiaoyu, Fazhan Jiaoyu Kexue</u>, p.32.
2. <u>Jiaoyu Yanjiu</u>, No.4, August, 1980, p.8.
3. <u>Renmin Jiaoyu</u>, No.1, January, 1981, p.41.

The strong emphasis on mastery of subject matter harbours the potential danger of teacher-training institutions losing their substantive teacher-training character. This is especially true of the higher level teacher-training institutes. There are already tendencies for these training institutes to devote a disproportionate amount of time and effort to research in specialised fields unrelated to school teaching. These institutes pride themselves on the findings of such research.[63] This tendency to neglect their major role of training teachers and devote their efforts to training research workers in other fields has been observed and criticised in several places.[64] Other educators, however, support this tendency and maintain that "curriculum should not be limited to those areas concerned with secondary school classes... The research tasks and research organisation of a keypoint normal college must likewise not be limited to areas concerned with secondary-school training."[65]

This tendency, if continued and further strengthened, will have the unfortunate effect of preventing the best students of teacher education from becoming school teachers. As mentioned above, most students of teacher education have not entered the training institutions willingly. They are always looking for ways to escape teaching. This attitude is reinforced by the policy of some of the higher teacher-training institutes of keeping their best students as researchers in specialised fields. Sometimes outstanding research workers are recommended by the teacher-training institutes to other sectors of the economy.[66] To many students, teacher education is nothing more than a second rank higher education through which they can further their studies in their own specialised fields.

While national standardised secondary teacher-training curricula have been developed,[67] there has been no talk about a standardised curriculum for higher teacher-training institutes. In the higher teacher-training institutes, each faculty designs its own training programmes. Even within the same institute, there is no central overall curriculum planning process.[68] Until a standardised curriculum is set up, the institutes are given the freedom to interpret and adopt whichever part of the official directives they see as appropriate to set up programmes "suitable for their local conditions".

THE STRUCTURE AND ORGANISATION OF TEACHER EDUCATION

The organisational provisions and structure of teacher education reveal the extent to which the achievement of stated aims has been facilitated. To be sure, the institutional structure and organisational provisions are closely related and in many cases the two terms are used interchangeably. For the purpose of analysis in this paper, however, it seems desirable to distinguish between the two. 'Structure' in this paper refers to the levels and kinds of training intended for different groups of teachers. 'Organisation' refers to the control and responsibilities different authorities exercise over teacher training. Two groups are directly concerned with the organisation of teacher training in China: the central government, and local authorities.

The Three-Tiered Structure of Teacher Education

Teacher training in Communist China after 1949 developed along lines of a dual system in which secondary school teachers were trained in higher teacher-training institutes and primary schools teachers in secondary teacher-training schools. This dual system evolved progressively into a three-tiered structure in the early sixties as an intermediate type of training became available to potential lower secondary school teachers.[69]

Teacher Education

This structure was destroyed in the Cultural Revolution.

Since 1977 the educational authorities have been clear about their intention to restore this three-tiered structure, which is illustrated in Figure 6.1. In the national conference on teacher education held in June, 1980, training institutions were described to be of three levels and their tasks specified as follow:

> Higher teacher-training institutes train teachers for secondary schools; teacher-training schools train teachers for lower secondary schools; secondary teacher-training schools, including schools for kindergarten teachers, enroll lower secondary school graduates and young people with the same level and train them to be primary school and kindergarten teachers.[70]

It was stressed that this structure should not be altered without the approval of higher educational authorities.

Figure 6.1

THE THREE-TIERED STRUCTURE OF TEACHER EDUCATION

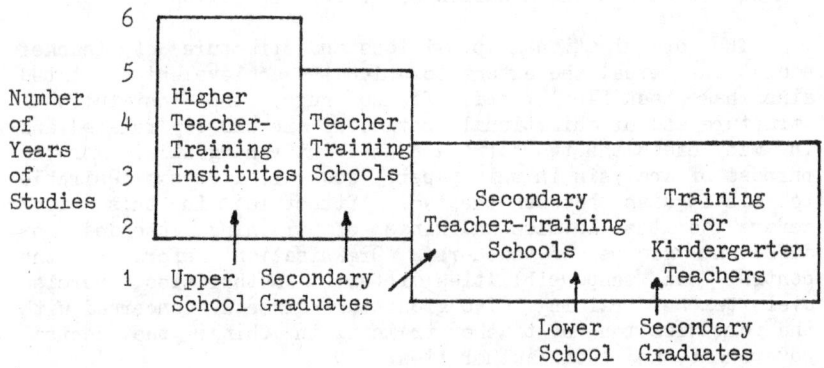

Thus, teacher training as proposed by the authorities is carried out on three levels;

1) *Gaodeng Shifan Yuanxiao* (higher teacher-training institutes)
2) *Shifan Zhuanke Xuexiao* (teacher-training schools)
3) *Zhongdeng Shifan Xuexiao* (secondary teacher-training schools)

The latter include training schools for kindergarten

teachers. Higher teacher-training institutes offer a four-year curriculum to intending upper secondary school teachers.[71] Teacher-training schools offer a three-year curriculum to intending lower secondary school teachers. Both types of training institutes recruit students from upper secondary school graduates. Secondary teacher-training schools and schools for kindergarten teachers recruit their students from lower secondary school graduates. The period of training is generally three or four years. Some secondary teacher-training schools also enroll upper secondary school graduates and train them for one to two years.[72]

However, this three-tiered structure of teacher education has not always been very clear. The intermediate level of training, the teacher-training schools, have so far not developed into a clearly identifiable category. They are sometimes considered as one form of the higher teacher-training institute. In fact, the official figure for higher teacher-training institutes has always included the number of teacher-training schools.[73] Official figures for the number of training institutions are given in two categories, namely, higher teacher-training institutes and secondary teacher-training schools instead of three.[74] This shows a tendency for a dual, rather than the intended three-tiered structure of teacher-education to persist in China.

A description of teacher education in China must also take into account a proliferation of in-service training courses offered in the above-mentioned training institutes as well as institutes established for the purpose. The large number of unqualified teachers teaching in schools makes it imperative to provide in-service training to improve their standards. In 1977, a document entitled 'Opinions on strengthening In-service Training for Primary and Secondary School Teachers' was issued.[75] Since then, a network of in-service training courses of varying lengths has been organised. In-service training is mostly provided on a part-time basis. A small proportion of teachers, however, are given one to two years to study full time with pay.[76]

Special kinds of training institutes called *Jiaoyu Xueyuan* (colleges of education) and *Jiaoshi Jinxiu Xueyuan* (schools for teacher refresher courses) have been established to provide in-service training to teachers. In 1980, 30 national-level colleges of education and over 2,000 county-level schools of education were reported to be in operation.[77] Another more recent report quotes a figure of 4,000 such colleges and schools at provincial, prefectural and county levels providing training for on-the-job teachers.[78] At present, the total number of existing regular teacher-training institutions is 1,189 (172 higher teacher-training institutes and 1,017 secondary teacher-training schools).[79] The number of colleges and schools of education established to provide in-service training is more than three times the number of pre-service training institutes. Together with the other kinds of in-service training provided also by the pre-service training institutes,[80] the emphasis given to in-service training of teachers is quite phenomenal.

The much larger number of colleges and schools of education of course also train more people. At present, one million secondary school teachers (of a total of three million) and 2.5 million primary school teachers (of a total of 5.5 million) are enrolled in some kind of in-service training;[81] whereas only 790,000 future teachers[82] are being trained in the 1,189 pre-service training institutes.

Efforts are being made to ensure high status to these colleges and schools of education. It has been officially announced that all colleges of education at provincial level are of an equal status with regular higher teacher-training institutes; all colleges of education at regional level are of equal status with pre-service teacher-training schools; and all schools of education at prefectural level are given the same status as the pre-service secondary teacher-training schools.[83]

The Organisation and Control of Teacher Education

In China, educational administration takes place at four levels: the Ministry of Education, the Provincial Education Bureau, the County and Municipal level Education Office, and the Urban and Commune Education Committee.[84] It is now necessary to clarify the responsibilities and control that educational authorities of different levels have in teacher education.

The official plan proposed in 1980 is that the Ministry of Education will directly administer the six higher teacher-training institutes affiliated to the Ministry.[85] All provinces, municipalities and autonomous regions are to plan their own networks of teacher-training institutions. The proposal is for every province, municipality and autonomous region to establish one or more higher teacher-training institutes. In economically more advanced places, each region should establish a teacher-training school and a few secondary teacher-training schools (including training schools or classes for intending kindergarten teachers).[86] As far as in-service training is concerned, provinces, counties and municipalities should each establish a college of education, and each prefecture should establish one school of education.[87]

Organisational provisions for teacher education are thus intended to be localised. As Gao Yi pointed out in the 1980 national conference on teacher education:

> Training institutions should be localised. They
> should be orientated to their own provinces and
> their own regions. They should train teachers

for their local use, forming a network of teacher training suitable for educational development in their own areas.[88]

Provincial-level and county-level educational authorities are entrusted with most of the responsibilities. They are responsible for the establishment and running of regular training institutions as well as colleges and schools of education for in-service training. Essentially, except for the six higher teacher-training institutes affiliated to the Ministry of Education, all teacher-training institutions are the responsibility of the local educational authorities.

Figure 6.2

THE ORGANISATION AND CONTROL OF TEACHER-EDUCATION

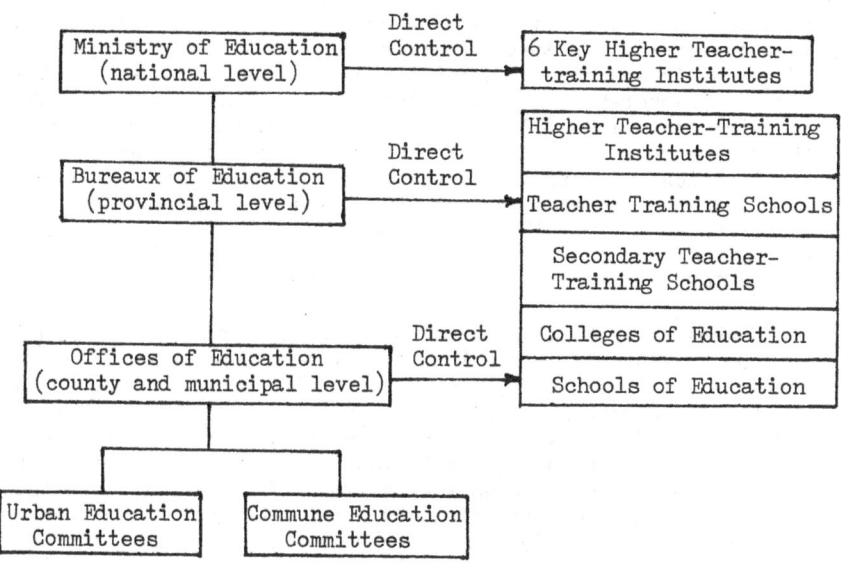

Thus, while teacher training has increasingly become recognised as a national concern, local authorities still shoulder much of the responsibility for the actual provision of teacher training. The role of the Ministry of Education in teacher education is intended to be that of guidance. It holds conferences to discuss problems; it issues directives and guide-lines. In short, it points out the general direction towards which teacher training is to be developed. The direct administration of the six affiliated higher teacher-training institutes is also intended to set a standard which other higher training institutes should strive to attain.[89]

Localising provisions for teacher training means that local educational authorities retain a considerable amount of autonomy in the actual running of teacher-training programmes. This tends to encourage variations among different provinces. So far, official directives issued concerning teacher education are of an advisory nature.[90] These 'guide-lines' and 'directives' issued by the Ministry of Education are often interpreted differently in different places. Some local authorities may choose to follow some policies but ignore others. However, local modifications of or even deviations from central policies are tolerated. Allowances are always made for local variations. The phrase 'if the local situation allows' is found in almost all official directives and policy guide-lines.

Allowances made for local variations, if not handled properly, may hinder the realisation of national educational goals. This has been reflected in the structural aspects of teacher education. In many provinces, educational authorities "adapt policies to local situations" and train secondary school teachers in secondary teacher-training schools instead of the higher teacher-training institutes. This has disrupted the structure of teacher education and caused great confusion among the teacher-training institutions.[91] In this case, the localisation of provision for teacher training has adversely affected the three-tiered structure favoured by the central authorities.

CONCLUSION

Four aspects of teacher education both from inside and outside of the training institutions have been examined. Unlike previous studies on the same subject[92] which adopt a historical-descriptive approach, the approach of this chapter is more sociological. The basic assumption is that forces outside of the training institutions play an important role in shaping reforms and changes inside. Thus, I have approached the subject of teacher training by first looking at how the authorities conceive the teacher's role. These conceptions of the teacher's role form the basic aims for teacher education. Social and economic forces conducive to or acting against achieving the aims of teacher education are then examined. Attention is then turned to the inside of the training institutions to examine the precise means of achieving these aims (i.e. the curriculum) and the conditions under which these aims are to be achieved (i.e. the organisation and structure).

It is my intention to conclude this study by discussing the question of relevance as set out in the beginning. The central questions asked were: has teacher training been reformed to reflect the overarching goal of raising educational standards? How well are teachers being equipped for their more demanding and altered functions. Although firm conclusions may not be possible, certain trends are identifiable.

First of all, there is the tendency to rely heavily on non-formal in-service training. Over the years, formal teacher-training has not expanded at a rate fast enough to provide enough teachers for the rapidly expanding primary and secondary levels of education. To quote some statistics, the number of secondary-school students increased by 60 million between 1965 and 1977. Using a teacher-student ratio of 1 to 30,[93] the number of teachers should have increased by 2 million. However, higher teacher-training institutes were only able to turn out 210,000 graduates in the same period, 30% of whom were assigned to jobs unrelated to teaching. As for primary schools, the number of students increased by 30 million between 1965 and 1977. The number of teachers should have increased by 1 million, but the total number of secondary teacher-training school graduates was only 400,000 in the same period.[94] Thus, the majority of teachers recruited during this period were untrained. Not only were these teachers untrained professionally, they were and many remain 'unqualified' in terms of their levels of education.

To improve the standards of these unqualified teachers, the authorities have developed various types of in-service training programmes. Expansion of in-service provision has been impressive during the past few years, with the establishment of a large number of special colleges and schools for the purpose. While the number of higher teacher-training institutes has increased substantially within the past few years, the number of secondary teacher-training schools has actually decreased.[95] If the rate of expansion of formal training institutions continues to be slow, schools will have to continue to recruit untrained and unqualified teachers. The need to rely on in-service training programmes to up-grade these teachers will then persist.

Since the chief aim of these in-service training programmes is to raise the educational level of teachers already in the profession, they are heavily subject-matter orientated. Even for formal pre-service training institutions, courses in academic subjects are emphasised above all other courses. The trend for teacher training in China to be heavily subject-matter orientated is pronounced.

The control of teacher training is localised. Except for the six keypoint higher teacher-training institutes which are directly under the Ministry of Education, all other kinds of pre-service and in-service training programmes are organised by the educational authorities at the provincial and county levels.

To summarise: teacher training in China can be described as localised, subject-matter orientated and mostly in the form of non-formal in-service training programmes. The question which remains is: it this kind of teacher training capable of preparing teachers for their now more demanding roles? Under this kind of training, will teachers and prospective teachers be able to develop the requisites desired by the authorities?

It seems quite obvious that training provisions other than those for proficiency in school subjects are generally not made. While the emphasis on subject matter reflects the official goal of raising educational standards, the demands for different kinds of teachers (e.g. teachers for secondary technical and specialised schools)[96] and teachers with other kinds of qualifications (e.g. teaching skills and social consciousness) cannot be satisfied by this single-track training.

Granted that the emphasis on subject-matter is absolutely necessary to raise the educational level of those under training, the need for teacher education to develop in teachers other requisites should also be recognised. At least some provision should be made for the development of other teaching skills. The danger of putting all the emphasis on subject-matter proficiency is that teacher training will lose its teacher-training nature and become a kind of second-class education.

The authorities have realised the urgent need to provide more teacher training and have 'quickly and economically' run many in-service training courses. To be sure, these in-service training courses are necessary to help unqualified teachers acquire a minimum level of competence in the subjects they teach. These courses are, however, basically remedial in nature and should not be allowed to take the place of pre-service teacher training. This seems to be inadequately recognised by the educational authorities. At present, the tendency is towards a rapid expansion of in-service training provision to the extent that development of formal pre-service training has been curtailed. This may form a vicious cycle: as less pre-service training can be provided to intending teachers, the chance is that more teachers will enter the profession 'unqualified'; as there are more 'unqualified' teachers, more in-service training will be needed; and as more resources are channelled towards non-formal in-service teacher training, less will be available for the development of pre-service training.

The intention to put even more emphasis on in-service training in the future can be seen in a move to 'institutionalise' in-service teacher training. Educators in China are now advocating the institutionalisation of non-formal in-service teacher training. This is to be combined with a system of assessment. Teachers may pursue their studies in various ways and take assessment examinations for one or more subjects. For each subject they pass, they are awarded a certificate of competence. When a student passes all the required subjects, he will be given a diploma and will be considered a college graduate.[97]

If by taking various in-service courses and passing assessment examinations teachers can eventually attain the status and qualification of college graduates, then the fear that teacher training will become a kind of second-class higher education is not at all unjustified.

Localised control and provision of teacher training probably makes a lot of sense in a vast country like China. However, the mere appeal to local authorities to pay more attention to teacher training will not suffice to provide the nation with an adequate supply of teachers well-qualified for their tasks. More definite policies from the central authorities are necessary if teacher training is to be more effectively developed in the direction desired.

In the same way, the mere call for society to respect People's Teachers will not suffice as a means of raising teachers' social status. More wide-ranging policy commitments are obviously required: there is a need to raise the level (both absolute and relative) of teachers' income; extensive measures ought to be taken to given more social benefits to teachers, and to ensure more sophisticated development in the professional aspects of education.[98]

Chapter Seven

ADULT EDUCATION IN URBAN-INDUSTRIAL CHINA: PROBLEMS, POLICIES, AND PROSPECTS

David I. Chambers

INTRODUCTION

Previous chapters have discussed the education of those who enter the work-force upon completion of their schooling. This chapter is concerned with the education of those already in employment in China's urban industrial enterprises. Adult education occupies a prominent position in modern China's educational history and particularly in those education programmes conducted under Chinese Communist Party (CCP) supervision. During the 1920's the Party devoted considerable efforts to the operation of night schools in order to provide China's nascent proletariat with a rudimentary political and cultural education. Following the Party's shift to rural China, CCP spokesmen called repeatedly for expanded educational facilities for working cadres and peasants. As the nationwide victory of 1949 approached, so one of the first actions taken in cities and town which came under Red Army control was the establishment of networks of schools for urban employees.[1]
Throughout this period the CCP regarded the education of children as an important political and economic investment. However, it was seen as one which could only yield its full returns when children had matured and entered into employment. By contrast, investment in adult education appeared to offer more immediate returns. If local cadres could be educated, then the integrity and efficiency of the Party's mechanisms of rule might be improved. If ordinary workers and peasants could receive carefully guided political education, then active mass support for the CCP's revolutionary programme might expand. If they could receive education which improved their vocational skills, then the economic viability of CCP-controlled areas might become less precarious. These were compelling reasons for conducting programmes of adult education alongside those geared to children: CCP policy-makers sometimes went so far as to suggest that the former should take precedence over the latter in the allocation of desperately scarce educational resources.[2]

The results of pre-1949 adult education programmes in CCP areas did not always match these declarations, but they provided experience upon which educational planners built in the years which followed. Adult education followed the same convoluted path between 1949 and 1966 as that of other sectors of China's education system. Policy and practice both reflected and contributed to elite debate and consequently never developed smoothly or in a unilinear direction.[3] The end of the Great Proletarian Cultural Revolution (GPCR) in 1976 provided China's educators with an opportunity to evolve new policies and now, seven years on, it is possible to examine their efforts to date. This chapter is divided into four sections. The first considers the official aims and objectives of employee education. The second discusses the national administrative system which is expected to realise these objectives and the third examines the critical area of employee education funding. The fourth section presents an overview of the various curricula available to employees and the institutional settings within which they receive their education.

AIMS AND OBJECTIVES

The current strategic aims and objectives of employee education are two-fold: to improve labour productivity and, via political education, to cultivate compliance with and commitment to the policies of the CCP. In the political lexicon of the 1980's, these aims are set within the Party's preoccupation with establishing the material and spiritual civilisation upon which Chinese socialism should rest.[4]

Since 1976 Party and State planners in China have been anxious to modernise the urban-industrial sector of the national economy. Yet in pursuit of this objective they have been confronted with a classic 'policy-resources contradiction'[5] since the education-skills profile of the work-force and its political characteristics are far from conducive to the conduct of socialist modernisation. This contradiction between ends and means lies at the heart of current specific official aims of employee education.

Economic modernisation rests to a large extent upon the existence of a suitably educated, skilled, motivated and adaptable work-force. Article after article in Chinese media have demonstrated that the work-force in urban-industrial China falls short of fulfilling these criteria. In early 1980 the All China Federation of Trade Unions (ACFTU) conducted a major survey of educational and skill attainment amongst some 19.8 million employees in twenty-six provinces. The results were depressing for, as Table 7.1 indicates, over 40% of the sample were found to have received no secondary education and less than 20% had received an upper secondary education. Moreover, as Vice-Minister of Education Zang Boping stressed later, these

Table 7.1

EDUCATIONAL ATTAINMENT AMONGST EMPLOYEES, January 1980

From an ACFTU survey of 19,825,990 employees in twenty-six provinces, municipalities and autonomous regions.

Level of Attainment	Number of employees	(%)
1. University	607,136	3.06
2. Upper secondary/ Secondary Specialised School Graduate	3,152,087	15.90
3. Lower secondary School Graduate	8,087,943	40.80
4. Primary School Graduate	6,352,434	32.04
5. Illiterate/Semi-literate	1,626,207	8.20
(Not Recorded	183	- -)
TOTAL	19,825,990	100.00

Source: Wang Shou'an & Wang Xianrun, Zhi Gong Jiaoyu Jingji Gailun, Changchun: Jilin Renmin Chubanshe, 1981, p.30.

data presented a flattering picture, since almost half of those in employment had been appointed during the GPCR and had thus received incomplete or sub-standard schooling at the levels indicated.[6] The same ACFTU survey also revealed that there were barely 20 engineers and technicians per 1,000 employees and that over 70% of employees worked in grades 1-3, i.e. they were essentially unskilled. As Zang pointed out, these distributions compared very poorly with equivalent data for advanced states and those clearly at the threshold of economic development.[7]

The results of a further survey published in 1982 indicated that leading cadres in industry and communications were similarly bereft of education and vocational skill. 70% of management had received but a lower secondary school education or less; only 11% had received a university education and 60% had never studied economics or management systematically. This survey of management found that the majority were elderly political appointees given office in the 1950's in the light of their contribution to the revolution rather than because they possessed any demonstrable managerial competence. The survey analysts commented acidly:[8]

> Many (cadres) have a low cultural level and an inadequate knowledge of economics, management and science. This sort of leadership is extremely incompatible with the establishment of modernised industry... the problems of ageing and worn-out knowledge are universal.

The profile of those who have entered the work-force since 1976 is hardly better. As Stanley Rosen has indicated in Chapter Four, the majority of those entering the urban labour pool lack any systematic pre-employment grounding in basic vocational skills and enterprises commonly recruit on the basis of performance in formal academic examinations and/or family connections with existing or retiring employees. Few enterprises recruit on the basis of vocational testing.[9]

Between 1976 and 1978 PRC media carried relatively few articles on the role and mechanics of political education in any sector of the country's education system.[10] In Spring 1979 this situation changed and a steady stream of hortatory directives, editorials and articles since then has urged educators to recognise the importance of political education, not least that directed at urban employees. This renewed emphasis derives from the perception of CCP leaders that many employees are ill-disposed or indifferent towards the demands of modernisation. Some are 'political recidivists' who continue to identify with the discredited norms and policies of the GPCR and exploit their positions to block reformist policies of the post-Mao regime. Others resent new policies imposing strict divisions of labour, quality controls, disciplinary codes etc., having become acclimatised to the egalitarianism and indiscipline which characterised much of the GPCR.[11] Potentially most disturbing to the CCP is the frustration, cynicism, apathy and disillusionment of workers below the age of 35. Socialised in the idealistic atmosphere of the GPCR, they have seen their ideals abused or ignored by officials before and since 1976 and have concluded that there is little to be gained from activism and hard work to build China into a powerful socialist state.

It is against this back-drop that the official aims of employee education have been formulated and against which the long-run performance of the system will be judged. Until mid-1978 officials were concerned with rewriting the recent history of employee education and it was not until August 1978 that the first skeletal statements of aims and objectives emerged in official media.[13] These have since been amplified after experimentation and discussion, a process which culminated in the February 1981 publication of a Joint CCP Central Committee-State Council 'Decision on strengthening work in employee education', launched publicly at the March 1981 national work conference on employee education. The February 'Decision'[14] formalised previous draft documents and post-1976 experience and is intended to guide the development of employee education until at least 1985. It specifies that until 1983-1984 the key objectives of employee education are to be the training of leading cadres and the conduct of political education and remedial cultural and technical classes *(bu ke)* for young workers. Within these priorities, the 'Decision' defined the particular objectives of employee education as follows:

Political Objectives:

- "Employees should be educated in communist ideals and their consciousness should be raised".
- "A sense of responsibility and dedication to work should be cultivated".
- Employees should "become concerned about state finances and dare to struggle against embezzlement and extravagence".
- "Labour discipline should be strengthened".
- "Backward thinking and unhealthy work-styles should be overcome".
- "The activism, initiative and creativity of employees" should be brought into full play.

Cultural Objectives:

- Illiteracy amongst young workers should be eliminated by 1985.
- 60% - 80% of employees with an educational level beneath that of a lower secondary school graduate should be educated to that level by 1985.
- One third of employees with the educational level of a lower secondary school graduate should reach the level of an upper secondary/secondary specialised school graduate by 1985.
- "A part" *(yi bufen)* of those with the educational level of an upper secondary/secondary specialised school graduate should reach the level of a university graduate by 1985.
- All university graduate technicians and management personnel should have study programmes to enable them to acquire knowledge of modern science, technology and management techniques.

Vocational Objectives:

- All workers should be organised to study technical theory, standards and operating procedures to the levels required for their jobs.
- By 1985 the practical operating skills of all young workers should be raised by one or two grades.
- The proportion of engineers and technicians to employees

should be significantly increased (no specification offered).
- Al leading cadres should attend at least one rotational training (*lun xun*) course by 1985 to study management and specialised technical knowledge.

So much for the detailed aims of employee education and their background. The remainder of this chapter is concerned with the ways in which they have been put into effect.

ADMINISTRATION.

At present there is no single integrated or nationally comprehensive administrative system for employee education. Administrative control is exercised by an almost baffling and constantly shifting array of governmental and non-governmental agencies, most of which have considerable autonomy over education programmes conducted under their auspices. Moreover the principle 'adapt policy to local conditions' (*yin di zhi yi*) means that many major issues (e.g. detailed curriculum development) are resolved by the sub-national levels of each agency. In addition the CCP exercises a critical role in the administration of employee education.

Governmental Agencies

1. The National Employee Education Administrative Committee (NEEAC)

China's State Council is formally the senior government body responsible for the formulation, implementation and administration of employee education policy. In practice, these powers have been devolved to the State Council's NEEAC ('Quanguo Zhi Gong Jiaoyu Guanli Weiyuanhui') which was established in 1980 under the chairmanship of State Economic Commission (SEC) Director Yuan Baohua.[15] Unfortunately, the NEEAC has maintained a relatively low public profile since its inception and it is not easy to determine precisely its administrative responsibilities. Nevertheless NEEAC directives and work conferences, as well as the activities of Yuan and NEEAC inspection groups, suggest that the committee is intended to play a major role determining strategic national policy, assessing its implementation by individual agencies and attempting to ensure that their efforts are coordinated and compatible with national economic requirements.[16]

2. State Council Ministries

Subject to the policy framework of the February 1981 'Decision', all government ministries and commissions under the State Council are required to provide education for employees within their systems (*xitong*) throughout China. At central (i.e. national) level, each ministry has a specialist employee education department which is responsible for defining core curricula and teaching plans and assessing their implementation by equivalent government offices at provincial level. These provincial offices are in turn responsible for the line administration of specialist employee education institutions which enrol those employed locally in a given system. In addition, these offices are concerned directly with the administration of extra-mural programmes provided for employees by formal universities under the control of their parent ministry and for the management of 'in-house' employee education programmes provided by individual factories and enterprises within the system concerned.

The Ministry of Labour and Personnel exercises some supra-ministerial powers in that it is responsible for establishing and reviewing general norms for the assessment of technical/vocational competence amongst apprentices and workers and for determining appropriate job titles and rates of pay for those who have completed courses of education.[17]

The administrative responsibilities of the <u>Ministry of Education</u> are discharged by the Ministry's Bureau of Worker-Peasant Education and the Bureau's Employee Education section and Correspondence and Evening Universities section. In addition it has been customary for the Bureau's work to be the specialist responsibility of a Vice-Minister of Education. Until recently this role (which includes championing the cause of the Bureau inside and outside the Ministry as well as administrative supervision) was discharged by Zang Boping. However since Zang's retirement in 1982 the number of Vice-Ministers within the Ministry has been drastically reduced and the resultant pattern of ministerial responsibility is unclear.

The Ministry of Education is only <u>directly</u> concerned with employee education administration in that it is responsible for the operation of the Central Broadcasting University and the extra-mural facilities offered by national key-point formal universities under its control. At provincial level the Ministry is represented by government Bureaux of Education or Higher Education, each with specialist employee education sections which directly administer some employee education institutions, self-study networks and oversee the extra-mural activities of universities under provincial education bureaux control.[18]

The exact lines of administrative demarcation between other agencies and the Ministry of Education and provincial education bureaux are extremely difficult to establish, not least because they are currently the subject of reform. From formal directives, media reports and interview data it would appear that the Ministry and provincial bureaux act as 'first amongst equals'. Thus once other agencies have devised and begun particular programmes within the framework of general CCP, State Council and NEEAC guidelines they are expected to take heed at national and provincial level of the 'professional' advice offered by the Ministry and provincial education bureaux. At provincial level, for example, the employee education sections of provincial education bureaux exercise substantial control over pedagogic matters related to the definition and maintenance of academic standards, the validation of employee education institutions and qualifications and the appointment, remuneration and professional development of full-time teaching staff.[19]

Non-Government Agencies

The central and local branches of several non-governmental mass organisations are concerned with the administration of employee education. Some act as providing agencies in their own right; others support programmes conducted by ministries and other mass organisations. Amongst the mass organisations the ACFTU is currently both the largest and fastest growing direct provider of employee education: in 1981 enrolment in trade union-administered schools was 1.3 million; by 1983 it had risen to 3.3 million, including some 51,000 employees attending 66 trade union universities.[20] Whilst this enrollment amounts to much less than 10% of national union membership, it accounts for approximately half of total national registered enrollments in employee education programmes. Schools and universities for unionists are administered in much the same way as those operated by ministries. Thus core curricula and teaching plans are determined by central education departments of the ACFTU and its constituent unions and then passed down for implementation by provincial and municipal unions in 'in-house' programmes or special institutions for union members in cities and large towns. As well as rendering administrative support (e.g. mobilisation of students, location of premises) to programmes conducted by other agencies, trade unions are required according to the February 1981 'Decision' to ensure that employees' rights to study time are observed by management. However, official media comment indicates clearly that this right and its defence by trade unions in the face of managerial recalcitrance is not fully exercised.

In addition to the ACFTU, the Chinese Communist Youth League (CCYL), National Womens' Federation (NWF) and Chinese Scientific and Technical Association (CSTA) also support employee education programmes. The principal role of the CCYL's central Propaganda Department and local league branches is to mobilise young workers to study, just as the NWF encourages female employees to join classes. The CSTA, whose membership is based upon academic and research scientists and engineers, operates a modest programme of direct provision, but its main role is to organise lectures and symposia upon specialist aspects of engineering and technology, particularly concerning new equipment and techniques.

These organisations all made significant contributions to

employee education before the GPCR and their current activities may be seen as an attempt to restore and develop their former roles. They have recently been joined by a new organisation which, whilst not a direct provider of employee education, can be seen as intended to tighten the administration of a particular component of employee education - political education. The Chinese Association For The Study of Ideological and Political Work Amongst Employees ('Zhongguo Zhi Gong Sixiang Zhengzhi Gongzuo Yanjiu Hui') was established in January 1983 during a national conference on employees' political education. The purpose of the conference was to receive and discuss a major programmatic document on political education which had been prepared under the direction of the CCP's Propaganda Department head Deng Liqun.[21] Presented in draft form, the document contained many detailed provisions regarding forms, contents and methods of employee political education. When the Association was established it was announced that its work would be "devoted to theoretical studies and the exchange and popularisation of practical experiences in ideological and political work amongst employees".[22] In practice the Association has played a more prominent role than this would suggest. During the first six months of its existence under the Presidency of ACFTU vice-Chairman Gu Dachun it was particularly responsible for monitoring initial experimental implementation of the document by agencies concerned with employee education and for helping to convey preliminary results to the CCP Propaganda Department so that the document might be refined, a process which concluded in July 1983 when the CCP formally published the document as the 'Programme for ideological and political work amongst employees in state-owned enterprises'.[23] In this context the Association had clearly acted as an important executive arm of the CCP and its Propaganda Department.

Given the PRC's political system the CCP, not surprisingly, plays a major role in the administration of employee education. Formally, the role of the Party is to decide policy and supervise its implementation by other non-Party bodies. In recent years this classic 'vanguard' role has been reasserted and the Party as a whole has been enjoined not to bog itself down in the minutiae of day-to-day administration. Nonetheless the central and local organs of the CCP and its individual members are directly involved in policy administration. The Party is concerned, for example, with the direct control of the national network of Party schools (*dang xiao*) which provide academically and vocationally oriented courses as well as politics courses for employees (particularly cadres) who are CCP members.[24] Similarly, the Party has exclusive control over employees' political education and a recent document envisages that a network of Party political and ideological reporters (*zhengzhi sixiang baogaoyuan*) will be established in the near future to tighten such control.[25]

The central CCP organ principally concerned with the determination of national education policy is the CCP Central Committee's Propaganda Department and its head Deng Liqun is known to take an active interest in employee education. In addition to supervising the drafting of policy documents, Deng has delivered many major formal public speeches calling for the development of employee education and on occasion has conducted less formal 'question and answer' sessions with employee education officials to elucidate the goals and administration of new policies. Once a policy receives the approval of the Propaganda Department, the CCP maintains control over its administration via the existence of Party committees *(dang wei)* and groups *(dang zu)* in all employee education institutions. These meet privately before a policy enters the public domain to discuss policy administration in the unit concerned and thereafter they are expected to meet regularly to consider its implementation. Reports of their observations are then channelled upwards through the national CCP network until, ultimately, they reach the Propaganda Department. Additionally, the majority of leading administrative posts in employee education at national and provincial level are occupied by Party members who are responsible as individuals to the relevant local and national organs of the CCP. Ideally the Party therefore commands its own autonomous channels of communication and control over the administration of employee education.

FUNDING

The principles governing the funding of employee education now are essentially the same as those which prevailed during the 1950's and 1960's. Funding is thus derived from (i) individual enterprise budgets (ii) local trade union funds and (iii) provincial education bureaux budgets.

According to a 1981 Ministry of Finance regulation, enterprises are expected to devote 1.0% of their total wage bill towards employee education. Additional funds may be allotted at the discretion of management once an enterprise has met its financial commitments to the state. This subvention is supplemented within enterprises by money drawn from trade union branch funds. Under PRC union law, management is required to remit a sum equivalent to 2.0% of the wage bill to union branches and according to the 1981 regulation 25.0% -37.5% of this is to be spent on the education of union members. These funds provide direct support for 'in-house' employee education programmes and are also drawn upon if an enterprise chooses to send an employee to an outside employee education institution, for example one run by a provincial education bureau. In such cases fee payments from employing enterprises are added to funds drawn from education bureaux budgets to provide the operational budget of the institution concerned. Regrettably neither the 1981 regulation, provincial budgetary reports nor the briefings given to foreign delegations provide consistent data as to the proportion of the national education budget which is devoted to employee education.[26]

It is clear that this pattern of funding leaves much to be desired and is currently creating difficulties similar to those of the 1950's and 1960's. According to the February 1981 'Decision' it is envisaged that in "several years" each employee education institution will have a floor-space equivalent to 0.3-0.5 square metres per student and that there will be three to five full-time teachers per 1,000 employees. This must remain a distant objective for some years, for the institutions which feature on the current itineraries of foreign delegations (it can be assumed that these are amongst the best) are commonly under-staffed and desperately short of books, teaching equipment and premises, particularly for laboratory and computer-based subjects. Many buildings formerly used for employee education but occupied by other organisations during the GPCR have not been returned and no compensation has been offered to their original users. Some institutions are able to overcome resource shortages by employing teachers from local formal education institutions who offer their services voluntarily; more commonly outsiders are employed on a fee basis. Some institutions are afforded free use of laboratory and computing facilities in formal schools; most have to choose between teaching with no access to the relevant equipment or else devoting up to a fifth of their budget to rental charges, thus reducing book budgets etc.

Funding problems also contribute to problems of student drop-out and the disinclination of employees to embark upon long courses of study. Employees may study on a full-time block-release basis, during working hours or after work. Provided that an employee has enterprise approval to take a course, tuition fees are generally paid by the employer. In the first two modes of study employees continue to receive a wage, but it usually excludes bonuses which might normally have been earned. The short-run financial opportunity cost of study is therefore high for such employees and even higher for the after-work student who, apart from losing overtime payments, has to renounce spare time for rest and recreation in order to pursue his studies.

These problems point to the major flaw in current funding arrangements - they discriminate in favour of the larger and more profitable enterprises at the expense of those smaller and less profitable whose employees are arguably in greater need of education. A further problem is that notwithstanding official regulations, management and unions have sometimes diverted educational funds to non-educational but highly popular uses, e.g. dormitory improvements and wage supplements. A measure of the seriousness of this problem is the fact that the ACFTU, Bank of China and Ministry of Finance were compelled to issue a special notice in December 1980 reminding those concerned of their obligations to provide employee education funding.[27] Similar recalcitrance on the part of provincial and municipal education bureaux sometimes leads to only the most meagre funds being allocated to employee education, but whilst the Ministry of Education is aware of the problem, it has limited powers to intervene given employee education's decentralised pattern of funding and administration.[28]

The peculiar sensitivity of the funding issue may be illustrated by the treatment of Vice-Premier Yao Yilin's summing up speech at the March 1981 national work conference on employee education. Delegates had offered several concrete suggestions to improve the slender financial base of employee education. Some directly attacked the Ministry of Finance for its miserliness; some suggested that wage bill subventions should be aggregated and redistributed at national level so as to reduce disparities between large and small enterprises. Others had suggested that a National Employee Education Funds Association should be established to solicit donations from home and abroad. In response, Yao defended the Ministry of Finance's argument that budgetary pressures meant that only 1.0% of the wage bill could be devoted to employee education. This was disappointing since the February 'Decision' had suggested a subvention equivalent to 1.5% of enterprise wage bills. Thus a major component of the employee education budget had been cut at a stroke by one third. Nevertheless, Yao was not unsympathetic to suggestions that alternative sources of funds should be explored urgently and directed the NEEAC to do so, going so far as to encourage an exploration of funding patterns in capitalist states.

All this was reported fully in the May 1981 issue of Renmin Jiaoyu. However when a conference volume was published six months later the 'meat' of Yao's response to delegates' had been excised, leaving only a bland bowdlerisation in its place.[29] The impact of this censoring has been unmistakeable since then, for there has been no detailed media discussion of funding and questions on the topic raised by foreign delegations are clearly a matter of some embarrassment to most Chinese employee education officials, although some express open dissatisfaction that the largest share of past World Bank loans has been directed into formal universities.[30] In the meantime they are able to satisfy only a fraction of current demand and that only with considerable difficulty and at some cost in terms of academic quality. It is within this context that local Party and State leaders have recently been encouraging the development of small private employee education institutions run by retired teachers and skilled workers, relying for their finances solely upon fees paid by students.[31]

FORMS, CONTENT AND METHODS IN EMPLOYEE EDUCATION

China's education does not 'walk on two legs'. Leo Orleans suggested in 1972 that it walked on the legs of a centipede and it is not unreasonable to argue that it now walks on the legs of an exceptionally well-endowed millipede.[32] This is especially so in the field of employee education where programmes range in level from literacy to post-graduate education, in modes of attendance from full-time to (very) part-time and in content from classical Chinese to computer programming. However for the purpose of this analysis the various programmes may be conveniently grouped according to their orientation towards the political, cultural and vocational objectives considered above.

Political Education

Political education is provided for employees in three ways: as a curricular component of cultural and vocationally oriented education programmes, as part of the CCP's established strategy of political mobilisation and counter-socialisation and thirdly via special 'politics only' courses directed at young workers. Of these three the second is the most common.

With regard to the first category, the GPCR has had a profound impact upon curriculum design. During the early 1970's politics as a subject in its own right took up an inordinate share of time on many curricula and also intruded extensively into other subjects. In recent years this approach has been rejected in favour of the view that since employees receive political education in other settings and teaching time is scarce, there is little need to include politics in culturally and vocationally oriented curricula unless it is academically relevant. One of the principal lessons drawn from the GPCR, in the words of an employee education text published in 1981, is that "political education must not be allowed to take the place of cultural and technical education."[33] Thus, to cite an apparently typical example, 11.8% of the Guangzhou Municipal Spare-Time University Law course for judicial-public security workers is devoted to Political Economy, Party History and Philosophy and 12.2% of its Chinese course for journalists and report writers is taken up by courses in Political Economy and classical Marxist texts. By contrast, the University's courses in Industrial Automation and Mechanical Engineering Technology and Design contain no provision for politics teaching.[34]

The vast majority of political education therefore takes place under the auspices of enterprise CCP committees, using the forms of Party-led lectures and talks by full-time political work cadres (zheng gong ganbu) and small group discussions amongst employees based upon current CCP and enterprise policies. These forms of political education are currently in a sorry state, having been "crippled, destroyed and ruined" during the GPCR according to Zhao Yinhua, Deputy Director of the SEC.[35] The basic problems is that this <u>medium</u> of political education which proved highly effective in the early 1950's has been damaged by the <u>message</u> which it carried in the 1960's and 1970's and the styles in which the message was conveyed. It became discredited since its messianic and 'radical' content frequently bore no relation to the reality of employees' lives and aspirations and it was often used as a forum for unpopular humiliation of 'backward' employees before their peers. Attempts to revive it and gear it to the attitudinal demands of modernisation have been stymied by employees' indifference, refusal to engage in mutual criticism and the poor quality of political work cadres. These cadres often lack credibility; they know little of the technical work of their enterprises and are abused by employees as unprincipled 'wobbly men' (budaoweng) for their previous zealous prosecution of successive and mutually contradictory Party policies. Many now refuse to perform their duties because they disagree with current policies, feel that their jobs have no future in an era of technological change or simply because they prefer a quiet life. As a group, over 70% of them have received only a lower secondary education or less and most have had no formal education in Marxism or pedagogic techniques.

It was to these problems that the CCP's July 1983 programme for political work was addressed. No substantial changes in the content of general political education are envisaged, for its main components are to remain (i) the domestic and international situation (ii) Party and State policies (iii) enterprise rules and regulations (iv) task fulfilment and (v) the deeds of model workers, all to be taught less didactically and more closely related to the actual situation prevailing in enterprises. Political work cadres themselves are all to receive rotational training within three to five years and the more elderly or politically suspect are to be retired or dismissed. It is envisaged that in the long run all cadres will be graduates of specialist political work courses provided by formal universities and secondary specialised schools.[36]

The success of this policy will be tested in the future. In the meantime desperate problems of attitude remain amongst young employees. One of the July 1983 programme's innovations is the suggestion that <u>all</u> young employees should attend short full-time courses of systematic education (xitong jiaoyu) to develop their patriotism, collectivism and faith in socialism and communism. The particular topics for study on such courses are (i) Chinese Modern History (ii) Scientific Socialism and (iii) The Chinese Working Class. After their courses, younger employees are to return to their enterprises for further education on (i) Basic Marxism-Leninism-Mao Zedong Thought (ii) Socialist Democracy and the Legal System (iii) Communist Morality (iv) Marxist Aesthetics (v) China and the World and

(vi) the fruits of modern science and technology. This education will be governed by a national teaching plan drawn up by the CCP Propaganda Department and Secretariat, SEC, Ministry of Education, Chinese Academy of Sciences, the ACFTU, CCYL and the CSTA.[37]

In practice, this scheme is already underway for experimentation began following a January 1982 national meeting on enterprise political work.[38] Recent reports from Shanghai suggest that some remarkable transformations have been brought about. Absenteeism and indiscipline have been replaced by voluntary overtime; insolence and greed by courtesy and collectivism, the 'blind pursuit of Western fashions' and decadent capitalist habits by glowing patriotism, socialist zeal and applications to join the CCYL and CCP.[39] Such reports are, naturally, selected to show newspaper readers the method in its best light; the depth and permanence of the attitudinal change which they describe must be a matter for speculation. For older (34+) employees there are to be no special courses, even though anxious press reports indicate that they are as jaundiced and alienated as their younger colleagues and their political education in therefore likely to remain a pressing concern of the CCP for some time to come.[40]

Cultural and Vocational Education

Recent official data on the performance of employee education are presented in Table 7.2 and 7.3. Regrettably, they leave much to be desired. For higher education it is unclear whether they include correspondence and self-study students; for this and other levels it is unclear whether student figures refer to those taking complete courses or single subjects at the levels indicated. Moreover, by dwelling upon longer courses designed to provide education equivalent to that available in the formal sector, they exclude the massive range of 'quick-fix' short and highly specific skill-training courses, professional refresher courses and the contribution of the Party school network to vocational education. In some senses this exclusion is unsurprising since it has probably proved impossible to aggregate coherent national data. Partial data for 1979 and 1981 suggest that total employee education enrollment (i.e. including short-term vocational training) may be 80% - 100% higher than the figures shown in Tables 7.2 and 7.3.[41]

The dominant theme running through employee education discussion since 1978 has been the need for 'regularisation' (zhengguihua), meaning the adoption of fixed standards determining access to and progress within the system and the establishment of clearly articulated teaching plans and curricula. As such, regularisation clearly implies a degree of modelling upon the formal education system. However several educationalists have argued strongly that modelling should not

Table 7.2: DEVELOPMENT OF EMPLOYEE EDUCATION ENROLLMENT, 1979 - 1981

INSTITUTION	1979 enrollment	(%)	1980 enrollment	(%)	1981 enrollment	(%)
Broadcasting Universities	n.a.	–	324,000	5.04	268,000	4.10
Employee Universities	211,000	4.15	440,000	6.85	486,400	7.45
Secondary Technical Schools	n.a.	n.a.	2,013,500	31.34	1,964,600	30.08
Upper Secondary Schools	2,131,000	41.94	n.a.	n.a.	701,000	10.73
Lower Secondary Schools	1,748,000	34.40	2,906,400	45.23	2,431,000	37.22
			n.a.	n.a.		
Primary Schools	606,000	11.93	493,800	7.68	472,600	7.24
Literacy Classes	385,000	7.58	247,900	3.86	208,500	3.19
	5,081,000	100.00	6,425,600	100.00	6,532,100	100.00

n.a. = not available   (differences due to rounding)

Sources:
1979 - Wang Shou'an & Wang Xianrun, p.39
1980 - Zhongguo Baike Nianjian 1981 Beijing & Shanghai: Zhongguo Dabaike Chubanshe, 1981, p.481.
1981 - Zhongguo Baike Nianjian 1982, p.579 & State Statistical Bureau Statistical Yearbook of China 1981 (English Edition) Hong Kong: Economic Information & Agency, 1982, p.460.

Adult Education

Table 7.3: EMPLOYEE EDUCATION INSTITUTIONS AND PERFORMANCE, 1981

Types of Institution	Number of Institutions	Number of Graduates	Number of New Admissions	Total Enrollment	Full-Time Teaching Staff
Institutions of Higher Education	1,383	70,000	168,000	486,000	17,000
Full-Time/Part-Time	879	20,000	34,000	100,000	14,000
After-Work	504	50,000	134,000	386,000	3,000
Secondary Technical Schs.	13,807	568,000	880,000	1,965,000	13,000
Full-Time/Part-Time	2,248	107,000	180,000	414,000	6,000
After-Work	11,559	461,000	700,000	1,551,000	7,000
Secondary Schools	21,825	654,000	2,066,000	3,132,500	32,000
Upper Secondary	6,499	125,000	474,000	701,000	10,000
Lower Secondary	15,326	529,000	1,592,000	2,431,000	22,000
Primary Schools	6,274	92,000	301,000	473,000	4,000
Literacy Classes	4,133	92,000	114,000	208,000	2,000
TOTAL	47,422	1,476,000	3,529,000	6,264,000	68,000

Source: Adapted from State Statistical Bureau, Statistical Yearbook of China 1981, p.460.

be slavish since employee education is and should continue to be qualitatively different in its objectives, settings, forms, clientele and teaching methods.[42] This points to a major debate between the so-called 'theoretical wind' (lilun feng) and 'practice wind' (shijian feng) which originated in university scientific and engineering education but has quickly spread to employee education.

During the GPCR employee education was based upon the pedagogic principle 'teach in conjunction with typical products'. Stripped of its political implications, the educational argument was that employee education's main role was the inculcation of current skills. Thus abstract theory, conceptual knowledge and the study of Western practices was an irrelevant luxury which the state could not afford and did not need. The best forms for employee education were therefore short training courses and these were powerfully advocated by the former de facto Vice-Minister of Education and associate of the 'Gang of Four' Chi Qun.

In the late 1970's this approach was condemned by the 'theoretical wind' for leading to academically incomplete education programmes for employees and for hampering economic growth and diversification in a period of technological change. Whilst a clear case existed for skills training, it had to be supplemented by education designed to equip employees with the ability to develop and work with new technology in the future. Thus curricula were to be remodelled comprehensively to include henceforth theoretical and conceptual matter not directly related to current production. Since then the 'practice wind' have guardedly suggested that this has led employee education to become a weak parody of formal education, largely divorced from urgent current needs. Some critics have invoked the old maxim 'Distant water will not extinguish a fire close at hand' (yuan shui bujiu jin huo). The programmes considered below can be seen as China's attempt to resolve the issue, one which is neither new in Chinese employee education nor unknown elsewhere.[43]

1. Employee Universities

During the GPCR the terms 'employee university' (zhi gong daxue) and 'workers university' (gongren daxue) were used freely to describe virtually all employee education institutions. Post-Mao planners therefore faced an awesome task of sorting the wheat from the chaff, but the result of their efforts is the existence at present of a varied group of institutions providing tertiary level courses broadly equivalent to vocationally-oriented courses in formal universities.

Employee universities are operated by provincial bureaux of education, formal universities, mass organisations and enterprises. Their size ranges from small institutions with less than 200 students to those with enrollments of 5,000. Employees may study on a full-time, part-time or after-work basis and take complete degree level courses or single subject tertiary courses lasting from six weeks to one year. Entry to all courses is selective and depends in the first instance upon gaining approval from one's employer. Employees attending full degree-level courses are further required to have an upper secondary school education, two years' work experience and to pass entrance examinations set at provincial level. This results in eight or nine out of every ten candidates being rejected, but the system is defended on the grounds that it ensures the academic quality of each intake.[44]

Each university determines its own curriculum, subject to the approval of provincial education bureaux and there is thus no standard national course structure. However, it is generally the case that complete degree-level courses involve c.2,000 class contact hours. Despite vast differences within and between institutions, such courses do have common characteristics. The first is that a substantial proportion (50% - 70%) of each is devoted to basic theory (jiben lilun). The second is that attempts are made to link study and employment via project work. Students are commonly required to prepare one or two projects, the topics of which are agreed jointly by their employers and the university. These are then subject to examination by outside assessors - formal university staff, local engineers etc. The third common characteristic is that degree-level curricula are modelled consciously upon those of local formal universities and students frequently use the same text-books.

External monitoring of curricula and examinations is intended to produce 'three same' students, i.e. employees who will receive the same pay, assignments and status as conventional graduates. Those working in employee education are convinced that this is justified. However the recurrence of official directives calling for observance of the 'three sames' indicates that not all are convinced of the quality and usefulness of employee university courses.[45] This situation may worsen, since the 1983 regulations for formal university entrance allow enterprises to send employees direct to formal universities - a provision which may cream off the more able employees and result in further scepticism about the quality of employee universities.[46]

2. Broadcasting Universities

Broadcasting universities began operation in China in the early 1960's, only to be closed like all employee education institutions in 1966.[47] Having reopened in 1979, their current (1982) enrollment is 270,000 and the majority of students are employees under the age of 35.[48] As in employee universities, students may take complete degree-level courses or single subject courses in a variety of disciplines related to their work. University entrance is also determined in a similar fashion: accepted students require their employers' approval and are obliged to pass a national entrance examination similar to but of a slightly lower standard than that for conventional universities. However, whilst this screens out over half af all applicants, non-registered employees may enter final examinations and received the same diploma as registered students if successful.

The Central Broadcasting University run by the Ministry of Education and Ministry of Radio and Television is the major body which prepares curricula, programme output and stipulates national examination standards. In addition virtually all provincial education bureaux add to its efforts by transmitting locally produced programmes and, subject to Ministry of Education approval, add to individual curricula. Classes are held variously in institutions directly managed by provincial education bureaux, within enterprises and other employee universities, generally according to a 3:3 daily schedule (i.e. three hours broadcast time, three hours classwork) comprising a total of 2,000 hours' tuition time spread over three to five years for complete degree-level courses.

Having completed national course examinations, employees are also expected to receive the 'three sames' treatment. However despite the fact that curricula and programmes are prepared by formal university staff, amongst the best in China, provincial education officials complain that widespread prejudice exists amongst those who regard broadcasting university graduates as graduate movie fans rather than 'real' university graduates *(bushi daxue biyesheng, shi yingmi biyesheng)*. Officials are also conscious that a severe shortage of local teaching staff, premises and equipment limits the amount of face-to-face tuition and laboratory work which is available to support broadcast material. Similarly, limited transmission capacity and competing demands for air-time mean that programmes are broadcast generally at times inconvenient for the majority of employees.[49]

3. Correspondence Education

Before the GPCR China possessed a well-developed system of higher education by correspondence. At its peak in 1965, 190,000 students were taking degree-level courses conducted by over 120 formal universities.[50] Some universities and provincial education bureaux recommenced correspondence education in 1973, but programme control soon fell into the hands of 'leftist' officials who sought to use the system as a covert weapon to foment local disorder and gather intelligence on 'revisionist' Party leaders.[51] Reconstruction of the current system began in earnest towards the end of 1980 following CCP Secretariat and Ministry of Education meetings which reaffirmed the achievements of the pre-GPCR system and called for its restoration.

Correspondence education is an acknowledged method of providing cost-effective education. Its recurrent costs are neglible and one Chinese source has indicated that the cost to the state of producing a graduate by correspondence education is but 4.5% of that of producing a graduate by conventional means.[52] In the best of universities offering correspondence courses a rigorous system of pre-admission screening, meticulous examinations and pastoral care combine to ensure the academic quality of the end product. Those admitted are required to have reached the academic level of an upper secondary school graduate and to pass a formal entrance examination. Individual syllabi are modelled closely upon those of intra-mural courses and sessional examinations are similar if not identical to those taken by conventional undergraduates.

According to 1980 data, some 177,000 correspondence students are supported by a mere 500 full-time specialist staff,[53] but their services are supplemented by assistance from internal university staff and part-time staff at correspondence stations. These stations play a critical role, providing facilities for discussion of assignments, laboratory work, revision and a few weeks of intensive face-to-face tuition each year. In the best of cases, participating universities also take it upon themselves to establish formal links with employers in order to guarantee their students' travel expenses for visits to correspondence education stations, study level for revision and to ensure that project work is linked to the needs of the enterprise.

The academic content of correspondence courses varies according to the speciality of each providing university. The Chinese People's University thus specialises in social science courses whilst Tongji University in Shanghai conducts engineering courses. Course length varies from three to five years and it is expected that successful students will have devoted 4,000 - 5,000 hours to their studies before attempting final examinations. This is a massive study load (c.15 hours a week) and student drop-out and failure rates are high. No recent data have been published but it is not unreasonable to assume that they may be in the 50% - 60% range reported before the GPCR. Cadres, who constitute around 80% of the student body, are particularly vulnerable given the demands on their time imposed by official meetings.

A further barrier to the development of correspondence education is what one educator recently called 'deeply ingrained bias' in favour of full-time schooling, with the result that:

> some comrades regard correspondence education as spare-time education. They think its demands are low and that it doesn't matter whether you

run it big or small, fast or slow, well or badly. They adopt a policy of letting things drift.[54]

The writer noted that such negative views were widespread, but drew particular attention to their prevalence in China's key point universities, i.e. those expected to operate correspondence education schemes. There is no reason to doubt his remarks, particularly since of the 120+ university schemes running in 1965 only 69 had resumed operations by the end of 1980.[55]

4. Self-Study Schemes

A major post-GPCR innovation ripe for development is the higher education self-study scheme for employees. The system owes its genesis to a 1980 Ministry of Education report which argued that the scarcity of employee education resources and limited capacity of existing institutions suggested that China should experiment with a system of organised self-study. Selected employees would be registered as students, receive details of curricula and suggested reading and subsequently submit themselves to an examination process. The registering bodies - provincial education bureaux and higher education self-study examination guidance committees (*gaodeng zi xue kaoshi zhidao weiyuanhui*) would provide no teaching. The report was later publicly promulgated in 1981 with an announcement that experimental implementation would begin in Beijing, Tianjin and Shanghai. The success of these experiments was such that in May 1983 the scheme was expanded to a further seventeen provinces.[56]

Formal regulations indicate that employees may be registered regardless of academic background or age. However phenomenal demand and early mishaps has led to the screening of candidates for registration. Employees may only register with their employers' approval and this is not automatically granted. Secondly, provincial registration bodies give priority to those who are relatively young and have already completed an approved secondary education. Shanghai Higher Education Bureau officials freely stated in 1982 that registration was restricted to those who had completed upper secondary schooling and data published on Beijing self-study students indicate that a similar practice has been adopted, since over 90% of those registered had received formal secondary schooling and were young employees under the age of 35.[57]

Once registered, employees study according to a curriculum devised by provincial bureaux of education, self-study guidance committees and local formal universities. The latter provide detailed syllabi and reading lists and sometimes publish self-study materials in their journals to supplement two national journals <u>Zi Xue</u> (Self Study) and <u>Zi Xue Daxue</u> (Self Study

University) oriented exclusively towards self-study students. Self-Study courses currently available are limited to arts and social sciences subjects, e.g. Chinese, Foreign Languages, Economics, Law, Dossier Management. However national and local discussions are considering the feasibility of adding science and engineering subjects to the curriculum.

Examination standards are determined by a national self-study committee currently headed by Minister of Education He Dongchang, but each province determines its own specific examination methods. Examinations are generally based on a credit system whereby students present themselves for examination in one subject of their discipline at a sitting; if successful they are awarded certificates and, having obtained the required number, they are then awarded diplomas which are intended to indicate that they have achieved the academic level expected of a conventional graduate. With no organised teaching and limited access to libraries, the failure rate amongst self-study students is high. Of 9,577 who sat single subject examinations in Beijing in 1981, only 3,985 (41.6%) were successful.[58] Nevertheless, self-study offers a further inexpensive route to higher education, for like correspondence education its recurrent costs are neglible.[59]

5. Secondary Technical Schools

In 1981 1.9 million employees were studying at 13,800 secondary technical schools, the majority of them operating on an after-work basis.[60] Secondary Technical Schools differ from the institutions of employee education discussed previously in that it is extremely rare for employees to take anything other than the standard full course. For full-time students, courses last two and a half to three years with 26 - 30 hours' teaching per week. The total number of contact hours regardless of mode of attendance is 2,700 for engineering subjects and 2,400 for non-engineering subjects. The average enrollment at each school is 142 and schools with enrollments over 200 are uncommon.

These schools match their formal counterparts to such an extent that apart from mode of attendance and students' ages there is little difference between them. Potential students under the age of 35 (exceptionally 40) with two years' experience as a regular worker and a lower secondary school education are nominated by their employers and have to pass entrance examinations in Politics, Chinese, Mathematics, Physics and Chemistry (engineering courses) or Politics, Chinese, Mathematics, History and Geography (non-engineering courses) to gain admission. According to a 1982 Ministry of Education document, the curricula of employee secondary technical schools are modelled closely upon their formal counterparts. Detailed curriculum and teaching plan development is the immediate responsibility of provincial government industrial bureaux which run the schools on a day to day basis, although they are required to submit copies for approval to the appropriate central industrial ministry and/or provincial education bureaux. Approximately 75% of class teaching is devoted to 'ordinary' (*putong ke*, i.e. academic subjects) and 'technical foundation' lessons (*jishu jichu ke*). Ideally these are taught by full-time university graduate staff so as to maintain continuity and quality and establish a broad base for the specialised skills which are taught in the remaining contact hours. Having passed final examinations almost identical to those in formal secondary technical schools, graduate students return to their enterprises and soon take up employment as skilled workers/technicians. Unlike the performance of other employee education institutions, that of secondary technical schools evokes a much less defensive and ambiguous response from employers and those working in formal education. Whilst not exclusively 'academic' institutions, they are widely regarded as providing a sound and useful training service to urban-industrial enterprises.[61]

6. Secondary and Primary Schools

The remaining institutions of employee education are devoted to remedial academic education, particularly at lower secondary school level. These secondary and primary schools, run largely by enterprises, are intended to compensate employees for the poor or incomplete school education which they received during the GPCR. Their raison d'etre is that skills training and political education cannot be conducted effectively unless based upon a foundation of literacy and numeracy comparable to that now provided by formal schools. At the lower level illiterate workers are expected to learn 2,000 Chinese characters before proceeding via 360 hours' teaching to primary school graduation. Thereafter lower and upper secondary school courses each last for 720 contact hours.

The development of these schools has been studded with pedagogic problems deriving from the official expectation that curricula should be modelled upon their formal counterparts in order to maintain standards. Some enterprises have succeeded in a highly selective exercise of modelling, emphasising language, mathematics and vocationally relevant science subjects. Employers and employees consequently perceive a direct relationship between available courses and the reality of work, a linkage emphasised by the use of customised teaching materials and methods in class. However in other enterprises the modelling is much less selective - even slavish - with the result that employers and students openly complain that there is little or no linkage between the education provided and the needs and demands of enterprises and employees. This may be illustrated by the fact that industrial workers attending some secondary schools are expected to learn classical Chinese and plant biology.[62]

Some educationalists have defended this approach, arguing that employee education should be at least partially concerned with cultural enrichment as well as vocational training and political education. But to others - probably the majority - it is unsatisfactory. Employees, anxious to advance their education in a way relevant to occupational improvement, are faced with a protracted and to them irrelevant stodgy diet of childrens' texts and teaching methods more suitable for ten year old children than mature workers. Not unnaturally, employees become bored, apathetic or impatient and drop-out rates of 30% have been reported. Investigations into drop-out reveal a common attitude, summed up in the following jingle:

> Study or not, it's all the same
> Study well, study poorly, it's all the same.

In an era when education has been officially identified as a lead sector of national economic growth it is paradoxical that this pessimistic jingle, reminiscent of the GPCR, should have gained such wide currency.[63]

CONCLUSION

There are no simple criteria by which the effectiveness of an education programme can be judged, particularly one as diverse as employee education in China and a programme which as yet has not run its full course. Since 1978 Chinese media have published scores of individual examples of the programme's success and there is no doubt that the education of China's urban-industrial work-force has improved and that employee education is contributing to economic growth and development. Equally, however, official media point to a number of recurrent problems.

Of these, the one which pervades virtually all media accounts and briefings to foreign delegations is the paucity of resources available to employee education at present. To some extent, this is an indicator of the fact that China is, by any definition, a poor developing country. At the same time it is symptomatic of a less than unanimous commitment to employee education which is exacerbated by its administrative system. As indicated above, most employee education is provided by agencies with other prime duties, be they the provision of formal education or the discharge of a commercial/production function. It is an inescapable fact that the central and local organs of some agencies do not share the commitment of national leaders and instead regard employee education variously as inferior to formal education, as an unwelcome burden subsidiary in importance to the fulfillment of their primary roles. This leads to inertia and, inevitably, the allocation of resources elsewhere. Yuan Baohua summed up this situation as follows:[64]

> One can generally say that in a great many units employee education still does not occupy its rightful position and that the needs of the objective situation are being overlooked. In the development of employee education, more often than not it's "When it's time to talk about it, it's very important; when it's time to do something about it, it's less important and if you're busy, it doesn't matter at all".

China's senior leaders may not share the myopia of some of their international contemporaries towards employee education, but the situation at lower levels is somewhat cloudy. At present a small Ministry of Education group is drafting a law governing employee education which is intended to guarantee compliance with state policy. In itself, this is partly an admission of the failure of existing control mechanisms to prevent evasion of responsibility, but it is difficult to imagine any law being more effective than directives issued with the full force of the CCP Central Committee. Thus the phenomenon which Yuan Baohua has described elsewhere as the issuing of 'silent commands' (wusheng de mingling) seems likely to continue for some time.

The development of employee education also reveals starkly a general problem inherent in the evolution of Chinese education policy since 1976. For all the failings - and these were massive - of the GPCR model of education, it was not without some merit. Regrettably, many sound principles were carried too far too fast and education policies were abused for political gain. Since the GPCR such maladministration and political interference with education has been roundly and justifiably condemned, but in 'black and white' terms which tolerate little if any defence of the merits of GPCR educational principles or their continuation in post-1976 education practice. Similarly the reflex return to the principles underlying education policies before the GPCR has stymied discussion of the failings of those policies and sincere attempts to avoid their shortcomings in post-1976 education practice. Such an approach to education policy-making is decided on high and is undoubtedly an appropriate method of convincing lower levels that there will never be a return to the educational chaos and luddism of the GPCR and that orderliness will prevail. Employee education suffered immeasurably during the GPCR from being proclaimed as a 'radical' non-formal alternative to a discredited and inferior formal education system. As the GPCR progressed, so employee education became the model upon which formal education, particularly at post-secondary levels, was based. The corollary of political change since 1976 has been that this relationship has been reversed with vengeance and with a lack of subtlety.

Adult Education

In contemporary employee education the insistence upon the establishment and maintenance of standards using methods borrowed from the formal school system is more than overdue. Planners have little choice but to concentrate the largest share of resources upon providing the work-force with something approaching a formal education. Unless the formal education system expands very greatly in the next decade it is inevitable that urban-industrial enterprises will be compelled to satisfy their own requirements for educated and skilled manpower. Equally, employee education will have a permanent task of updating skills and knowledge in the light of new technology and acquainting workers with the requirements of new Party-State policies. The future of employee education is therefore not at issue. What is at issue is whether in responding to these needs Chinese employee education will continue to model itself explicitly upon the formal system as at present, continuing to invite criticism that it is a 'second best' avenue to formal education, or whether it will move out of the shadow of the formal educational system and establish itself as a truly independent 'leg' of the national education system free from the political constraints of the past.

Chapter Eight

CHINESE-WESTERN SCHOLARLY EXCHANGE: IMPLICATIONS FOR THE FUTURE OF CHINESE EDUCATION

Ruth Hayhoe

INTRODUCTION

In this final chapter the situation of Chinese-western scholarly interaction in the early eighties will be described. China's present lively educational exchange with countries of the developed capitalist world is unprecedented since 1949. However such interaction was a significant feature of China's educational development between 1860 and 1949. Chapter Two has presented a historical and analytical framework within which the outcomes of pre-Liberation educational experiments could be evaluated. Y. C. Wang's celebrated study of the period, 'Chinese Intellectuals and the West',[1] may give too bleak a picture of the failure of western education to equip Chinese intellectuals for China's modernisation tasks, yet there can be little doubt that western educational patterns and values did not fulfil their promise in the pre-Liberation Chinese context. It may be that China is now in a position to make more profitable use of intellectuals who received their scholarly training in the West, and of selected aspects of western educational experience which Chinese leaders may wish to draw upon. This chapter offers a context for reflection on the implications of present ambitious scholarly exchange programmes for the future of Chinese education.

One future trend suggested in Chapter Four was a reinforcing of the hierarchical nature of the education system with keypoint institutions setting standards at all levels, a pattern whose values have some echoes of the Confucian examination system. Another trend suggested in Chapter Three was the rise of urban elites and an exacerbation of the urban-rural dichotomy with very little promise of social mobility within the rural education system, a pattern less consistent with the Confucian past. A third trend which has been discussed in Chapters Four and Five is the diversification of the secondary and higher education system and the development of a wide variety of types of institutions catering to differing needs within the formal system. A fourth trend that has been noted in several chapters is the reformulation of political education on a more strongly moral than ideological basis. What will the present interaction of China's scholars, teachers and students with their western counterparts contribute to these trends? Will the distinctive scholarly policies and practices of specific western nations have differing effects? On a more general level, will China's present gamble with western academia prove more worthwhile for the fulfilment of her modernisation tasks than was the case before 1949? These are questions that might be kept in mind while considering present scholarly exchange policies.

First the Chinese approach to scholarly exchange will be examined, their aims and policies, the bodies through which exchange relations are administered, financial arrangements, structure and curricular priorities. Then the aims and policies of select western countries which have large contingents of Chinese scholars and students will be analysed within the same taxonomy: USA, West Germany, France, Great Britain and Canada. This selection is broadly representative of distinctive approaches in North American and European countries, yet it is not intended to denigrate the importance of China's scholarly relations with other European countries and with Japan, where less information has been available. In addition to bi-lateral educational exchange with western nations, China's present involvement with international organisations is affecting educational development in a way unprecedented since Liberation. World Bank educational projects in China are undoubtedly the largest in scope and call for a brief discussion in this chapter. It will conclude with some reflections on the implications of this burgeoning exchange situation for the future of Chinese education and society.

CHINESE EXCHANGE POLICIES AND PRACTICES

The heart of Chinese scholarly exchange policy is expressed in this statement by Vice-Premier Deng Xiaoping at the 12th Congress of the Chinese Communist Party in August, 1982:

> We will unswervingly follow a policy of opening to the outside world and actively increase exchanges with foreign countries on the basis of mutual equality and benefit. At the same time we will keep a clear head, firmly resist corrosion by decadent ideas from abroad, and never permit the bourgeois way of life to spread in our country.[2]

This emphatic expression of determination to separate the advanced knowledge of western capitalist countries from the 'decadent ideas' and 'bourgeois way of life' which provide its social and ideological context may have overtones of the formula devised in China's early modernisation efforts: "Chinese learning as the substance, western techniques for their usefulness".[3] Chinese learning has since incorporated Marxism-Leninism and demonstrated the effectiveness of this combination both in the Liberation struggle and in nation-building, but can the 'techniques' of western capitalist science be disentangled from their social context and made useful in the service of China's socialist modernisation? This is the demanding task expected of Chinese scholars and students sent to study in the West. The large numbers working in fields of the applied sciences may find it fairly easy to fit their contribution into this paradigm set by Chinese policy makers. But what of those who are pursuing high level studies in the pure sciences and may be encouraged to adopt a quality of questioning, critical thought which is fundamentally at odds with the norms of their own society? And how can those working in the arts and social sciences gain an in-depth understanding of their field of study as pursued in the West without being contaminated by the 'bourgeois way of life' which these disciplines reflect?

In China's Sixth Five-Year Plan (1981-1985) one paragraph is devoted to the subject of sending scholars and students abroad. It gives concrete form, in terms of numbers and curricular orientation, to the general policy discussed above:

> Within these five years, efforts will be made to send 15,000 persons abroad, an average of 3,000 persons per year; within this period 11,000 persons will complete their studies abroad and return home. Students sent abroad major primarily in such specialties as the natural sciences and engineering technology, with emphasis on those fields and areas in which China is currently weak or which it needs to explore. At the same time, certain numbers of persons should be sent abroad to survey and study politics, economics, law, education and languages of foreign countries.[4]

The training of Chinese students and scholars in those fields of the natural sciences and engineering where Chinese education is weak is clearly intended to contribute directly to China's modernisation goals, and so implies a strong emphasis on the applied, production-related sciences. The much smaller numbers being sent to 'survey and study' various fields of the social sciences and humanities will be expected to provide an understanding of capitalist society and access to its information resources at the least, and in certain fields, such as management science, to bring back knowledge and skills which can be adapted to socialist modernisation needs.

Chinese scholarly exchange is largely administered by the Foreign Affairs Office of the Ministry of Education in Beijing, which processes most exchanges involving staff or students of higher learning institutions. The other central bodies of major importance in administering academic exchange are the Chinese Academies of Sciences and Social Sciences, which make their own arrangements for scholars and research students of their institutes on the basis of agreements with parallel scholarly bodies in western countries.[5] Research or graduate students are selected by these central bodies through nationwide graduate entrance examinations. In some case examinations are also used to select the mature scholars they send abroad, in others these scholars are sent on recommendation from the institutions to which they are attached. A spokesman for the Foreign Affairs Office of the Ministry of Education explained to the writer how this office sets quotas for both graduate students and research scholars according to curricular priorities based on manpower planning needs. The geographical distribution of opportunity is also taken into account in selecting candidates for study abroad. Key institutions are favoured, but some places are also given to scholars from non-key institutions.[6]

The Ministry of Education and the Academies are responsible for financing those students and scholars they send, and terms are negotiated as favourably as possible through the Education Section of the Chinese Embassy in the relevant foreign countries. This office also administers living stipends. These are spartan by the standards of western student life, but they are intended to harmonise with the salaries of Chinese diplomatic personnel, and Chinese living standards in general. Scholars who have received fellowships from the host country are sometimes expected to contribute what is in excess of a normal Chinese stipend to the Embassy, where it is redistributed for the benefit of all. This is not acceptable to western funding agencies, but it is justified from the Chinese side in that it enables more people to be sent, or the extension of the study period for those already there. In addition to scholars and students sent abroad by these central agencies, many are also going on the basis of institution-level agreements, where expenses are sometimes covered by a direct exchange of personnel. The Chinese are eager to increase this form of exchange and individual Chinese institutions are given considerable autonomy in making such arrangements.

The structure of exchange studies has reflected very clearly the changes that have taken place in the Chinese education system as a whole since 1976, changes which have been described in earlier chapters of this book. From 1977 to 1980, the emphasis was on undergraduates and mature scholars. The former were selected from secondary schools and sent for a three or four year study period in Europe or North America. Some of these young people were instructed only to audit courses they considered useful to China, while others did courses leading to degrees or certificates. Mature scholars from 35 to 50 in age were sent for one or two year periods to familiarise themselves with research in their field abroad and repair some of the damage of the Cultural Revolution interruption in their careers. Some graduate students were sent for doctoral degrees during this period, but there was not a large pool of qualified graduating students to draw from until 1982 when the first two higher education classes selected by competitive entrance examinations in 1977-8 received their degrees. From these two classes about 1,000 were selected to begin doctoral programmes in Europe and North America in 1982, and a further 1,000 were to be selected through graduate entrance examinations early in 1983.[7] In future it is expected that the number sent to follow postgraduate programmes will increase, while the numbers of mature scholars sent to upgrade their research abilities will decrease. There is already a moratorium on the sending of undergraduate students, except in the case of private sponsorship, as Chinese institutions are considered well able to provide facilities of equivalent quality.[8] As for the curricular emphasis, figures given below will demonstrate that the applied sciences are given highest priority, specially those which are seen as essential to present modernisation goals. The pure sciences are also considered important, a tendency that is reinforced by the policies of some western nations. Supportive social sciences such as economics, management and international law are given increasing attention, while the humanities and less pragmatically oriented social sciences have very small quotas.

So far the majority of scholars returning to China go back to their original working units and seek to apply what they have learned to raising standards of research and teaching.[9] However more dramatic changes may be expected in a few years when younger scholars who have gone through four or five years of rigorous doctoral training return, eager to put into action a whole new intellectual perspective. This group is more likely to bring fundamental changes to the Chinese education system than either the older scholars or the large contingent of western teachers who are now working in Chinese tertiary institutions and secondary schools attached to Foreign Language Institutes. In 1980 there were reported to be about 180 American teachers of English who had been directly hired by the Chinese government,[10] also much smaller numbers of Canadian, British, French and German language teachers working on similar terms. While these teachers are treated with great respect and their work is sincerely valued, it is unlikely that their presence will be a strong impetus for change in the Chinese education system.

AMERICAN-CHINESE SCHOLARLY EXCHANGE

The American scene will be dealt with first since there were an estimated 9,000 Chinese scholars and students in USA in

1983,[11] which represents about half of the whole contingent overseas. Also the United States differs from other western countries in the scrupulous self-examination which has accompanied this flowering of exchange with China and the many publicly commissioned studies that have been made on aspects of the exchange process.[12] In the American case, the objectives for exchange have been formulated with the greatest care by the Office of Science and Technology and the Committee for Scholarly Communication with the People's Republic of China and published for public discussion. The following useful summary is found in the Clough Report of 1981:

1. To provide scientific gain in certain areas.
2. To establish important contact with the younger generation of Chinese scientists and engineers who will likely furnish much of the future leadership of China.
3. To enable the United States to compete more easily in an expanding commercial market.
4. To enhance Chinese agriculture and facilitate the development and export of Chinese minerals and energy resources.
5. To contribute to the development of a 'strong, secure and peaceful China'.
6. To provide a better understanding of China's society, politics and government through research in China by American social scientists and China specialists.
7. To improve the Chinese leadership's understanding of the United States by exposing its scholars to the United States.
8. To make available to those Chinese turning toward Western ideas for economic development American techniques, such as management science.
9. To determine whether aspects of China's rural development policies may be applicable elsewhere in the developing world.
10. To create a network of personal and institutional links between the United States and China and to establish numerous ongoing programmes, making the trend toward closer relations difficult to reverse.[13]

The way in which these objectives are phrased indicates the strong thrust of the American government towards facilitating the entrance of Americans to China, both in order to deepen American scholarly understanding of Chinese society, and to encourage the transfer of knowledge from USA to China. In other western countries, government and educational leaders soliciting Chinese scholars and students have taken less seriously the opportunity to ensure research opportunities for their own scholars in exchange for facilities offered to the Chinese.[14] With regard to the flow of Chinese scholars and students to America, the American government has been in the fortunate position of being able to take a laissez-faire approach, and leave most of the administration to individual American universities, which have moved energetically towards forming ties with Chinese institutions of higher learning.

By 1981 there were reported to be 51 American universities having agreements with over 100 Chinese institutions[15] and many more have been added in subsequent years. The presence of many American-educated Chinese scholars in Chinese institutions has inclined younger Chinese to a favourable attitude towards American scholarship.[16] Also the network of sister relations that existed between Chinese and American institutions in the pre-Liberation period, linked to the 16 American missionary colleges,[17] was responsible for an ethos of scholarly cooperation which has been smoothly and quickly revived. In a few celebrated cases the actual ties between former American institutions and their sisters in USA have been revived, such as Yale-Hunan Medical School and Oberlin-Shansi Agricultural University. Most of the movement of Chinese scholars to the United States has taken place within these exchange relations at the university level, or through the applications of individual Chinese to American institutions, either sent directly by the individual or through the Chinese Ministry of Education. Both TOEFL and Graduate Record Examinations can now be taken in China, and these assist American institutions in the selection of Chinese candidates. The American government has done little to provide financial aid for Chinese scholars and students in the USA, but many American institutions have been able to provide scholarships or other forms of aid, sometimes raised from local business circles where interest in China is high, or from national foundations.[18]

The American government has focused rather on the sending of American scholars to China through a programme administered by the Committee for Scholarly Exchange with the People's Republic of China which provides research fellowships for over fifty American scholars to spend time in China each year. In addition the United States International Communications Agency administers a programme for ten American teachers of English to work in China on a Chinese salary supplemented by American funds, in some cases Fullbright scholarships.[19] The focus of their teaching work is increasingly on American studies rather than the English language. Another education project of the American government is the Dalian Training Centre for Industrial Science and Technology which was set up under a protocol between the State Science and Technology Commission and the U.S. Department of Commerce in 1980, and has given 6-month training sessions to Chinese managers and directors of enterprises each year since then.[20] It is significant to notice how these activities express a clear intention to disseminate American ideas in the humanities and social sciences, an approach that is welcomed by the Chinese in spite of their determination not to be influenced by 'decadent ideas'. Such American funding agencies as the United Board for Christian Higher Education in Asia, which takes the support of Chinese scholars in the humanities and social sciences as one of its objectives, contribute further to this effort to educate the Chinese in the social context of American science.[21]

The structure of studies of Chinese scholars and students in USA is represented in Table 8.1 but several points should be taken into account in interpreting this data. It draws on only a cross-section of the 9,000 scholars from China in the USA, and the fact that half of them are funded by the American Chinese community accounts for the relatively high number in the arts, social science, and language studies. No comprehensive figures are yet available for the structure of studies and the curricular orientation of the total Chinese scholar population in the USA.[22]

Table 8.1

PROFILE OF A CROSS-SECTION OF CHINESE SCHOLARS AND STUDENTS IN USA IN 1981-82

Level	Maths & Physical Sciences	Medical & Life Sciences	Engineering	Social Sciences	Arts	ESL	TOTAL
Undergraduates	84	24	42	37	44	96	327
Graduates	244	60	154	35	90	18	601
Visiting Scholars	108	44	187	14	12	20	385
TOTAL	436	128	383	86	146	134	1313

Since the autumn of 1982, the emphasis from the Chinese side has moved to the sending of graduate students for doctoral research, so that the proportion of these is likely to become even larger. Under the programme for sending graduates set up by the Chinese Ministry of Education, nearly half of the 1,000 being sent each year go to American institutions. This programme has been supplemented from the American side by the efforts of American scientists to provide for the training of talented young Chinese capable of working competitively at the top levels of pure scientific disciplines. Present arrangements set up from the American side are catering for 120 doctoral candidates in physics, about 100 in biology, and 40-60 in chemistry each year, beginning from the autumn of 1982.[23]

American-Chinese scholarly exchange policies are characterised, on the one hand, by the scope for individual initiative which has been manifested in these attempts to counterbalance the Chinese emphasis on the applied sciences with programmes emphasising the pure sciences, as well as many other programmes started up by individuals or small groups. Most of the organisation of exchange has been left to the universities in their institutional links with Chinese counterparts, a decentralised approach suited to the American higher education system. Both of these tendencies are rooted in historical precedents, which may be one reason for their remarkable success. On the other hand, the American government has put its weight behind efforts to disseminate knowledge about the United States in China, and to maximise opportunities for American Sinologists and other scholars to study contemporary Chinese development.

GERMAN-CHINESE SCHOLARLY EXCHANGE

The Federal Republic of Germany has taken an active and energetic role in encouraging German-Chinese scholarly relations, and this is reflected in the fact that it hosts the second largest contingent of Chinese scholars and students in the western world. In 1982 there were reported to be 1,393 Chinese in Germany, of whom 1,036 were on study terms longer than six months, the rest on shorter-term visits.[24] Germany began to receive Chinese scholars in 1974, and up to 1978, 94 were trained at German universities mainly as teachers and translators of the German language.[25] The first group of 8 scientists were sent in 1977, and in the same year a national agreement on cultural cooperation was signed which included details on scholarly exchange relations. Unlike the American case, the aims and objectives of scholarly exchange have not been clearly delineated, but German policies can be seen in the practical arrangements made for scholarly exchange from the German side.

The two most important organisations administering exchange programmes are the Deutscher Akademischer Austauschdienst (DAAD) and the Westdeutsche Rektorenkonferenz (WRK). Applications by Chinese scholars and students are usually processed through the Chinese Ministry of Education to the German Embassy, then through the German Ministry of Foreign Affairs to either the DAAD, which liaises with German higher institutions on behalf of mature scholars and graduate students, or the WRK, which is responsible for arranging the placement of Chinese undergraduates.[26] While university-level agreements have also flourished between German and Chinese institutions, with a count of 23 in 1983, they are of less importance in the actual administration of exchange than in the American case.[27] They are taken into account in the placing of Chinese scholars from specific Chinese institutions, and in short-term study and lecture tours both ways, but German institutions do not have the financial autonomy to initiate large scale programmes of their own with Chinese sister-institutions.

In the financing of Chinese scholars, the German side has provided far greater support than is the case in any other western country. Only 505 or 28% of the total in 1982 were financed by the Chinese government, and all the rest received stipends from German funding agencies, including the DAAD, the Alexander von Humboldt-Stiftung, the Deutshe Forschungsgemeinschaft, the Friedrich Ebert-Stiftung and others.[28] In addition to this generous financial support, the fact that no tuition fees are charged at German higher institutions provides an added incentive for Chinese students and scholars. The large concentration of Chinese in Germany may well be due to these favourable conditions, which demonstrate the importance placed on German-Chinese scholarly interaction by German authorities. Although there is some reciprocity from the Chinese side in making provision for German students of Chinese and other German scholars in China, the numbers are minimal by comparison.

The structure of studies and curricular orientation of the Chinese in Germany reflect the general patterns that have been described above. From 1980 to 1982 about 100 Chinese undergraduate students were sent each year after special preparation at a German college attached to Tongji University in Shanghai. The overwhelming emphasis of their studies has been on fields of the applied sciences, particularly engineering. The other large contingent has been young and middle-aged scholars going on two-year programmes to upgrade their teaching and research abilities. Of those in this category placed through the DAAD, ten percent were reported to have completed doctoral studies, quite a remarkable achievement under these conditions. The figures in Table 8.2 reflect the general emphasis which the Chinese have placed on the applied sciences, and to a lesser degree pure sciences, and the fact that funding agencies such as the DAAD have been able to make some provision for the humanities and social sciences.[29] Overall figures suggest that there is actually a rather higher percentage of Chinese in the social sciences than these three groups reflect. However German administrators responsible for placing Chinese students and scholars report that maximum effort is made to accomodate the scholars in the fields of specialty stated on their application forms, and that there are few restrictions of access to German institutions, even those dealing with sensitive fields of the applied sciences. Beginning from 1982, a new emphasis on the postgraduate education of newly graduating young Chinese scholars is expected to result in the presence of 500 Chinese doctoral students in Germany by 1985, and a parallel decrease in the undergraduate and mature scholar groups.[30]

Table 8.2

PROFILE OF THREE GROUPS OF CHINESE SCHOLARS IN GERMANY, 1980-82

Level	Pure Sciences	Engineering	Other Applied	Social Sciences	Arts	TOTAL
Undergrads (Tongji)	67	114	27	-	-	208
Scholars supported by Chinese Gov't	79	126	20	4	3	232
Scholars supported by DAAD	29	26	-	7	8	70
TOTAL	175	266	47	11	11	510

As in the American case, historical continuity is a significant feature of German-Chinese scholarly relations. This can be seen most notably in the revival of Tongji University and to a lesser degree Wuhan Medical College, as lively centres of German-Chinese scholarly interaction. Tongji University was founded by Germans in 1907, and administered jointly by German and Chinese leaders during its evolution over the turbulent years up till 1927 into a high level centre for medical and engineering studies. In 1927 it became a national university under the newly established Chinese University Council, and subsequently the Ministry of Education.[31] It remained an important Chinese educational institution over the pre-Liberation years. Then in 1952 its medical school was moved to Wuhan and its engineering school became a distinguished polytechnical institution within the Soviet-oriented patterns adopted at that time. In the Cultural Revolution period it was selected as one of the first nationally emulated models of a revolutionised university.[32] All through these changes, remnants of the German Technische Hochschule ethos were preserved through Chinese staff educated in Germany and fluent in the German language. As German-Chinese cultural relations began to flourish in the late seventies, the Chinese and Germans agreed on Tongji as an appropriate centre for German academic activities in China. In 1979 Tongji College was established with a staff of about 13 German teachers to prepare 100 Chinese young people each year for entrance to undergraduate studies in German higher institutes. Another five German teachers were placed at Tongji University in accordance with Chinese intentions to make it a centre for scholarly interaction with Germany, where German professors could lecture in German and be widely understood. Thus about half of all the German language teachers supported by the DAAD in China were located there.[33] On a much smaller scale Wuhan Medical College, where there is also a concentration of German-educated Chinese scholars, has been another focal point for German-Chinese scholarly interaction.

Between 1980 and 1982 about 300 Chinese students entered undergraduate programmes in Germany through the Tongji College project. Then from the autumn of 1982 it was changed into an orientation centre for Chinese graduate students aspiring to do higher degrees in Germany. A fourteen month preparation course is now offered, giving basic German language training in the first four months, then higher level language preparation under German teachers, and finally a five-month training period in German scientific method offered by German scientists. This is intended to give Chinese students a through intellectual preparation as well as the necessary language training for study in Germany. Prospective candidates are then required to take examinations administered by examiners sent through the WRK before they are placed in appropriate German institutions for their higher degree programmes.[34]

This brief review of the German scene draws attention to certain distinctive policies of German scholarly interaction with China. The central coordination of much exchange movement through the DAAD and WRK, and of links between German and Chinese institutions, is parallelled by the establishment of one major German academic centre within China at Tongji University. This makes possible a concentration of resources which is particularly important in view of the fact that the German language is not widely taught in China. While the general dissemination of German culture is clearly an important task of German teachers in China, even greater emphasis has been put on the task of giving to Chinese students preparing to study in Germany a through initiation into German scientific and intellectual culture. Finally high levels of funding have been made available to Chinese scholars in Germany with very little expectation of reciprocal provision from the Chinese side, and little attempt to interfere with or influence Chinese-set priorities with regard to the fields of study pursued.

FRENCH-CHINESE SCHOLARLY RELATIONS

French Chinese scholarly relations are carried out within the terms of agreements for cultural and scientific cooperation signed by representatives of the two governments in 1979, and renegotiated every two years. These agreements provide for the exchange of scholars in the natural and social sciences and humanities, in some cases within specific links such as that between the Chinese Academy of Sciences and the Centre Nationale de la Recherche Scientifique. Provision made for the 600 or more Chinese scholars and students in France and for a strong French presence in China demonstrate the importance which the French government attaches to scholarly relations with China, although the numbers of scholars involved are about half of those in West Germany.

Applications from Chinese scholars and students to study in France are mainly processed through the Foreign Office of the Chinese Ministry of Education, then the French Ministry of Foreign Affairs, and finally the Service des Affaires Internationales of the French Ministry of Education. It liaises with French institutions of higher learning in order to place Chinese scholars appropriately.[35] About twenty university-level agreements have been negotiated between French and Chinese institutions, but only a few of them have active programmes, due to the lack of financial autonomy of French institutions. However in the placing of Chinese scholars in France, these links are taken into account as far as possible. About 110 Chinese scholars and students are supported through French provided living stipends, 65 of them on the basis of an exchange with the equivalent number of places provided for French students in China, and 45 as direct grants from the French government. In addition all Chinese scholars and students benefit from the fact that there are no tuition fees in French higher institutions.[36]

The structure of studies and curricular orientation of the Chinese in France reflect similar patterns to those described above. In 1979, 100 Chinese students came to France for undergraduate studies, and another 50 followed in 1981. However no further students are expected in this category, as the focus is now mainly on higher studies for young graduates of China's own reformed higher education system.[37] The curricular orientation indicated in Table 8.3 suggests a somewhat stronger emphasis on pure sciences than in Germany, and some dissatisfaction has been noted on the Chinese side over what they perceive as restrictions on entry into applied, industry-related sciences.[38] This is defended on the French side in terms of the autonomy of French institutions over their enrollment policies. It is thus unclear whether or not this reflects a definite policy on the French side to strengthen Chinese exposure to the pure sciences, such as has been noted in the USA. The large number of visiting scholars in the arts may indicate a strong Chinese interest in French language and literature. Overall the figures in Table 8.3 represent the total Chinese scholar population in France in Spring, 1983, with the exception of a considerable group on short-term study visits, and about 50-60 Chinese students supported privately by relatives in France.

Table 8.3

PROFILE OF CHINESE SCHOLARS AND STUDENTS IN FRANCE, MARCH 1983

Level	Pure Sciences	Applied Sciences	Social Sciences	Arts	TOTAL
Undergrads	67	75	3	5	150
Graduates	64	80	9	7	160
Visiting Scholars	130	87	6	37	260
TOTAL	261	242	18	49	570

Just as in the German case, the French scholarly presence in China has a clear geographical focus, necessary in light of the limited development of French language teaching in China. There is less historical continuity, however, in that the French centre is at Wuhan University, which has no links either with the former Université Franco-Chinoise in Beijing of the twenties, or the former French Jesuit University, L'Aurore of Shanghai. The latter was transformed into Shanghai's No.2 Medical School in 1952, and the strong French background of many of its older staff is now being utilised. One class each year is being educated entirely in French, and strong links with French institutions are being formed.[39] However French efforts to establish a strong presence at Fudan University in Shanghai have not been welcomed, perhaps partly due to the mistaken suggestions of French journalists that Fudan was the former Aurore.[40]

Rather it was decided that a concentration of French teachers should be situated at Wuhan University, and an agreement was signed early in 1980 for a programme beginning in September of 1980.[41] About 17 of the 30-35 French teachers supported by the French government in China are working at Wuhan University, 7 language and literature teachers in the Department of French, 4 teachers of French for scientific purposes in various science departments, and about 6 scientists teaching and doing research within the faculty of sciences. Their work is supported by the provision of journals and books in French, and one of the aims of the project is to make French scientific research accessible to the Chinese. Another is clearly the dissemination of French culture and the preparation of well qualified Chinese teachers of French. The French language programme should ensure that Wuhan becomes a university where French professors can lecture in French and be widely understood. However it is not specifically linked with preparing Chinese students and scholars for study in France, a task carried out mainly in the French sections of the Foreign Languages Institutes in Beijing, Shanghai and Canton.[42]

French scholarly policies towards China thus are characterised by concerted efforts to make favourable provision for Chinese scholars and students in France and a centralised administration of much of the exchange movement, which is somewhat similar to the German scene. Like the Germans, the French have a strong focus on one Chinese institution and area, but unlike the Germans, their efforts there are directed mainly towards the dissemination of French culture and science within China rather than the intellectual preparation of Chinese scholars and students going to France. In the reception of Chinese students, French institutions may be somewhat more restrictive than German ones, resulting in a conscious or unintended bias towards the pure sciences, in contrast to German receptivity to Chinese in all fields of the applied sciences.

BRITISH-CHINESE SCHOLARLY EXCHANGE

British-Chinese scholarly relations are organised within the terms of the Agreement on Cooperation in the Fields of Education and Culture signed in November, 1979.[43] Under this general agreement there are three specific agreements between the Royal Society and the Chinese Academy of Sciences, the British Academy and the Chinese Academy of Social Sciences, and the Confederation of British Industry and the State Economic Commission. Most of the short-term academic visits are administered within these agreements, as well as some longer-term programmes for visiting scholars. The majority of longer-term exchange is administered through the British Council, which processes applications sent by the Chinese Ministry of Education and arranges placement for Chinese scholars and students at appropriate British academic institutions. There are only a few British universities that have institution-level agreements with Chinese counterparts, but these have very active exchange programmes involving the sending of British undergraduates to China and the reception of Chinese scholars in Britain with financing worked out reciprocally between the two institutions. The Leeds University-Fudan link, and the Polytechnic of Central London's link with the Beijing Languages

Institute are example of such ties.

The British Council's Academic Links Scheme provides funding for short-term scholarly exchanges, mainly covering international air travel for British scholars going to China, and living expenses for Chinese scholars in Britain. The British Council also provides scholarships and living stipends for 25 Chinese scholars each year in exchange for 25 British postgraduate students and scholars going to China, and two open scholarships. As of 1983, additional funding has been made available to Chinese scholars in Britain through 24 places financed by the Overseas Development Agency's Technical Cooperation Training Places Scheme, and 7 discretionary awards offered to the Chinese by the Foreign and Commonwealth Office.[44] A few scholarships are also offered by British universities and Chinese students may apply on a competitive basis for Overseas Research Student Awards, which reduce somewhat the otherwise heavy burden of overseas student fees in Britain.

The structure of studies and curricular orientation of Chinese in Britain is indicated in Table 8.4. The relatively low number of undergraduate and postgraduate students may reflect the high cost of formal study in Britain, although visiting scholars are also expected to pay bench fees for their use of scientific equipment. The relative stress on the applied sciences indicates Chinese interest in many aspects of British technology, and the considerable access given to them by the British to these areas of study.[45]

Table 8.4

PROFILE OF CHINESE SCHOLARS AND STUDENTS IN BRITAIN, MARCH 1983

Level	Pure Sciences	Applied Sciences	Social Sciences	Arts	TOTAL
Undergrads	14	27	–	7	48
Graduates	37	76	5	6	124
Visiting Scholars	93	278	32	27	430
TOTAL	144	381	37	40	602

The British presence in China is much more geographically diverse than that of the French and Germans, and the focus is on the training of Chinese teachers of English, with five centres having three British teachers in each: one in the Beijing Foreign Languages Institute, two in the Guangzhou Foreign Languages Institute, one for secondary school teachers and the other for advanced teachers, one in the Shanghai Foreign Languages Institute, and one in Shanghai's Jiaotong University. In addition there are another 10-12 British Council teachers working in other projects including the T.V. University in Beijing. In order to ensure that these courses and the short-term courses provided by British Council teams several times each year are used only by Chinese teachers of English rather than scholars preparing to come to Britain, the British Council is now planning to provide a five-month course in Beijing specifically for the latter group.

In general British policies of scholarly exchange with China are marked by increasing financial provision from the British side, and a centralised administration of exchange, supplemented by a few active institution-level links. There is a strong emphasis on the applied, production-related sciences in the curricular orientation of the Chinese in Britain. The training of Chinese teachers of the English language, with a special concern for television teaching, is also an important focus, providing a counter-balance to the otherwise overwhelming influence of American English in China.

CANADIAN-CHINESE SCHOLARLY EXCHANGE

Recent Canadian-Chinese scholarly relations have taken shape within the terms of a memorandum signed by educational leaders of the two sides in June, 1979. This document provided for a special programme administered by the Council of Ministers of Education, Canada, (CMEC) to assist Chinese scholars in being placed within Canadian institutions of higher learning for two-year periods of research and scholarly upgrading. In addition it was agreed that Chinese undergraduates and graduate students should seek places within Canadian institutions through normal channels and that Chinese institutions would equally be open to Canadian students and scholars. Direct university-level links between Chinese and Canadian institutions were also to be promoted.[46]

The main bodies administering scholarly exchange with China have been the CMEC, which relates to the Chinese Ministry of Education, the National Research Council (NRC) which relates to the Chinese Academy of Sciences (CAS), and the Social Science and Humanities Research Council of Canada (SSHRCC), which is linked to the Chinese Academy of Social Sciences (CASS). While the scholar programme under the CMEC deals with Chinese scholars coming on two-year terms, who are financed by the Chinese government, the CAS-NRC and CASS-SSHRCC agreements allow for short-term exchanges of scholars with reciprocity of numbers and funding from each side.[47] In addition the Canadian International Development Agency (CIDA) is linked with the Ministry of Foreign Economic relations and Trade (MFERT) in China. In September 1983 a Development Cooperation Agreement was signed between the two agencies establishing terms and conditions for substantial development assistance from Canada. CIDA projects within this agreement have a strong educational component and will lead to a very lively exchange of personnel, both Canadian professors and teachers going to China, and Chinese scholars, managers and technologists coming to Canada. The overall budget for 1983 to 1988 is 93 million Canadian dollars.[48]

The four major areas of emphasis for the CIDA programme are agriculture, forestry, energy and human resources development. Geographically there is quite a strong focus on the North Eastern province of Heilongjiang, where it is considered that similar needs and conditions to those of Canada provide a favourable setting for technology transfer in the areas of forestry, agriculture and agricultural management and teaching. In addition to geographically specific projects in energy, agriculture and forestry which include both scientific and management components, the large human resources development project is geared towards management education and English language training for those involved in all of CIDA's projects. CIDA is relying on institutional linkages which have been formed between 8 key Chinese universities with newly developing management programmes and 8 Canadian counterparts along with other supporting Canadian institutions. Within these links Canadian professors of management will teach for short periods within Chinese institutions and Chinese students will come to these Canadian institutions for MBA and PhD programmes or as visiting scholars. The first 25 were due to arrive in September of 1983.[49] CIDA also has a Human Development Awards programme which will provide 3000 man years of specialised training for mid-career mid-level personnel in Chinese ministries and state corporations. Probably the emphasis will again be on management, although not exclusively so.

The curricular orientation and structure of studies of Chinese scholars and students in Canada in 1981-2 is indicated in Table 8.5.[50] Special features include the large number of secondary school students and undergraduates in the arts, which represents the considerable group of privately sponsored Chinese students who are mainly supported by the Canadian Chinese community. The strong emphasis on the applied sciences already evident will be further strengthened by the CIDA programme described above. Management studies will come to dominate the social sciences sector, originally very small. With the statistics presently available, it was not possible to distinguish between the undergraduate and graduate student groups, but there is evidence that at present there are only 9 undergraduates among officially sponsored Chinese students,[51] and there is an increasing emphasis on postgraduate studies since 1982, as in other western countries.

Table 8.5

PROFILE OF CHINESE SCHOLARS AND STUDENTS IN CANADA, 1981-2

Level	Pure Sciences	Applied Sciences	Social Sciences	Arts	General	TOTAL
Visiting Scholars	54	166	6	-	-	226
Under-grads & graduates	108	149	38	197	-	492
Secondary Students	-	-	-	-	127	127
TOTAL	162	315	44	197	127	845

Canadian scholarly policies towards China fall somewhere between those of USA and Europe. Like Europe, the scholar programme is centrally administered by the CMEC and institution-level links are centrally coordinated in some cases. This is true for those within the CIDA programme, although they are intended to develop autonomously with individually distinctive programmes. On the level of graduate and undergraduate studies, however, the Canadian scene is closer to the American one, with Chinese students applying through normal university enrollment channels, and a large proportion of privately sponsored students making up the total group.

Unlike USA and France, there seems to be no stress on disseminating Canadian intellectual culture through scholarly programmes, and efforts to orient Chinese coming to Canada are concerned mainly with language skills rather than the initiation into scientific discourse which is part of German policy. The practical emphasis on the applied, production-related sciences which represents a consistent Chinese policy in scholarly exchange has been reinforced from the Canadian side, especially through the CIDA programme. The basic assumption of this programme seems to be that applied sciences linked to the areas of agriculture, forestry and energy provide a common area of interest for Canadians and Chinese which will assure the smooth transfer of advanced Canadian technology to the Chinese context. Evidently the principles and techniques of enterprise management, linked to these key resources, are thought also to be non-problematic in terms of culture or ideology and easily transferable to the Chinese context.

THE WORLD BANK AND CHINESE-WESTERN SCHOLARLY EXCHANGE

Besides the bi-lateral scholarly interaction between China and various western countries which has been discussed above, Chinese involvement with international organisations has been another feature of present educational development which is unprecedented since 1949. In this section we will consider briefly three contemporary educational projects in which the World Bank is cooperating with the Chinese. All of them involve substantial scholarly interaction with the West and in total they may represent the largest single input into the Chinese education system from outside China.

World Bank education policies can be summed up by reference to five broad principles: basic education for all; the widening of educational opportunity to ensure both productivity and social equity; internal efficiency in the management of educational resources; the use of education to promote knowledge and skills directly linked to work and the environment; and finally the importance of developing countries having their own institutional capacity for designing, managing and evaluating educational programmes.[52] In the three China projects that have been approved so far, the Bank has uncharacteristically focused exclusively on tertiary-level education, since China's achievements in basic education are regarded as more than adequate to justify this. (See the discussion of this issue in Chapter 5, pp.137-141.) The other four principles can be seen to a greater or lesser degree within the projects, with productivity probably taking precedence over social equity in line with the present Chinese policy of upgrading key institutions first.

The first project, initiated in 1980 and running from 1982 to 1986, is aimed at supporting a Chinese government decision to upgrade the teaching and research quality of 26 key higher institutions with emphasis on the pure and applied sciences which account for 75% of their enrollment. A second goal is improvement in resource management within the institutions so that a much larger student body can be accomodated. The overall cost of the project is 295 million U.S. dollars, and the Bank is loaning the Chinese 200 million of this. This assistance will take the form of advanced research equipment which cannot be purchased within China, and the provision of high level scientific expertise. A major concern is the development of graduate programmes in chemistry, physics, computer science and engineering. For this an internal Chinese advisory commission is being supported in its task by a foreign advisory panel able to offer expert consultation services. Another important part of the project is staff development and a total of 800 overseas fellowships, mainly tenable in western countries, are being provided. Half are for 2-3 year programmes in science and engineering, the other half for one year study visits by mature scholars. The improvement of internal management of five pilot universities is also a part of the project.[53]

A second World Bank project in China focuses on the improvement of agricultural education, and here a World Bank loan of 75.4 million U.S. dollars is combined with a Chinese input of 126.2 million. The project involves 11 key agricultural colleges, selected by the Chinese government and representing 25% of the whole agricultural enrollment in China, 6 research institutes and the founding of a new National Rice Research Institute. The objectives are to improve the quality of teaching and research, to expand enrollment and research capacity, and to strengthen the organisation and management of resources in agricultural education and research. World Bank funds will be used to finance equipment and research materials from outside China, and an even larger outlay will go to the provision of 633 fellowships for overseas study, including 3-year doctoral courses, 2-year masters courses, and study visits up to one year. 84% will go to English speaking countries, 13% to Japan, and 3% to other non-English speaking countries. In addition management expertise will be provided and short-term management training overseas for 100 Chinese administrators.[54]

The third and most recent educational project involves assisting in the development of a polytechnic and T.V. university system in China offering two to three year programmes at a somewhat lower level than the degree oriented programmes of the regular higher education system. (The polytechnics are termed 'higher technical colleges' in the discussion of this development in Chapter 5, p.125.) The total cost of the project is 206.2 million U.S. dollars, of which 85 million is to be loaned by the Bank. The objectives are to increase enrollment in post secondary institutions, to improve the quality of staff and to assist in the development of approriate curricula distinct from those used in the regular higher education system. It is mainly through this type of institution that the Chinese are attempting a major expansion in higher education enrollment, and some concern for social equity and the meeting of youth aspirations is a factor, alongside the need for mid-level technical manpower. However urban youth stand to benefit more from this system than those in the rural areas.[55]

One of the significant features of the World Bank's educational involvement with China is the tremendous boost that it is giving to the education of Chinese scholars and students in the West and Japan, with over 1,500 scholarships provided in the first two projects described above. This represents a larger movement of people than any of the bi-lateral exchange programmes that have been discussed except that of the USA and possibly Germany. Secondly the World Bank's focus on tertiary education indicates both the acceptance of Chinese-set priorities and a recognition of China's considerable achievements in basic education. The three projects combined suggest a balanced concern for issues of quality in the pure and applied sciences in China's top institutions, the recognition of the vital importance of sustained agricultural development for the success of the whole modernisation programme, and finally a willingness to support the new style polytechnic and television tertiary system which should meet mid-level technical manpower needs and satisfy the aspirations of Chinese youth for higher education.

IMPLICATIONS FOR THE FUTURE OF CHINESE EDUCATION

One of the most compelling trends of the present Chinese education system is the strengthening of hierarchy, resulting in an educational ladder that has some echoes of traditional China. This has been discussed in the chapters on primary, secondary and tertiary education. A system of national, provincial and local keypoint institutions sets a qualitative pace for all others and provides sure opportunities of social mobility for the few who succeed in entering them. The above review of China's scholarly exchange policies with western nations suggests, that these exchanges are almost certain to strengthen this hierarchical tendency. The top prize for those who succeed in climbing the educational ladder is the opportunity for study abroad, and possibly a teaching post in a tertiary institution that has close links with the West. The Foreign Affairs Office of the Chinese Ministry of Education has a policy of favouring keypoint institutions in selecting students and scholars for study abroad, and two of the three World Bank projects are designed to strengthen keypoint tertiary institutions. Non-keypoint institutions are not totally excluded, however, and in some cases deliberate efforts have been made from the western side, particularly from some American universities, to forge links with provincial level institutions in China that do not have wide foreign connections.[56]

Still the increasingly hierarchical nature of the education system is undeniably enhanced by scholarly exchange, and a historical perspective would suggest this is likely to harmonise with deeply held Chinese traditional values. The idea of young people achieving good positions in the bureaucracy on the basis of merit demonstrated in competitive examinations is easily accepted in Chinese society. What may be problematic, however, is the kind of knowledge which marks them for success. It is no longer a mastery of the moral values enshrined in classical texts, nor of the ideological principles expounded in Maoist texts and demonstrated through revolutionary activism rather than examination, but modern scientific knowledge, most of which is legitimated outside China through processes not easily understood or accepted by the Chinese masses. Much may depend on the success of present efforts to popularise scientific knowledge in China, on the one hand, and the kind of scientific training received by Chinese students in various western countries on the other.

A distinction has been made above between those western nations whose policies favour a strengthening of the pure sciences for Chinese graduates (USA and France), and those which accede to or reinforce the consistent Chinese emphasis on the applied sciences (West Germany, Britain and Canada). Pure scientific training is obviously important for the nurturing of creative Chinese scientists able to do self-initiated, self-generating scientific work, while an exclusive focus on the applied sciences could result in dependent scientific relations with the West. At the same time the type of iconoclastic thinking necessary for pure scientific research will not easily be accepted in the Chinese social and intellectual context, unless its value for production-related application can be demonstrated. A judicious balance between the pure and applied sciences might possibly satisfy the contradictory demands of the nature of pure scientific research on one side and the nature of Chinese society of the other. It remains to be seen whether or how western nations can achieve this balance in their scholarly policies towards China.

In the social sciences and humanities the success of western-educated Chinese scholars in critically evaluating western scholarship and making creative adaptations to the Chinese context is of vital importance. The uncritical introduction of western theory in these fields could result in Chinese scholars in keypoint institutions being alienated not only from the masses, but from students and colleagues who have not been abroad and are not easily able to understand or accept the scholarly views which have been assimilated from the West. The problem, then, is not so much the hierarchy itself, nor the way in which scholarly exchange enhances it, but rather the kinds of knowledge which legitimate the scholarly authority of those in the top echelons, and how acceptable these can be made to a wider Chinese society.

A second trend which has been noted in Chapters Three and Four above is the deepening of the rural-urban dichotomy, with rural education being geared towards local needs and having a lower mobility function than ever before in Chinese history. It is difficult to judge the degree to which this trend is being exacerbated by scholarly exchange, as World Bank and CIDA emphases on agricultural education should draw many rural Chinese into their programmes. All other scholarly exchange, however, is strongly urban-based, with an emphasis on large cities, especially those in coastal areas. Fifty-eight percent of a group of 530 Chinese scholars in Germany in 1981-1982 came from Beijing and Shanghai,[57] as did thirty-three percent of Chinese scholars on the scholar programme in Canada, 1979-1983.[58] Eighteen of the 26 institutions being upgraded by

World Bank funds in the university development project are located in major East Coast cities.[59] This urban bias is almost inevitable, given the highly urbanised nature of the developed societies with which China is interacting and the necessity of sending scholars and students able to benefit from the kind of study and research that is being done.

The crux of the matter may lie in the question of whether expert personnel in major Chinese cities will be able, as they have been in the past, to pass on their expertise to inland areas and the countryside, or whether their absorption with pursuing western scientific standards will distract them from this task. From the perspective of the rural areas, will the present dissatisfaction with the lack of possibility for social mobility in rural schools lead to a lowered level of scientific knowledge among rural youth? Or will the opportunities for individual and family prosperity provided by the responsibility system foster a thirst for scientific knowledge that can be applied to rural problems? Is a compromise possible between a rural curriculum suited to local needs, such as that called for in Chapter Three, and one that allows the modicum of social mobility necessary to gain parental support for rural schooling? The sustained success of present agricultural development is an essential element in the modernisation programme, and so far it is difficult to judge how far present educational policies are contributing effectively to it.

Perhaps the trend which offers greatest hope both in terms of widening youth educational opportunities and the realistic service of education to social and economic modernisation is the diversification of the secondary and tertiary education systems, discussed in Chapters 4 and 5. It is here that the Maoist vision of uniting theory and practice, mental and manual labour, may be finding more effective institutional form than in the Cultural Revolution experiments. How is scholarly exchange with the West likely to affect this trend? Are western countries able to provide successful exemplars of this type of institution at the secondary and tertiary level? The possibility of diversification at the secondary level falling into a pattern similar to the pre-comprehensive British secondary system or parallel European patterns is a real one. It is unlikely, however, that there will be enough interaction on this level for any direct influence to be felt, though Chinese interest in studying western patterns of vocational education offers a possible channel of influence.

Rather it is on the tertiary level that the most interaction is taking place. One wonders how well the Chinese will succeed in creating new style tertiary institutions which are not second-class universities following a watered-down university curriculum, but dynamic institutions unhampered by traditional views of knowledge in their service to the perceived problems of the local community. It is fascinating to reflect on how far interaction with western academia in general and with specific nations in particular has anything positive to contribute to this trend. Scholarly exchange already facilitates some Chinese involvement with North American community colleges, British polytechnics, and German Fachhochschule, and it remains an open question how appropriate the distinctive values associated with these institutions are to the Chinese context.

Finally the reformulation of political education on a more strongly moral than ideological basis has been noted in Chapters Three and Seven as an important contemporary trend. The moral values to be inculcated through the education system include discipline, honesty, respect for law and order, social responsibility, patriotism, and a love for socialism and the Communist Party. There can be little doubt that these have more in common with values implicit in the western educational institutions hosting Chinese scholars abroad than Maoist educational values. These returning scholars are therefore likely to contribute to this trend. One of their tasks will be to distinguish between the knowledge needed for China's modernisation and those western values which are regarded as decadent from the Chinese point of view and to be rejected. Presumably there are some values such as discipline and social responsibility which span both societies and are not viewed as a threat to the purity of Chinese socialism.

The question worth serious reflection here is whether the distinctive constellations of values associated with specific western academic traditions, the German, the American, the French, the British, will have differing effects in the Chinese situation. Which will encourage the already evident trend of a return to traditional Chinese values, and which may support and give substance to present attempts to reformulate creative aspects of Maoism in a more acceptable way than that of Cultural Revolution extremism? The input of western returned scholars to Chinese political thought will probably be minimal. Still it could be one of the factors which make the difference between a falling back on traditional solutions, only too tempting in a society with such rich traditional precedents as those provided by Chinese civilisation, or the seeking of creative new solutions to China's social and economic problems.

NOTES AND REFERENCES

Chapter One

1. The methodological approach used in this chapter has been exemplified in the author's contribution to the World Yearbook of Education over the years from 1954 to 1974, as well as in other writings. See for example:
    'Teacher Education in a Changing World', in Bereday, G. and Lauwerys, J. (eds.), The World Yearbook of Education 1963: The Education and Training of Teachers, London: Evans, 1963;
    'Education in Cities', in Lauwerys, J. and Scanlon, D. (eds.), The World Yearbook of Education 1970: Education in Cities, London: Evans, 1970;
    'Universities, Higher Education and Society', in Holmes, Brian and Scanlon, D. (eds.), The World Yearbook of Education 1971-72: Higher Education in a Changing World, London: Evans, 1971;
    'Postscript', in Foster, P. and Sheffield, J. (eds.), The World Yearbook of Education 1974: Education and Rural Development, London: Evans, 1974;
    Homes, Brian, Diversity and Unity in Education, London: George Allen and Unwin, 1980;
    Holmes, Brian, Comparative Education: Some Considerations of Method, London: George Allen and Unwin, 1981.
    For the author's writing on Soviet education, see 'Soviet Education in Transition', in Phi Delta Kappa, Vol.42, No., November, 1960; 'Polytechnical Education in the USSR', in Bulletin of the Institute of Physics and the Physical Society, March, 1961; 'Education in the Soviet Union', in Ignus, E. and Corsini, R. (eds.), Comparative Educational Systems, Ithaca, Ill.: F.E.Peacock, 1981; also reports in the University of London Institute of Education Library on annual educational visits to the Soviet Union which he has led over many years.
2. Statistical data on Chinese education and society is available in English in such publications as:
    Wu Yuanli (ed.), China: A Handbook, New York: Praeger, 1973; The China Official Annual Report 1981 and 1982-3, Hong Kong: Kingsway International Publications Ltd., 1981 and 1982; Scherer, John L., China: Facts and Figures Annual, Volumes 1 - 6, Florida: Academic International Press, 1978-83.

Chapter Two

1. Teng Ssu-yu and Fairbank, John, China's Response to the West: A Documentary Survey 1839-1923, Cambridge, Mass:

Harvard University Press, 1954, p.271.
2. Sun Yat Sen, SAN MIN CHI I: The Three Principles of the People, Shanghai: The Commercial Press, 1929.
3. The Selected Works of Mao Tse-tung, Vol.I-V, Peking: Foreign Languages Press, 1975-1977.
4. Higginson, J. H. (ed.), Selections from Michael Sadler, Liverpool: Dejall and Meyorre International Publishers, 1979, p.49.
5. Hans, Nicholas, Comparative Education, London: Routledge and Kegan Paul, 1971.
6. Two pioneering studies of modern Chinese education are: Tsang Chiu-sam, Society, Schools and Progress in China, New York: Pergamon Press, 1969, and Price, Ronald, Education in Communist China, New York: Praeger Publisher, 1970.
7. Holmes, Brian, Comparative Education: Some Considerations of Method, London: George Allen and Unwin, 1981, p.29-34.
8. Franke, Wolfgang, The Reform and Abolition of the Traditional Chinese Examination System, Cambridge, Mass: Harvard University Press, 1960.
9. Chen Hsi-en, Theodore, The Maoist Educational Revolution, New York: Praeger Publishers, 1974. This book gives a clear exposition of Maoist educational values and institutions in the Cultural Revolution period.
10. Wang Feng-gang, Japanese Influence on Educational Reform in China from 1896 to 1911, Peiping: Authors Book Store, 1933. (Stanford University doctoral dissertation, 1931).
11. Keenan, Barry, The Dewey Experiment in China, Cambridge, Mass: Harvard University Press, 1977.
12. Becker, C. H., Langevin, P., Falski, M. and Tawney, R. H., The Reoganisation of Education in China, Paris: League of Nations Institute of Intellectual Cooperation, 1932.
13. Orleans, Leo, Professional Manpower and Education in Communist China, Washington, D. C.: U.S. Gov't Printing Office, 1960.
14. Galt, Howard, A History of Chinese Educational Institutions, London: Arthur Probsthain, 1951.
15. Ho Ping-ti, The Ladder of Success in Imperial China, New York: Columbia University Press, 1962.
16. Menzel, Joanna (ed.), The Chinese Civil Service: Career Open to Talent?, Boston: D.C. Heath and Co., 1963.
17. Miyazaki, Ichisada, China's Examination Hell: The Civil Services Examinations of Imperial China, New York and Tokyo: Weatherhill, 1977.
18. Levenson, Joseph, Confucian China and Its Modern Fate, Vol.II, London: Routledge and Kegan Paul, 1964, p.73.
19. Martin, W.A.P., Hanlin Papers, London: Trubner and Co., 1880, p.114.
20. Chang Chung-li, The Chinese Gentry: Studies in Their Role in the Nineteeth Century, Seattle, Washington: University of Washington Press, 1955, pp.201-2

21. Meskill, John, Academies in Ming China, Arizona: University of Arizona Press, 1982.
    Liu Boji, Guangdong Shuyuan Zhidu (The Shuyuan System in Guangdong), Taiwan: Zhonghua Congshu, Taiwan Shudian, 1958.
    Sheng Langxi, Zhongguo Shuyuan Zhidu (The Chinese Shuyuan System), Shanghai: Zhonghua Shuju, 1934.
    Jiang Liuquan, Zhongguo Shuyuan Shihua, (A History of the Chinese Shuyuan), Beijing: Jiaoyu Kexue Chubanshe, 1981.
22. Chen Dongyuan, Zhongguo Jiaoyu Shi, (A History of Chinese Education), Shanghai: The Commercial Press, 1937, pp.446-454.
23. Rawski, Evelyn Sakakida, Education and Popular Literacy in Ch'ing China, Michigan: University of Michigan Press, 1979; Borthwick, Sally, Education and Social Change in China: The Beginning of the Modern Era, Stanford, California: Hoover Institution Press, 1983, chapters 1 & 2.
24. Needham, Joseph, The Shorter Science and Civilisation in China, edited by Colin Ronan, Cambridge University Press, 1978.
25. Folsom, Kenneth, Friends, Guests and Colleagues: The Mu-fu System in the Late Ch'ing Period, Berkeley and Los Angeles: University of California Press, 1968.
26. Lindsay, Michael, Notes on Educational Problems in Communist China, 1941-1947, New York: Institute of Pacific Relations, 1950, p.55.
27. Mao Tse-tung, 'On Practice', The Selected Works of Mao Tse-tung, Vol.II, pp.295-310.
28. Wang Hsueh-wen, Chinese Communist Education: The Yenan Period, Taiwan: Institute of International Relations, 1975.
29. Selden, Mark, The Yenan Way in Revolutionary China, Cambridge, Mass: Harvard University Press, 1971. p.187ff describes the attempts to break down this hierarchy in the rectification campaign of 1942.
30. Wang Hsuen-wen, Chinese Communist Education, p.99.
31. Mao's admiration for the *shuyuan* is discussed in Jiang Liuquan, Zhongguo Shuyuan Shihua, p.135.
32. Wang Feng-gang, Japanese Influence on Educational Reform in China, p.135
33. Kuo Ping Wen, The Chinese System of Public Education, New York: Teachers College, Columbia, 1915, pp.79-80.
34. Bastid, Marianne, Aspects de la réforme de l'enseignement en Chine au Debut de XXè siècle d'après des écrits de Zhang Jian, Paris: Mouton, 1971, p.76.
35. The China Year Book, Tientsin: Tientsin Press Ltd., 1921, p.2.
36. Zhou Yutong, Zhongguo Xiandai Jiaoyu Shi (Recent Chinese Educational History), Shanghai: Liangyou Tushu Yinshua Gongsi, 1934, p.29.
37. Djung Lu-dzai, A History of Democratic Education in Modern

China, Shanghai: The Commercial Press, 1934, pp.59-61.
38. Ibid. pp.72-75.
39. Chen Qingzhi, Zhongguo Jiaoyu Shi (A History of Chinese Education), Vol.11, Shanghai: Commercial Press, 1936, pp.728-732.
40. Duiker, William, Ts'ai Yüan-p'ei: Educator of Modern China, University Park and London: The Pennsylvania State University Press, 1977, pp.54-68.
41. Chow Tse-tsung, The May Fourth Movement, Stanford: Stanford University Press, 1960.
42. Hsiao, Theodore E. The History of Modern Education in China, Shanghai: The Commercial Press, 1935, p.102.
Shu Xincheng, Jindai Zhongguo Liuxue Shi (A History of Recent Chinese Overseas Study), Shanghai: Zhongguo Shuju, 1927.
43. Chuang Chai-hsuan, Tendencies Toward a Democratic System of Education in China, Shanghai: The Commercial Press, 1922.
Yin Chiling, Reconstruction of Modern Educational Organisations in China, Shanghai: The Commercial Press, 1924.
Cheng, Robert Yu Soong, The Financing of Public Education in China, Shanghai: The Commercial Press, 1935.
See also Kuo Ping Wen (1915), Wang Feng-gang (1931), Djung Lu-dzai (1934), and Theodore Hsiao (1935).
44. Keenan, Barry, The Dewey Experiment in China.
45. American fears over Chinese nationalism and militarism come across most clearly in Peake, Cyrus, Nationalism and Education in Modern China, New York: Columbia University Press, 1932.
46. Zhou Yutong, Zhongguo Xiandai Jiaoyu Shi, pp.30-33.
47. Yin Chiling, Reconstruction of Modern Educational Organisations in China, p.97.
48. Djung Lu-dzai, A History of Democratic Education in Modern China, p.57.
49. Chen Qingzhi, Zhongguo Jiaoyu Shi, p.700.
50. Israel, John, Student Nationalism in China 1927-1937, Stanford: Stanford University Press, 1966, pp.12-13.
51. Zhou Yutong, Zhongguo Xiandai Jiaoyu Shi, pp.34-35.
52. Sun Yat Sen, SAN MIN CHU I; Tsao, Y.Y., The Constitutional Structure of Modern China, Australia: Melbourne University Press, 1947.
53. Linden, Allen B., 'Politics and Education in Nationalist China: the Case of the University Council, 1927-1928', Journal of Asian Studies, Vol.27, no.4, August, 1968, p..763-776.
54. Becker, C.H., et. al, The Reorganisation of Education in China.
55. Chen Qingzhi, Zhongguo Jiaoyu Shi, p.775.
56. Israel, J., Student Nationalism in China, pp.24-38.
57. Pepper, Suzanne, The Chinese Civil War, Berkeley:

University of California Press, 1978, pp.42-93
58. Alitto, Guy, The Last Confucian: Liang Shuming and the Chinese Dilemma of Modernity, Berkeley: University of California Press, 1979.
59. Yen, Y. C. James, The Ting Hsien Experiment in 1932, Peking, 1934, republished in the Philippines: Institute of Rural Reconstruction, 1975.
Buck, Pearl, Tell the People - Talks with James Yen About the Mass Education Movement, New York: The John Day Co., 1942.
Chang Yen-chi, Pre-Communist China's Rural School and Community, Boston: The Christopher Publishing House, 1960.
60. Education in China, Compiled by the Education in China Group of the Ministry of Education, Beijing, 1975, p.28.
61. Scherer, China Facts and Figures Annual, Vol.1, 1978, Florida: Academic International Press, 1978, p.92
62. Price, Education in Communist China, pp. 132ff.
63. Chung Shih, Higher Education in Communist China, Hong Kong: Union Research Institute, 1953.
64. Orleans, Professional Manpower and Education in Communist China.
65. Lee Hong Yung, The Politics of the Chinese Cultural Revolution, Berkeley: University of California Press, 1978.
66. Hawkins, John, Mao-Tse-tung and Education: His Thought and Teachings, Conneticut: Linnet Books, 1974.
67. Urban, George, The Miracles of Chairman Mao: A Compendium of Devolutional Literature 1966-1970, London: Tom Stacey Ltd., 1971.
68. Hinton, William, Hundred Day War, New York and London: Monthly Review Press, 1972. This book gives a graphic description of the revolutionising of one of China's major polytechnical universities along Maoist lines.
69. Chen Qingzhi, Zhongguo Jiaoyu Shi, pp.803-810.
70. Chapter eight will deal with this subject.
71. Xinhua News Agency Special, Dec. 6, 1982, p.8

Chapter Three

1. See Borthwick, Sally, Education and Social Change: The Beginnings of the Modern Era, Stanford, California: Hoover Institution Press, 1983, chapters one and two for an analysis of these 'two tracks' in traditional China, where a distinction was made between *yucai* (cultivating talent) and *jiaohua* (improving customs and reforming manners among the masses).
2. Renmin Jiaoyu, No.11, 1951, pp.53-54.
3. Survey of China Mainland Press, No. 726, 1954.
4. Renmin Ribao, 14 December, 1953, editorial.
5. Survey of China Mainland Press, No. 711, 1953.

Notes and References

6. Montaperto, Ronald N., (ed.), China's Schools in Flux, New York: M. E. Sharpe Inc., 1979, p.19.
7. Union Research Service, Vol.17 No.12, pp.158-161.
8. Chen, Theodore, 'Elementary Education in Communist China', The China Quarterly, No.10, 1962, p.103.
9. Text of the directive in Collection of Laws, Beijing: Law Press, 1957, Vol.5, pp.316-317.
10. 'Chronology of the Two-Road Struggle on the Educational Front in the Past Seventeen Years' translated in Seybolt, Peter (ed.), Revolutionary Education in China: Documents and Commentary, White Plains, N.Y. : International Arts and Sciences Press Inc., 1973, pp.5-60.
11. Ibid., p.53.
12. Hongqi, No.8, 1980, pp.31-35.
13. Chen, Theodore H.E., The Maoist Educational Revolution, New York: Praeger Publishers, 1974, p.42.
14. Guangming Ribao, 10 June, 1978, p.1.
   NeiMenggu Jiaoyu, No.5-6, 1982, pp.5-8.
15. Hongqi, No.8, 1980, pp.31-35.
   Jiaoyu Yanjiu, No.1, 1982, pp.44-47.
16. Daily Report, No.141, 1979, p.L8.
17. Daily Report, No.171, 1979, p.L15.
18. Renmin Jiaoyu, No.12, 1980, p.3.
19. Jiaoyu Yanjiu, No.1, 1982, pp.2-7.
20. Ibid., p.2.
21. China Report, No.178, 1981, p.43.
22. Jiaoyu Yanjiu, No.1, 1982, pp.2-3.
23. Guangxi Jiaoyu, No.6, 1982, p.6.
24. Daily Report, No.31, 1978, p.E13.
25. Peking Review, No.8, 1978, p.14.
26. Renmin Jiaoyu, No.1, 1982.
   Hebei Jiaoyu, No.4, 1982, p.3.
27. Daily Report, No.31, 1978, pp.E12-13.
28. Pepper, Suzanne, 'Chinese Education After Mao: Two Steps Forward, Two Steps Back and Begin Again?' The China Quarterly, No. 81, 1980, p.34.
29. Beijing Review, No.32, 1979, p.8.
30. Wenhui Bao, 4 January, 1982, p.1.
31. Renmin Ribao, 12 August, 1979, p.1
32. Renmin Jiaoyu, No.12, 1980, p.3.
33. Hubei Jiaoyu, No.4, 1982, p.3.
34. Daily Report, No.140, 1978, p.E13.
35. Beijing Review, No.1, 1980, p.20.
36. Beijing Review, No.49, 1980, p.6.
37. China Report, No.161, 1981, p.80.
38. Yunnan Jiaoyu, No.4, 1982, p.3.
39. Daily Report, No.113, 1978, p.G3.
   Hubei Jiaoyu, No.4, 1982, p.3.
40. Peking Review, No.8, 1978, p.14.
41. Pepper, Suzanne, 'Chinese Education After Mao: Two Steps Forward, Two Steps Back and Begin Again?', p.35.

Notes and References

42. Guangming Ribao, 13 and 25 January, 1978, p.1.
43. Zhongguo Baike Nianjian 1980, (The China Encyclopedic Yearbook 1980), p.541.
44. Renmin Jiaoyu, No.1, 1982, p.15.
    Zhongguo Qingnian, No.2, 1982, p.26.
45. Renmin Ribao, 23 April, 1978, p.2.
46. Guangming Ribao, 15 January, 1982, p.1.
    Renmin Jiaoyu, No.1, 1982.
    Daily Report, No.31, 1979, p.E11.
47. Translations on People's Republic of China, No.530, 1979, p.49
48. Daily Report, No.141, 1979, p.L7.
    Daily Report, No.107, 1979, p.L18.
49. Daily Report, No. 141, 1979, p.L7.
50. Renmin Jiaoyu, No.1, 1982, p.15.
    NeiMengu Jiaoyu, No.5-6, 1982, pp.6-7.
51. China Report, No.243, 1981, p.100.
52. Sichuan Jiaoyu, No.12, 1981, p.2.
53. Zhongguo Qingnian, No.2, 1982, pp.26-27.
54. Wenhui Bao, 4 January, 1982, p.1.
55. Ibid.
56. NeiMenggu Jiaoyu, No.5-6, 1982, p.5.
57. Renmin Ribao, 12 August, 1979, p.1.
58. Renmin Jiaoyu, No.2, 1981, p.11.
59. Ibid.
60. Zhongguo Baike Nianjian 1981, p.469.
    Renmin Jiaoyu, No.12, 1980, p.4.
61. Renmin Ribao, 12 August, 1979, p.1.
62. Renmin Jiaoyu, No.12, 1980, p.5
63. Hubei Jiaoyu, No.4, 1982, p.3.
64. Jiaoyu Yanjiu, No.6, 1981, p.8.
65. Renmin Jiaoyu, No.12, 1980, p.4.
66. Zhongguo Baike Nianjian 1981, p.470.
67. Guangxi Jiaoyu, No.6, 1982, p.6.
68. Guangxi Jiaoyu, No.6, 1982, pp.6-7.
    Guangxi Jiaoyu, No.3, 1982, pp.2-5.
    Yunnan Jiaoyu, No.4, 1982, p.2.
69. Renmin Jiaoyu, No.11, 1981, pp.37-38.
70. Renmin Jiaoyu, No.12, 1980, pp.47-48.
71. Ibid.
72. Renmin Jiaoyu, No.11, 1980, p.48.
73. Jiaoyu Yanjiu, No.3, 1980, p.69.
74. Jiaoyu Yanjiu, No.2, 1982, p.56-57.
75. Beijing Review, No.1, 1980, p.20.
76. Beijing Review, No.49, 1980 p.6.
77. Jiaoyu Yanjiu, No.4, 1982, p.11.
    Jiaoyu Yanjiu, No.4, 1982, p.83.
78. Daily Report, No.50, 1981, p.L8
79. Daily Report, No.107, 1978, p.E19.
80. Daily Report, No.37, 1981, p.L9.
81. China News Analysis, No.332, 1960, p.5.

82. Chen, Theodore H.E., 'Elementary Education in Communist China', The China Quarterly, No.10, 1962, p.103.
83. Beijing Review, No.1, 1980, p.20.
84. Tianjin Jiaoyu, No.2, 1982, p.9.
85. Wenhui Bao, 4 January, 1982, p.1.
    Beijing Ribao, 25 December, 1981, p.2.
    Beijing Jiaoyu, No.2, 1982, p.4.
86. Renmin Jiaoyu, No.1, 1981, p.41.
87. Daily Report, No.37, 1981, p.L9.

Chapter Four

1. Gu Mingyuan, 'Lun zhongdeng jiaoyu de renwu he jiegou', (On the Task and Structure of Secondary Education), in Beijing Shifan Daxue, No.5, 25 August, 1982, p.1.
2. Beijing Review, No. 28, 13 July, 1979, p.7.
3. Shirk, Susan, Competitive Comrades, Berkeley: University of California Press, 1982; Unger, Jonathan, Education Under Mao, New York: Columbia University Press, 1982; Rosen, Stanley, Red Guard Factionalism and the Cultural Revolution in Guangzhou, Boulder: Westview Press, 1982.
4. For detailed accounts of the secondary school structure before the Cultural Revolution, see Unger, Shirk, and Rosen, all cited in footnote 3.
5. In China, those of good class origin include the so-called 'five red categories,' i.e., revolutionary cadre, revolutionary military, worker, poor and lower middle peasant, and revolutionary martyr. Those of bad class origin include capitalist, 'rightist', rich peasant, landlord, 'bad element', and counter-revolutionary. Those of middle class origin include both non-intelligentsia middle class (peddlers, store clerks, and so forth) and intelligentsia middle class (teachers, professionals, office workers, and so forth). These class designations, inheritable through the male line, were based on a man's employment three years prior to Liberation. They have been an important factor in determining a student's prospects for educational advancement. By 1979, in a series of policy changes, China's moderate leaders made the role of class in Chinese life much less important. First, the 'rightist' label, which had given bad class status to 400,000 families, was entirely expunged. Second, the middle-class professionals were designated mental labourers, thus becoming part of the working class. Third, the class designations of former exploiters "who had worked honestly and done no evil" were removed. In the countryside, this meant former landlords and rich peasants - and their children - were now classified as 'commune members.' The most detailed account of the evolving concept of class in Chinese life is Kraus, Richard, Class

Notes and References   Pages 69 to 76

   Conflict in Chinese Socialism, New York: Columbia University Press, 1981.
6. The Cultural Revolution educational reforms have been discussed in Unger, *Education Under Mao*, pp. 139-206; Chen Hsi-En, Theodore, *Chinese Education Since 1949: Academic and Revolutionary Models*, New York: Pergamon, 1981, pp.63-152; and Pepper, Suzanne, 'Education and Revolution: The "Chinese Model" Revisited', *Asian Survey*, Vol.XVIII, No.9, September, 1978, pp.847-890. This section draws from Rosen, Stanley, 'Obstacles to Educational Reform in China', *Modern China*, Vol.8, No.1, January, 1982, pp.11-13.
7. *Zhongguo Baike Nianjian 1980*, p.536.
8. I have dealt in detail with the evolution and politics of keypoint school policy in 'Restoring Keypoint Secondary Schools in Post-Mao China: The Politics of Competition and Educational Quality, 1978-1983', paper presented at the SSRC Conference on Policy Implementation in Post-Mao China, Ohio State University, June 20-24, 1983.
9. *Guangming Ribao*, 13 January, 1978, and 25 January, 1978, both p.1; Pepper, Suzanne, 'Chinese Education After Mao: Two Steps Forward, Two Steps Back and Begin Again?' *The China Quarterly*, No.81, March, 1980, p.35.
10. *Renmin Ribao*, 25 January, 1978, p.1.
11. *Zhongguo Baike Nianjian 1980*, p.541.
12. On the various pressures in the urban school system in this period see, Chan, Anita, Rosen, Stanley and Unger, Jonathan, 'Students and Class Warfare: The Social Roots of the Red Guard Conflict in Canton', *The China Quarterly*, No.83, September, 1980, pp.397-446 and Rosen, Stanley, *The Role of Sent-Down Youth in the Chinese Cultural Revolution*, Berkeley: Center for Chinese Studies, University of California, Berkeley, 1981.
13. Feng Lanrui and Zhao Lükan, 'Urban Employment in China', *Social Sciences in China*, No.1, 1982, pp.123-139.
14. *Jiaoyu Yanjiu*, No.8, August, 1981, p.27.
15. For provision regarding vocational schools in Jilin province, see *Summary of World Broadcasts* FE/7073/BII/12-13 July, 1982, (Radio Changchun, July 3).
16. On hiring practices in factories, see Shirk, Susan, 'Recent Chinese Labour Policies and the Transformation of Industrial Organisation in China', *The China Quarterly*, No.88, December, 1981, pp.576-579.
17. For more detail on the university enrollment regulations and the characteristics of candidates and successful enrollees, see Rosen, Stanley, 'Secondary and Higher Education in the People's Republic of China', paper prepared for the conference entitled 'The Relation Between Secondary and Higher Education: An International View', UCLA, July 25-28, 1983.
18. This analysis is based on the following local newspapers: *Guangzhou Ribao*, 19 May, 18 June, 16 July, 4 and 11

Notes and References   Pages 80 to 83

August, 20 and 30 October, 1981 and 5 January, 8 June and and 22 July, 1982; Yangcheng Wanbao, 10 August, 23 November, 1981 and 4 January, 20 May, 5 June, 14 and 22 July, and 9 August, 1982; Nanfang Ribao, 5 August, 1981.

19. In Beijing in 1982, there were only twice as many applicants as there were openings for vocational classes, while specialist schools attracted 29.3 times as many applicants as openings, teacher training schools attracted 17.9 times as many applicants as openings, and workers' training schools attracted 4.6 times as many applicants as openings. See Beijing Ribao, 28 July, 1982, p.1.
20. This issue is discussed in Pepper, Suzanne, China's Universities: Post-Mao Enrollment Policies and their Impact on the Structure of Secondary Education, Centre for Chinese Studies, University of Michigan, forthcoming; For comments on this in the Chinese press, see Guangming Ribao, 11 August, 1982, p.2; Guangzhou Ribao, 24 June, 1981, p.4; Zhongguo Qingnian Bao, 12 April, 1983, p.1.
21. Pepper, China's Universities, Table 20.
22. Peking Review, No.30, 28 July, 1978, p.18. It was admitted, however, that the number of students from families of intellectuals "was greater in proportion to the total population than in previous years".
23. Zhongguo Baike Nianjian 1980, p.538.
24. For example, Fudan University in Shanghai, one of the country's top schools, took only '20-odd' of its 1,342 freshmen in 1980 from the countryside. See Pepper, China's Universities, p.139 (draft).
25. Rosen, Stanley, 'Education and the Political Socialisation of Chinese Youths', in Hawkins, John N., Education and Social Change in the People's Republic of China, New York: Praeger, 1983.
26. Hebei Jiaoyu, No.4 April, 1982, p.9.
27. Beijing Keji Bao, 22 February, 1982, p.1.
28. For university promotion rates from 1949-1983, see Rosen, 'Restoring Keypoint Secondary Schools in Post-Mao China: The Politics of Competition and Educational Quality'.
29. Renmin Ribao, 7 July, 1983, p.3, and Guangming Ribao, 4 August, 1981, p.1.
30. Zhongguo Baike Nianjian 1980, p.538.
31. For examples of the problem, see Renmin Jiaoyu, No.3, March, 1982, pp.30-33 and Guangming Ribao, 6 March, 1983, p.2, for Hubei province; Guangming ribao, 7 October, 1982, p.2 for Shandong province. The county report is from Zhejiang Jiaoyu, (secondary school edition), No.6, June, 1982, pp.10-13.
32. The figures are for 1980. Interview, Naomi Woronov, Manhattan Community College, New York, March 1982, cited in Mark Sidel, 'University Enrollment in the People's Republic of China, 1977-1981: The Examination Model Returns', Comparative Education, Vol.18, No.3, 1982,

p.226. Also see Pepper, China's Universities, Tables 13-19 (draft).
33. This section draws from Rosen, 'Restoring Keypoint Secondary Schools in Post-Mao China'.
34. Dagong Bao, (Hong Kong), 6 December, 1982, p.2.
35. Renmin Ribao, 12 March, 1983, p.3.
36. Interview at the Ministry of Education, 17 August, 1982, and Daily Report, 8 July, 1982, pp. K9-10, (China Daily, 7 July).
37. Renmin Jiaoyu, No.3, March 1982, p.34.
38. Guangdong Jiaoyu, No.2, February, 1981, p.3.
39. Liaoning Jiaoyu, No.1, January 1982, p.2 and No.3, March 1982, p.2; Lau Wing Fong, 'Zhongguo nongcun jiaoyu zhi yanjiu: Taishanxian jiaoyu fazhan zhi xiankuang', (Research on Chinese Rural Education: The Current Situation of Educational Development in Taishan County, Guangdong), M.A. Thesis, Chinese University of Hong Kong, 1982, footnote, 33, p. A16.
40. Neimenggu Shehui Kexue, No.3, 1983, pp.27-30.
41. Pepper, Suzanne, China's Universities, p.139 (draft).
42. China trip notes, anonymous, spring 1980.
43. Guangdong Jiaoyu, No.2, February 1981, pp.5-6.
44. Daily Report, 1 July, 1983, p. K17, (Renmin Ribao, 29 June).
45. Brown, Hubert O., 'Recent Policy Towards Rural Education in the People's Republic of China', Hong Kong Journal of Public Administration, Vol.3, No.2, December, 1981, p.171, citing Dagong Bao Weekly Supplement, No. 698 (Hong Kong), November 8-14, 1979, p.1.
46. Brown, 'Recent Policy', pp.176-177, citing Deputy Minister of Education, Zang Boping, in Renmin Jiaoyu, No.1, January 1980, pp.37-39, 52.
47. Central control and support is not completely lacking, however. Subsidies are provided for locally-recruited teachers; textbooks in basic subjects like Chinese and mathematics are prepared at the centre, and so forth.
48. Peter Mauger, 'Changing Policy and Practice in Chinese Rural Education', The China Quarterly, No.93, March, 1983, pp.139-140.
49. Banyuetan, No.5, 10 March, 1983, p.13.
50. Zhongguo Baike Nianjian 1982, p.642.
51. Renmin Jiaoyu, No.8, August, 1980, p.11.
52. Yangcheng Wanbao, 4 January, 1982, p.1; Guangzhou Ribao, 19 May, 1981, p.1 and 8 June, 1982, p.1.
53. Renmin Jiaoyu, No.3, March 1982, pp.29-31. I have discussed the attitudes of youths in the countryside in 'Education and the Political Socialisation of Chinese Youths'.
54. Xin Guancha, No.18, 25 September, 1982, pp.24-27.
55. Banyuetan, No.21, 10 November, 1982, p.40. In part because of the relatively small numbers promoted to upper

secondary the drop-out rate at that level is only 4.8% in Shaanxi.
56. For these reasons and many others, see the series in Heilongjiang Qingnian, Nos. 4 to 8, April to August, 1982. Some of these reasons are also given for primary school drop-outs by Billie L. C. Lo, elsewhere in this volume.
57. Beijing Review, No. 10, 7 March 1983, pp.10-11; The Asia Record, June, 1982, p.16.
58. Daily Report, 18 March, 1983; pp. K9-10, (NCNA, 16 March).
59. Renmin Ribao, 19 May, 1983, p.1.
60. Zhongguo Qingnian Bao, 31 March, 1983, p.1. and Daily Report, 1 July, 1983, p. K21, (Renmin Ribao, 29 June).
61. Mauger, 'Changing Policy and Practice in Chinese Rural Education', pp.140-141; New York Times, 10 April, 1983, pp.1, 8; Jiaoyu Yanjiu, No.12, December, 1982, pp.7-10, 28; Renmin Jiaoyu, No.3, March 1982, pp.29-31.
62. Guangming Ribao, 8 March, 1983, p.1.
63. Guangming Ribao, 15 November, 1982, p.2. This has also been suggested in Guangdong. See Yangcheng Wanbao, 23 February, 1983, p.1.
64. Renmin Ribao, 3 July, 1983, p.3.
65. Beijing Review, No.28, 11 July 1983, pp.4-5; Yangcheng Wanbao, 23 February, 1983, p.1.
66. Zhongguo Jingji Nianjian 1982, p. V-389; Zhongguo Baike Nianjian 1983, p.595.
67. This draws primarily from Jiaoyu Yanjiu, No.8, August, 1981, pp.30-31 and Beijing Review, No.22, 30 May, 1983, p.X (from the Sixth Five Year Plan).

Chapter Five

1. Franke, Wolfgang, The Reform and Abolition of the Traditional Chinese Examination System, Cambridge, Mass.: Harvard University Press, 1960;
Bielenstein, Hans, The Bureaucracy of Han Times, Cambridge: Cambridge University Press, 1980, pp.132-142.
2. Franke, The Reform and Abolition of the Traditional Chinese Examination System, p.7. The Song Dynasty lasted from A.D. 907 - A.D. 1279.
3. Ho Ping-ti, The Ladder of Success in Imperial China, New York and London: Columbia University Press, 1962, p.8.
4. Levenson, Joseph H., 'The Amateur Ideal in Ming and Early Ch'ing Society: Evidence from Painting', Fairbank, John (ed.), Chinese Thought and Institutions, Chicago & London: The University of Chicago Press, 1957, p.321.
5. Munro, Donald J., The Concept of Man in Early China, Stanford, Cal.: Stanford University Press, 1969, p.11.
6. Ibid., pp. 16, 55.
7. Cited in Miyazaki, Ichisada, China's Examination Hell: The Civil Service Examinations of Imperial China, New York:

John Weatherhill, 1976, p.17.
8. Fung Yu-lan, A History of Chinese Philosophy, Princeton, New Jersey: Princeton University Press, 1952. (Seventh Printing, 1973), p.52.
9. So far as the issue of 'equality' is concerned "we find that in the course of centuries the dominant trend of Chinese opinion has continued for the most part to recognise the need for equal opportunity in the examinations. In defining the desirable form of 'equal opportunity', however, political conditions of different periods have led to shifting formulations, which have stressed variously equality for the individual, the racial group, or the region. Regional equality has in turn assumed the various forms of equality among administrative areas, among populations of similar size, or among similar numbers of potential candidates." Kracke, E.A., Jr., 'Region, Family, and Individual in the Chinese Examinations System', Fairbank (ed.), Chinese Thought and Institutions, p.268.
10. Hsu C. Y., Immanuel, 'The Reorganisation of Higher Education in Communist China', The China Quarterly, No.19, 1964, p.128; Kun, Joseph C., 'Higher Education: Some Problems of Selection and Enrollment', The China Quarterly, No.8, 1961, pp.135-148.
11. Hsu, 'The Reorganisation of Higher Education', p.139.
12. 'The Policy and Tasks of Higher Education', as translated in Hu Shi Ming and Seifman, Eli (eds.), Towards a new World Outlook, New York: Ams Press, 1976, p.51.
13. See Emerson, John Philip, Administrative and Technical Manpower in the People's Republic of China, Washington, D.C.: U.S. Department of Commerce, 1973, pp.72-85.
14. See Shirk, Susan L., Competitive Comrades: Career Incentives and Student Strategies in China, Berkeley, Los Angeles & London: University of California Press, 1982, pp.41-47;
Rosen, Stanley, Red Guard Factionalism and the Cultural Revolution in Guangzhou (Canton), Boulder, Colorado: Westview Press, 1982, pp.11-60.
15. Beijing Review, No. 26, 24 June, 1966, p.3.
Reprinted in Hu and Seifman, Towards a New World Outlook, p.202.
16. See Renmin Ribao, 29 March, 1969. English translations appeared in Current Background, No.881, 26 May, 1969 and following issues, No.890, 18 September, 1969, No.903, 17 March, 1970, No.916, 10 October, 1970. Comprehensive bibliographical documentation is given in Dilger, Bernhard, and Henze, Jürgen, Das Erziehungs- und Bildungswesen der VR China seit 1969: Eine Bibliographie, Hamburg: Institut für Asienkunde, 1978.
17. Wen Hui Bao, 6 October, 1966. A translation of this article as well as other materials used in an exhibition

on Kangda which was organised in various cities throughout China from August 1966 is given in 'Shanghai Municipality Holds Exhibition of Memorabilia Relating to the History of the Former Chinese People's Anti-Japanese Military and Political College in Yenan', <u>Union Research Service</u>, Vol.46, No.2, 6 January, 1967, pp.16-30.
18. <u>Current Background</u> (Hong Kong), No.885, 31 July, 1969; Hu and Seifman, <u>Towards a New World Outlook</u>, p.201
19. See the discussion of the politics of 'radical' and 'conservative' elites during the Cultural Revolution in Lee Hong Yung, <u>The Politics of the Chinese Cultural Revolution</u>, Berkeley, Los Angeles & London: University of California Press, 1978.
20. <u>Renmin Ribao</u>, 22 July, 1968; <u>Beijing Review</u>, 2 August, 1968. The experiences of the Shanghai Machine Tools Plant were first widely distributed through the publication of an investigation report 'The Road for Training Engineering and Technical Personnel Indicated by the Shanghai Machine Tools Plant' <u>Renmin Ribao</u>, 22 July, 1968. A translation is available in Hu and Seifman, <u>Towards a New World Outlook</u>, p.218-224.
21. Hu and Seifman, <u>Towards a New World Outlook</u>, p.223-224; Mao Zedong, 'On the Correct Handling of Contradictions among the People', <u>Selected Works of Mao Tsetung</u>, Vol.V, Beijing: Foreign Languages Press, 1977, p.405.
22. See 'Strive to Build a Socialist University of Science and Engineering', originally published in <u>Hongqi</u>, No.8, 1970 pp.5-19; translated in <u>Chinese Education</u>, Vol.IV, No.1, 1971, pp.7-35.
23. <u>Ibid.</u>, pp.26-27.
24. In order to make the Chinese experience internationally comparable in the following section the term 'system of higher educaion' is used with reference to the 'Guidelines for Country Studies', as given in Eurich, Nell P., <u>Systems of Higher Education in Twelve Countries: A Comparative View</u>, New York: Praeger, 1981, pp.149-152. What should be understood by using the term 'higher education'? As a guiding frame of reference throughout our analysis the term 'higher education' is used in accordance with a definition which recently was published by the European Centre for Higher Education (Bucharest) which spoke of
> higher education as that level of education requiring as a minimum condition of admission the successful completion of education at the second level, or evidence of attainment of a level of knowledge equivalent to what is considered satisfactory experience. It covers both public and private institutions and includes: (1) programmes leading to an award not equivalent to a first university degree; (2) programmes leading to a first university degree or equivalent qualifica-

tion; and (3) programmes leading to a post-graduate university degree or equivalent qualification.
See The European Centre for Higher Education, Access to Higher Education in Europe, Bucharest: CEPES, 1981, pp.11-12. Although this definition would imply institutions of the adult education system too, we restrict its scope to those higher education institutions not belonging to adult education which is dealt with in Chapter Seven.

25. The term 'reactivated' is strictly used to identify only those higher education institutions which accepted students on the basis of full-time study for at least two years. The majority of university programmes lasted between two and three years. This definition stands in contrast to widely published information that Chinese universities were reopened as early as 1967. (See for example Kan, David, The Impact of the Cultural Revolution on Chinese Higher Education, Hong Kong: Union Research Institute, 1971.) The difference is that we do not accept mere reports of the Chinese media on reopening and instead use information on planned and implemented admission as an indicator of 'reactivation'.

26. Information of the group's involvement in educational reform is given in Lee, The Politics of the Chinese Cultural Revolution, pp.82-83.

27. See Lamb, Malcolm, Directory of Chinese Officials and Organisations, 1968-1978, Canberra: Australian National University, 1978; Bartke, Who's Who in the People's Republic of China, Armonk, N.Y.: M.E. Sharpe, 1981.

28. One of the very rare detailed descriptions of the administrative structure of universities during this period is offered in Liu, William H., 'University Administration in Post-Cultural Revolution China', China Report (N.Dehli), Vol.X, No.1/2, 1974, pp.27-35.

29. In accordance with the educational terminology used by the 'European Centre for Higher Education' the following definition will be used throughout our analysis: Access to higher education, as "the process by which individuals, groups, sections of age groups etc. 'enter' as students into higher education"; Admission as a term which "describes the rules, procedures, etc. by which states and institutions of higher education determine the terms of access and thus influence the quantitative aspects. It also describes the positive decision to give an individual the status of student;" Recruitment base as a term "for the group of potential students, that is the group of people who, in accordance with the regulations in force in the given country, have the right to become students in an institution of higher education, or the right to seek admission to such an institution." See Access to Higher Education in Europe, edited by the European Centre for Higher Education (CEPES), Bucharest: CEPES, 1981, pp.13-

Notes and References Pages 107 to 115

14.
30. See the author's study Bildung und Wissenschaft in der VR China zu Beginn der achtziger Jahre, Hamburg: Institut für Asienkunde, 1983, pp.53-68.
31. For relevant population and enrollment statistics see Statistical Year Book of China 1983, Hong Kong: Economic Information and Agency, 1983.
32. Unger, Jonathan, Education Under Mao: Class and Competition in Canton Schools, 1960-1980, New York: Columbia University Press, 1082, p.171.
33. Renmin Ribao, 30 December, 1977. A translation appeared in Chinese Education, Vol.XII, No.1, 1979, pp.33-34.
34. Ibid., p.36.
35. Ibid., p.40.
36. Ibid.
37. Ibid., p.43.
38. See Deng Xiaoping's speech at the National Science Conference, in Beijing Review, No.18, 24 March, as discussed and cited in Suttmeier, Richard P., Science, Technology and China's Drive for Modernisation, Stanford, Cal.: Hoover Institution Press, 1980, pp.45-47.
39. See note 24.
40. Fingar, Thomas, China's Quest for Independence: Policy Evolution in the 1970's, Boulder, Colorado: Westview Press, 1980, p.42.
41. Bowles, Frank, Access to Higher Education, Vol.1, Paris: Unesco, 1963, p.61f.
42. See note 30.
43. Renmin Ribao, 21 October, 1977; as translated in Summary of World Broadcasts, Far East, (SWB/FE), 5648/BII 2/24.10.77.
For the 1977 entrance examinations see the following sources: Renmin Ribao, 21, 22, 23 and 26 October, 1977; SWB/FE/5648/B II 1-6, 24.10.1977; No.5651/B II 1-2, 27.10.1977; No.5652/B II 2-16, 28.10.1977; No.5653/B II 1-2, 29.10.1977; No.5657/B II 2-3, 3.11.1977; No.5661/B II 4-5, 8.11.1977; No.5671/B II 14, 19.11.1977; No.5673/B II 13-15, 22.11.1977.
44. Renmin Ribao, 22, October, 1977; as translated in: SWB/FE /5652/B II 13, 28.10.1977.
45. See Renmin Ribao, 22 October, 1977 (SWB/FE/5652/B II 13-14, 28.10.1977) for a detailed description of the administration of enrollment.
46. Swetz, Frank, 'Science Education in the People's Republic of China: Observations and Impressions', Science Education, Vol.63, No.1, 1979, pp.119-129, gives an example of 'Science Topics Listed in the Review Programme for 1977 Entrance Examinations to Higher Educational Institutes and Vocational Schools in Kwangtung (Guangdong) Province'.
47. For the 1978 examinations see the excellent study by

Barendsen, Robert D. (ed.), The 1978 National College Entrance Examination in the People's Republic of China, Washington, D.C.: U.S. Department of Health, Education and Welfare, 1979. In addition: SWB/FE/ 5824/B II 10, 27.5.1978; No. 5846/B II 14, 23.6.1978.

48. Developments since 1980 are documented in: SWB/FE 6419/ B II 1-5, 14.5.1980; No.6426/B II 1, 22.5.1980; No.6678/B II 14,20.3.1981; No.6751/B II 7-8, 17.6.1981; No.7002/B II 3-5, 15.4.182; No.7031/b II 14-15, 20.5.1982; No.7249/B II 5-7, 4.2.1983; No.7285/N II 11-12, 18.3.1983; No.7295/B II 3-4, 30.3.1983; No.7305/B II 5, 12.4.1983; Xinhua New Agency (London), 21 January, 9, 16 March; 5, 10, 20 May; 14 June, 15, 21, 23 July, 1983. Chinese texts appeared in Zhonghua Renmin Gongheguo Guowuyuan, No.351, 25 April, 1981; No. 381, 10 May, 1982; No.402, 10 May, 1983.

49. See Gu Mingyuan, 'Lun zhongdeng jiaoyu de renwu he jiegou', in Beijing Shifan Daxue Xuebao, No. 5, 1982, pp.1-11, reprinted in Zhongxiaoxue Jiaoyu, No.9, 1982, pp.9-19. Table according to page 14. Figures for 1981 and 1982 are given in Statistical Yearbook of China 1981,1982. For 1983 estimates of graduates and number of admitted students, see Xinhua News Agency, (London), 2 September, 1983. It must be noticed however, that the term 'transition rate' in an international context may be somewhat misleading. The statistical prerequisite for significant figures would be that the population of entrants into higher education institutions at a rate of 100%, but in reality this is far from being so. Throughout the 1950s a great number of accepted entrants did not come from the related yearly population of graduates, a great number of persons who already had been working for some years were accepted, as well. Similar remarks must be made for the situation after 1976. Only at the beginning of the 1980s were the majority of entrants taken out of the population of the same year's graduates at upper secondary schools. Before that a considerable proportion of entrants had graduates some years earlier, so that as a final conclusion the 'transition rate' may only serve as a rough indicator for demand and supply of candidates.

50. It may be interesting to note that in July 1981 the Ministry of Education had issued the document 'Explanation of Terms Concerning the Status of Students in Institutes of Higher Education' in order to standarise important terms of higher education, including 'suspension of schooling', 'College leaver', and 'dropout student'. See China Official Annual Report 1982/83, edited by New China News Photos Company, Hong Kong: Kingsway International Publications, Ltd., 1982. pp.666-667; Gaojiao Zhanxian, No.1, 1982, in Joint Publications Research Service (JPRS), No.82440, 12 December, 1982, pp.77-78.

51. Zhongguo Baike Nianjian, 1980, p.539.

52. The institutional distribution was as follows:

	1978 Enrollment	%	1980 Enrollment	%	1980 Entrants	%	1983 Entrants	%
Universities & Colleges	8396	77	17728	82	2964	82	12674	84
Institutes of the Chinese Academy of Sc.	1381	12	1393	7	193	5	1144	8
Institutes of the Chinese Academy of Social Sciences	405	4	594	3	40	1	192	1
Other Research Institutes Administered by Ministries & Commissions under the State Council	753	7	1577	7	328	9		
Research insts. administered by provinces, municipalities, autonomous regions	--		312	1	95	3	1124	7
TOTAL	10934	100	21604	100	3620	100	15134	100

Sources: Zhongguo Baike Nianjian 1980, 1981; Zhongguo Jiaoyu Bao, No.12, 22 September, 1983.

53. Xinhua (Chinese), 31 October, 1982, as translated in Joint Publications Research Service (JPRS), No.82347, 30 November, 1982, p.90. A general introduction is given in Sidel, Mark, 'Graduate Education in the People's Republic of China: New Steps, New Challenges', Higher Education, Vol.12, 1983, pp.155-170. For regulations in 1981 and 1982, see Xinhua (Chinese), 9 January, 1982 in JPRS, No.79954, 27 January, 1982, p.37 and JPRS, No.78640, 30 July 1981, pp.18-20 for a translation of Guangming Ribao, 16 June, 1981.
54. An institutional profile of Beijing University is described in Sidel, 'Graduate Education in the PRC', P.161.
55. Xinhua News Agency (London), 28 May, 1983. For general information, see Barendsen, Robert D., Doctoral Degree Programs offered by China's Colleges and Universities, Washington, D.C.: Office of Postsecondary Education, U.S. Department of Education, Nov., 1982; by the same author, Doctoral Degree Programs at China's Research Organ-

isations, Washington, D.C.: Office of Postsecondary Education, U.S. Department of Education, July, 1983. In addition JPRS, No.79938, 26 January, 1982, pp.101-102; JPRS, No.80272, 9 March, 1982, pp.47-48; JPRS, No.80461, 31 March, 1982, pp.92-94; JPRS, No.80461, 31 March, 1982, pp.95-95, all translations from Guangming Ribao. Guangming Ribao, 16 January 1982, gives the figure of 458 institutions qualified to give degrees. It is expected that a new enlarged list of institutions approved to confer degrees will be issued by the State Council in 1984.

The 'Provisional Methods of Implementing Regulations Concerning Academic Degrees of the People's Republic of China', state the following basic requirements for degrees:

Bachelor's Degree *(xueshi)*: Undergraduates of institutions of higher learning who have fulfilled the requirements of a teaching project; who have been permitted to graduate after being examined and verified; whose achievements in the study of the courses and whose graduation theses (graduation projects or other graduation practical work) indicate that they have acquired a fairly good grasp of the fundamental theory of their major, specialised knowledge and some basic skills; and who have gained a preliminary ability to engage in scientific research or carry out specialised technical work will be given a bachelor's degree.

Master's Degree *(shuoshi)*: Examination courses and requirements for a master's degree applicant: 1.Marxist theory course. The requirement is a good grasp of basic Marxist theory. 2. Basic theory course and speciality course which normally cover either three or four subjects. The requirement is a good grasp of solid basic theory and a systematic speciality knowledge. 3. One foreign language. The requirement is a relative proficiency in reading the foreign materials pertinent to the particular speciality.

Doctorate *(boshi)*: Courses to be examined and requirements for the doctorate: 1. Marxist theory course: It is required that the candidate master the basic theories of Marxism fairly well. 2. Basic theory course and speciality courses. It is required that the candidate have a solid and broad knowledge in basic theories and study the speciality courses systematically and profoundly. The range of the examination is determined by the Degree Assessment Committee of the degree conferring unit....3. Two foreign languages. To meet the requirement of the first foreign language, the candidate must be able to proficiently read reference materials of his speciality in that

language and have achieved a certain competency in writing. To meet the requirement of the second foreign language, the candidate must be able to basically read reference materials of his speciality in that language.
See: Guangming Ribao, 13 June, 1981; Renmin Ribao, 14 February, 1980; an English translation appeared in China Official Annual Report 1982/3, edited by New China News Photos Company, Hong Kong: Kingsway International Publications Lt., 1983, pp.661ff.

56. Xinhua News Agency (London), 28 May, 1983.
Of the reported total of 21,284 research students in 1982 20,910 are candidates for masters' degrees and 374 are candidates for the doctorate. See Education in China: The Past Five Years, p.35.
In the Chinese media there are a number of conflicting figures for entrants and enrollment of research students. For a discussion of that issue see Orleans, Leo A., The Training and Utilization of Scientific and Engineering Manpower in the People's Republic of China, Washington, D.C.: U.S. Government Printing Office, 1983, pp.31-34.

57. Figures up to 1981 are found in the Statistical Yearbook of China 1981, p.456.

58. See Scharping, Thomas, Umsiedlungsprogramme für Chinas Jugend 1955-1980, Hamburg: Institut für Asienkunde, 1980. This is by far the best analysis in the international field of research. Another explanation could be that the proportion of students which had been enrolled in universities and colleges outside the region increased, but this seems unlikely.

59. The following sources give information on private schools: Bray, Mark, 'The Re-emergence of Private Education in China', International Review of Education, Vol.28, No.1, 1982, pp.95-97; Li Yongzeng, 'Privatschulen in Beijing', Beijing Rundschau, Vol.20, No.17, 26 April, 1983, pp.20-21, 29; Provincial developments are documented in SWB/FE 6467/B II 13, 10.7.1980 and No.6481/B II 8, 26.7.1980; No.7198/B II 6, 2.12.1982; Xinhua News Agency (London), 7, 30 December, 1982, 26 January, 1983; JPRS, No.76253, 19 August, 1980, p.64, No.76272, 15 January, 1981, pp.121-122; No.77730, 1 April, 1981.

60. Renmin Ribao, 14 June 1950, p.1; translated in Hu and Seifman, Towards a New World Outlook, 1976, p.12.

61. Xinhua News Agency (London), 26 January, 1983.
62 Ibid.
63. Hebei provincial service, 20 November, 1982, in JPRS, No.82449, 13 December, 1982, p.90.
64. Ibid.
65. China Daily, 29 July, 1983.
66. Ibid.
67. China Daily, 17 August, 1983; Xinhua News Agency (London),

16 August, 1983.
68. China Daily, 2 September, 1983.
69. Xinhua News Agency (London), 12 September, 1983.
70. Xinhua News Agency (London), 15 April, 1983. In addition see Lee, Mary, 'Self-reliance on campus', Far Eastern Economic Review, 22 May, 1981.
71. Xinhua News Agency (London), 15 April, 1983.
72. The analysis is based on the following sources: China Daily, 9 September, 1983; Ming Bao (Hong Kong), 6 December, 1982, as translated in JPRS, NO. 82615, 11 January, 1983, pp.87-88; Dazhong Ribao, 19 January, 1983, as translated in JPRS, No. 83105, 3 March, 1983, pp.131-132; Renmin Ribao, 7 May, 1983; Xinhua News Agency (London), 19,20 May and 27 April, 1983 as well as 24 September, 1983; Guangming Ribao, 11 June, 1983; Jiefang Ribao, 19 May, 1983; Education in China: The Past Five Years, 1983, p.30; Heilongjiang provincial service, 27 May, 1983, in SWB/FE/BII 6, 4.6.1983.
73. Statistical Yearbook of China 1983, p.515. The forerunner of these universities was the recruitment of 100,000 nonresident students (zoudusheng) at a number of universities and colleges in 1978. As it turned out later a lot of problems with this new type of student arose and some universities cancelled this practice. It now looks as if nonresident students in future only will be admitted at regular higher education institutions on a minor scale. Instead they will be enrolled in these new types of institution. See Renmin Jiaoyu, No.8, 1980, pp.6-9.
74. See Henze, Bildung und Wissenschaft, pp.212-215 for a list of keypoint universities and colleges.
75. We do not discuss priority schools in detail because a number of excellent studies have appeared recently, and the issue has been discussed in Chapters Three and Four of this book. See Rosen, Stanley, 'Restoring Keypoint Secondary Schools in Post-Mao China: The Politics of Competition and Educational Quality, 1978-1983', Paper prepared for the SSRC Conference on Policy Implementation in Post-Mao China, Ohio State University, 20-24 June, 1983; Seifman, Eli, 'China's Key Schools: A New Educational Mandate', Asian Affairs, Vol.10, No.1, 1979, pp.42-50; Hu Shi-ming and Seifman, Eli, 'On the "Key" Colleges and Universities in the People's Republic of China', Asian Thought and Society, Vol.6, No.1, 1981, pp.25-35; and the author's study 'Begabtenförderung im Bildungswesen der VR China: Das System der Schwerpunkt-Schulen', ASIEN, No. 4, 1982, pp.29-58.
76. For a general introduction see Orleans, Leo A., Professional Manpower and Education in Communist China, Washington, D.C.: U.S. Government Printing Office, 1961, pp.57ff. A list of higher technical colleges for 1965 appeared in Barendsen, Robert D., The Educational

250

Revolution in China, Washington, D.C.: U.S. Department of Health, Education, and Welfare, 1975, pp.47-48.
77. See OECD, Classification of Educational Systems in OECD Member Countries, Finland, Germany, Japan, Paris: Organization for Economic Co-operation and Development, 1972, p.54.
78. The reader who is interested in examples of curricula in various specialities is refered to the author's study: Bildung und Wissenschaft, pp.239-253, where materials concerning the study of chemistry and mathematics at universities directly administered by the Ministry of Education have been translated.
79. Beijing Ribao, 29 May, 1980, in JPRS, No.76141, 30 July, 1980, p.105.
80. Zhongguo Qingnian Bao, 2 February, 1980, in JPRS, No.75448, 7 April, 1980, p.39.
81. Ibid., p.41.
82. See Henze, Bildung und Wissenschaft, pp.73ff., Appendix pp.239ff.
83. Guangming Ribao, 25 June, 1981, in JPRS, No.78733, 12 August, p.42.
84. Jiefang Ribao, 22 July, 1980, in JPRS, No.76366, 4 September, 1980, p.72.
85. Gaojiao Zhanxian, No.5, May, 1982, pp.13-16, translated in JPRS, No.82347, 30 November, 1982, pp.51-58. Cited from p.58.
86. Pepper, Suzanne, 'China's Universities: New Experiments in Socialist Democracy and Administrative Reform', Modern China, Vol.8, No.2, 1982, p.196.
87. Guangming Ribao, 8 August, 1980, in JPRS, No.77238, 26 January, 1981, p.92.
88. By far the best analysis of administrative reforms on the basis of empirical research is that of Pepper, 'China's Universities: New Experiments in Socialist Democracy and Administrative Reform'. For a translation of relevant articles see: Ogden, Suzanne,'The Politics of Higher Education in the PRC', Chinese Law and Government, Vol.XV, No.2, 1982, pp.4-117. In addition see Ogden, Suzanne, 'Higher Education in the People's Republic of China: New Directions in the 1980's', Higher Education, Vol. 11, 1982, pp.85-109. Historical perspectives of China's bureaucratic culture are discussed in Baum, R., Scientism and Bureaucratism in Chinese Thought: Cultural Limits of the "Four Modernizations", Lund: Research Policy Institute, 1981.
89. The historical dimension is discussed in Pepper, 'China's Universities', pp.174-179, and in Gaojiao Zhanxian, No.3, March, 1982, pp.4-7, translated in JPRS, No. 81992, 15 October, 1982, pp.100-107.
90 Guangming Ribao, 6 December, 1980, translated in Ogden, 'The Politics of Higher Education in the PRC', p.29.

91. Pepper, Suzanne, 'Chinese Universities: Experiments in Democracy', The Asian Wall Street Journal, 2 September, 1981. For a discussion of the tension between theory and reality as well as further consequences arising out of this new ideal see Pepper, 'China's universities'. For examples of reforms of Shanghai Jiaotong University, Shanghai Normal University, Shanghai Tongji University and Tianjin's Nankai University, see Renmin Ribao, 26 February, 1983, in JPRS, No.83181, 4 April, 1983, pp.52-57; Guangming Ribao, 27 April, 30 June, 1980 and 14 November, 1979, as translated in JPRS, NO.75962, 30 June, 1980; Ogden, 'The Politics of Higher Education in the PRC', pp.31-32; JPRS, No. 74875, 7 January. 1980, pp.93-95; Renmin Ribao, 25 February, 1983, in JPRS, No.83231, 8 April, 1983, pp.127-128.
92. The following analysis is based on the maximum of sources that have been available to the author. Besides interview data, it is based on Zhongguo Gaodeng Xuexiao Jianjie, Beijing, 1982; Quanguo Zhongdian Gaodeng Yuanxiao Jieshao, Beijing, 1982; Fingar, Thomas, Higher Education and Research in the People's Republic of China: Institutional Profiles, Washington, D.C.: U.S. - China Education Clearinghouse, 1981. Figures for national totals are in Zhongguo Gaodeng Xuexiao Jianjie, 1982, p.2.
93. Ibid., p.5, 17.
94. Ibid., p.21.
95. Renmin Ribao, 8 April, 1983, as translated in JPRS, No.83638, 9 June, 1983, pp.109-112.
96. For an interesting case study on the economics of higher education administration see Gaodeng Jiaoyu Yanjiu, No.1, 1981, pp.73-79, reprinted in Daxue Jiaoyu, No.10, 1981, pp.47-52.
97. Ogden, 'The Politics of Higher Education in the PRC', p.50.
98. Ibid.
99. Gaojiao Zhanxian, No.3, March, 1982, as translated in JPRS, No.81992, 15, October, 1982, pp.100-101.
100. Ibid., p.103.
101. Ming Bao, 14 November, 1982, translated in JPRS, No.82540, 27 December, 1982, p.108.
102. Pepper, 'China's Universities', p.189.
103. Renmin Ribao, 23 August, 1980; Wen Hui Bao, 23 August, 1980.
104. Pepper, 'China's Universities', pp.191ff.
105. See Lardy, Nicholas (ed.), Chinese Economic Planning, White Plains, New York: M.E. Sharpe, 1978; Klenner, Wolfgang, Ordnungsprinzipien im Industrialisierungsproze der Volksrepublik China: Planung, Organisation und Unternehmenskonzept, Hamburg: Verlag Weltarchiv, 1979.
106. Lardy, N., Chinese Economic Planning, pp.61-76, 221-228, 256-267.

Notes and References   Pages 133 to 140

107. References are given in Henze, Bildung und Wissenchaft, p.157ff.
108. Xinhua News Agency (London), 5 and 10 May, 1983. Zhonghua Renmin Gongheguo Guowuyuan Gongbao, No.406, 30 June, 1983, pp.492-495.
109. Ibid.
110. As examples see articles in: SWB/FE/6165/B II 3-4, 12.7.1979; No. 6858/B II 2-3, 20.10.1981; No. 7064/B II 6-7, 29.6.1982; JPRS, No.79865, 15 January, 1982, pp.46-47; No.79635, 10 December, 1981, pp.139-140; No.79743, 28 December, 1981, pp.65-66; No.82590, 5 January, 1983, pp.161-162; No.80272, 9 March, 1982, pp.51-53; No.83059, 11 March, 1983, pp.184-5. All translations from Guangming Ribao; Beijing Ribao, 28 September, 1981, JPRS, No.79557, 1 December, 1981, pp.85-87; Jiefang Ribao, 18 Debember, 1981, JPRS, NO. 80461, 31 March, 1982, pp.89-91.
111. In 1985 it is estimated that "Shanghai's national economy will need a reinforcement of 90,000 plus college graduates.., yet its higher schools can only supply 50,000 to the city." See Guangming Ribao, 7 November, 1982, in JPRS, No. 82590, 5 January, 1983, p.161.
112. We have to remind the reader of the fact, that even during the coming years the Chinese economy is far from having its manpower needs met. Calculated in mere quantitative terms, assuming a constant 5% increase in entrants into higher education institutions for every year between 1966 and 1976, we would estimate the Cultural Revolution's loss of graduates at about 2,400,000. Assuming a constant increase of 10%, it would have caused a loss of 3,300,000.
113. Renmin Ribao, 23 August, 1980, p.4
114. Renmin Ribao, 22 August, 1982, in JPRS, No.82025, 20 October 1982, p.33-34.
115. Jinqi Ribao, 1 February, 1983, in JPRS, No.83105, 21 March, 1983, p.65.
116. Guangming Ribao, 8 August, 1980, p.2.
117. Renmin Ribao, 22 August, 1982, in JPRS, No.82025, 20 October, 1982, p.33.
118. For sources see Note 110. An example of a graduate losing his assignment due to his objections is given in Xizang Regional Service, 13 January, 1982, in JPRS, No.79954, 27 January, 1982, p.36.
119. Translated in SWB/FE/7375/B II 13-15, 2.7.183.
120. Ibid., pp.B II 14-15.
121. The following sources give an overview on recent measures and discussions: SWB/FE/7274/B II 15, 5.3.1983; No.7295/B II 5, 30.3.1983; No.7302/B II 13, 8.4.1983; No.7373/B II 14, 30.6.1983; No.7375/B II 13-15, 2.7.1983; No.7391/B II 12-13, 21.7.1983,No.7397/B II 13-14,28.7.1983. Xinhua News Agency (London), 30 April, 15, 18 and July, 9 August, 1983.
122. Education in China: The Past Five Years, p.28.

123. See Psacharopoulos, George, 'Returns to Education: An Updated International Comparison', in Comparative Education, Vol.17, 1981, p.333; See also Psacharopoulos, Returns to Education, Amsterdam-London: Elsevier Scientific Publishing Co., 1973; and Higher Education in Developing Countries: A Cost-Benefit Analysis, Washington, D.C.: World Bank, 1980.
124. Psacharopoulos, George, 'Returns to Education', p.333
125. Pasacharopoulos, G, 'The Economics of Higher Education in Developing Countries', Comparative Education Review, Vol.26, 1982, pp.139-159.
126. Henze, Bildung und Wissenschaft, p.XI
127. 'Education Reform in the People's Republic of China', China Notes, Vol.VIII, No.3, 1970, p.37.
128. Ibid.
129. Ibid.
130. Ibid.
131. Ibid.
132. See Domes, Jürgen, 'The Gang of Four" -and Hua Kuo-feng: Analysis of Political Events in 1975-76', The China Quarterly, No.71, Sept., 1977, pp.473-497; Bradsher, Henry, 'China: The Radical Offensive', Asian Survey, Vol.XIII, 1973, pp.989-1001.
133. Crombag, Hans F.M., 'On Defining Quality of Education', Higher Education, Vol.7, 1978, p.390.
134. Ibid., p.392.
135. For an interesting analysis on the planning of higher education in developing countries see: Sanyal, Bikas C., 'Alternative Structure of Higher Education and the World of Work', International Review of Education, Vol.XXVIII, 1982, pp.239-257.
136. Farrell, Joseph P., 'Educational Expansion and the Drive for Social Equality' in Altbach, P., Arnove, R. and Kelly, G. (eds.), Comparative Education, New York and London: Mac Millan, 1982, p.43.
137. Statistical Yearbook of China 1981, p.458; Statistical Yearbook of China 1983, p.518.
138. See Rosen, Stanley, Red Guard Factionalism and the Cultural Revolution in Guangzhou (Canton), Boulder, Colorado: Westview Press, 1982; Unger, Jonathan, Education Under Mao: Class and Competition in Canton Schools, 1960-1980, New York: Columbia University Press, 1982; White, Gordon, The Politics of Class and Class Origin: The Case of the Cultural Revolution, Canberra: The Australian National University, 1976.
139. Zhongguo Baike Nianjian 1982, p.573. The percentage of new female students in 1979, 1980 and 1981 in the same source was reported as 22.51%, 23.57% and 25.12%.
140. Xinhua News Agency (London), 27 October, 1982.
141. Renmin Ribao, 6 March, 1981, in JPRS, No.77613, 18 March, 1981, p.73.

142. See the following sources: Heberer, Thomas, 'Das Erziehungswesen der nationalen Minderheiten in China', ASIEN, No.6, 1982, pp.67-89; Hawkins, John, N., 'National-Minority Education in the People's Republic of China', Comparative Education Review, Vol.26, 1982, pp.147-162; Dilger, Bernhard, 'The Education of Minorities', Comparative Education, Vol.20, No.1, 1984.
Regional statistics appeared in Mingzu Tuanjie, 22 December, 1980, p.9 cited in Heberer, p.73.
SWB/FE/6539/B II 5, 3.10.1980, and No. 6528/B II 8-9, 20.9.1980; No. 6847/B II 8, 7.10.1980; Beijing Rundschau, No.46, 18 November, 1980, pp.8-9; Xinhua News Agency (London), 30 August, 1980; Xinjiang regional service, 11 June, 1982, in JPRS, No.81432, 3 August, 1982, p.53; Sichuan regional service, 28 March, 1981, in SWB/FE/6698/B II 4, 13.4.1981;
Zhongguo Baike Nianjian 1980, Beijing-Shanghai, 1980.
Zhongguo Baike Nianjian 1981, Beijing-Shanghai, 1981.
Zhongguo Baike Nianjian 1982, Beijing-Shanghai, 1982.
Zhongguo Baike Tongji 1981, Beijing, 1982.
For population figures see Scharping, Thomas, Chinas Bevöl Kerung 1953-1982. Teil I: Statistik, Koln: Bundesinstitut für ostwissenschaftliche und internationale Studien, 1983; The 1982 Population Census of China (Major Figures), compiled by the Population Census Office under the State Council and the Department of Population Statistics of the State Statistical Bureau, Hong Kong: Economic Information and Agency, 1982.

143. Mingzu Tuanjie, No.6, 15 June, 1980, p.11, in JPRS, No. 76699, 27 October, 1980, pp.57-58.

144. These statistics are based on the assumption that the information which is given in Zhongguo Tongji Nianjian 1981, p.26, for 'other' institutions of higher learning may be related to minority colleges. The same assumption has been made for figures given in Zhongguo Baike Nianjian 1981, pp.474, 475, for 1980.

145. Guangming Ribao, 12 March, 1982, in JPRS, No.80792, 12 May, 1982, pp.117-118.

146. Ibid. For a very rare document on enrollment work in minority areas see Ningxia Ribao, 20 May, 1981, p.3, in JPRS, No.78678, 8 August, 1981, pp.42-47. Besides Chinese official statements concerning minority education, the reader should take into account some more critical information from the Dalai Lama's report on two visits to Tibet: Tethong, Tenzin N., 'Report on the Second Delegation to Tibet', and Gyalpo, Jetsun Pema, 'Three Months in Tibet: A Personal Viewpoint', From Liberation to Liberalization: Views on 'Liberated Tibet', Dharamsala (Himachal Pradesh): The Information Office of His Holiness the Dalai Lama, 1982, pp.100-112; 113-126.

147. Warnock, Mary, 'The Concept of Equality in Education',

Oxford Review of Education, Vol.1, No.1, 1975, p.4.
148. Xinhua News Agency (London), 6 December, 1982, pp.7,10.
149. Coleman, James, 'What is Meant by "An Equal Educational Opportunity"?', Oxford Review of Education, Vol.1, No.1, 1975, pp.27-29.
150. See Sauvy, Alfred, Access to Education, The Hague: M. Nijhoff, 1973, p.25: "We can discern in the upheavals of public education structures under socialist regimes two phenomena which are unequal but complementary. The primary and ideological concern has been to rapidly improve the education of the previously underprivileged classes - working class and peasant class - but this aim very quickly came into conflict with the immediate demands of the economic structure for managers and technicians."

Chapter Six

1. Daily Report, Vol.1, No.79, 24 April, 1978, pp. E1-4.
2. FBIS -- China Report (Political, Sociological & Military Affairs), No.123, 3 October, 1980, pp.88-89. For reasons for reorganising secondary schools, see Guangming Ribao, 17 October, 1980, p.1, 24 Oct., 1980, p.1 and Renmin Ribao, 24 Oct., 1980, p.1. For examples of reorganisation, see Renmin Ribao, 14 Oct., p.3, Guangming Ribao, 11 Oct., 1980, p.1, Beijing Ribao, 27 Oct., 1980, p.1, and Nanfang Ribao, 16 Oct., 1980, p.1.
3. The approach of this paper is adopted from Lynch, James and Plunkett, H. Dudley, Teacher Education and Cultural Change - England, France, West Germany, London: George Allen and Unwin Ltd., 1973. Lynch and Plunkett use this analytical framework to compare teacher education in three countries.
4. Confucius used different methods to teach different students. This can be seen in the intellectual discourses he had with his students in the Analects. It is particularly obvious in passages like 'On the Superior Man' and 'On Filial Piety'.
5. Mencius elaborated on the subject, stating: The good teacher (who is the moral man) will use the following five methods according to the special individual characteristics of his pupil:
   (i) Some he influences like a seasonable rain - these are the pupils who are ready and alert and receive instruction eagerly and joyfully.
   (ii) Some he leads into higher paths of virtue and righteousness - these are the pupils who show real ethical aptitude and are amenable to guidance.
   (iii) Some he encourages to specialise - these are the pupils who show particular interest and talent in some branch of learning.

(iv) Some he trains in disputation - these are the pupils who show critical powers and awareness.
(v) Some he cultivates as companions - these are the pupils who will learn by personal influence and emulation.
Richardson, Thomas A., 'The Classical Chinese Teacher', in Bereday, George Z.F., and Lauwerys, Joseph (eds.)<u>The Year Book of Education, 1963: The Education and Training of Teachers</u> London: Evans Brothers Ltd., 1963, p.33.

6. See for example <u>Renmin Jiaoyu</u>, No.12, Dec., 1981, pp.57-58, No.8, Aug., 1980, p.4, <u>Jiaoyu Yanjiu</u>, No.4, April, 1981, pp.14-16, No.5, May, 1981, pp.78-81 and <u>Guangming Ribao</u>, 29 Aug., 1981, p.2 and 24 Aug., 1981, p.2.
7. Peking Institute of Educational Administration, School Management Research Unit, <u>Xuexiao Guanli</u>, (School Management), Beijing: Science Press, 1981, p.21.
8. Teachers complained that they could not make enough to feed and clothe themselves. Another complaint was that teaching had no future. <u>Renmin Jiaoyu</u>, Vol.2, No.4, Feb., 1951, p.52.
9. Teachers wrote to the editor to complain that their expertise was not being used correctly. In their opinion, they should be assigned to more 'appropriate' jobs other than teaching. <u>Renmin Jiaoyu</u>, No.12, Dec., 1952, pp.52-55.
10. <u>Renmin Jiaoyu</u>, No.7, July, 1952, pp.19-21; <u>Renmin Jiaoyu</u>, No.10, Oct., 1952, p.53.
11. <u>Guangming Ribao</u>, 22 Oct. 1969, p.4.
12. <u>Jiaoyu Yanjiu</u>, No.3, March, 1981, pp.7-12; <u>Renmin Jiaoyu</u>, No. 10, Oct., 1980, p.7.
13. <u>Guangming Ribao</u>, 12 Jan., 1981, p.2, <u>Renmin Jiaoyu</u>, No.10 Oct., 1980, pp.10-11.
14. <u>Renmin Jiaoyu</u>, No.4, April, 1979, p.27.
15. <u>Renmin Jiaoyu</u>, 2 Sept., 1980, p.3.
16. <u>Renmin Jiaoyu</u>, 2 Sept., 1980, p.3; <u>Renmin Jiaoyu</u>, No.10 Oct., 1980, p.7.
17. <u>Renmin Jiaoyu</u>, No.5, May, 1981, p.52.
18. <u>FBIS - China Report</u> (Political, Sociological & Military Affairs), No.28, 25 Oct., 1979, pp.38-39.
19. <u>Nanfang Ribao</u>, 2 Nov., 1980, p.2; <u>Guangming Ribao</u>, 12 Jan., 1981, p.2.
20. <u>Renmin Jiaoyu</u>, No.10, Oct., 1980, pp.8-9.
21. <u>Renmin Jiaoyu</u>, No.4, April, 1980, p.30.
22. <u>Ibid</u>.
23. <u>Ibid</u>. There are approximately three Chinese yuan to the English pound, two Chinese yuan to the American dollar.
24. <u>Hupeh Chiaoshi</u>, 1 August, 1956, p.3.
25. <u>Monsoon</u> (Hong Kong), Vol.3, No.7, August, 1980, p.31.
26. Rural Teachers *(minban jiaoshi)*, who have permanent rural residential status *(nongmin hukou)* are allocated plots for cultivation. Most rural teachers teach during the day and work on the private plots in the mornings and evenings. This information was collected on one of my visits to the

Canton Delta. Scholars from other parts of China have also confirmed this information.
27. Ming Pao (Hong Kong), 6 October, 1980, p.3
28. FBIS -- Daily Report, Vol.1, No.225, 23 Nov., 1981, pp.K11-12.
29. Guangming Ribao, 23 January, 1981, p.1.
30. Examples of this are seen in Guangming Ribao, 23 November, 1980, p.2, 12 December, 1980, p.2, 12 January, 1981, p.2, and Renmin Ribao, 5 March, 1981, p.3.
31. Renmin Jiaoyu, No.5, May, 1981, p.50; Jiaoyu Yanjiu, No.4, Aug., 1980, p.31.
32. Jiaoyu Yanjiu, No.4, August, 1980, p.31.
33. Renmin Jiaoyu, No.8, August, 1980, p.4.
34. Renmin Jiaoyu, No.4, april, 1979, p.27.
35. Jiaoyu Yanjiu, No.4, August, 1980, p.31.
36. Renmin Jiaoyu, No.4, April, 1979, p.29.
37. Renmin Jiaoyu, No.5, May, 1981, p.50.
38. Renmin Jiaoyu, No.12, December, 1981, p.56.
39. Guangming Ribao, 9 July, 1981, p.3, 7 April, 1981, p.1. Renmin Ribao, 4 Nov., 1980, p.3, Renmin Jiaoyu, No.10, Oct., 1980, pp.10-11.
40. Renmin Jiaoyu, No.10, Oct., 1980, p.41.
41. Ibid.
42. Renmin Jiaoyu, No.5, May 1981, p.51.
43. Ibid.
44. Banhao Shifan Jiaoyu, Fazhan Jiaoyu Kexue, (Manage Well Normal, Develop Pedadogical Science), Beijing: People's Education Press, 1979, pp.11-12.
45. Ibid., p.35.
46. This information was obtained on a visit to Beijing Teacher Training University.
47. Jiaoyu Yanjiu, No.4, August, 1980, p.9.
48. Banhao Shifan Jiaoyu, Fazhan Jiaoyu Kexue, p.35.
49. Ibid., p.49.
50. Ibid., p.45.
51. Ibid., p.37.
52. Ibid.
53. Ibid.
54. Jiaoyu Yanjiu, No.4, August, 1980, p.10.
55. Jiaoyu Yanjiu, No.4, August, 1980, p.9.
56. FBIS -- Daily Report, Vol.1, No.41, 1 March, 1978, p. E17.
57. Gu Mingyuan, 'Teacher Training in China', Journal of Education for Teaching, Vol.7, No.3, Oct., 1981, p.249; Renmin Jiaoyu, No.4, April, 1979, p.28.
58. Jiaoyu Yanjiu, No.4, August, 1980, p.11.
59. China Daily, 27 November, 1981, p.3.
60. Renmin Jiaoyu, No.6, June, 1979, pp.49-50.
61. Renmin Jiaoyu, No.11, November, 1980, p.41 and No.10, October, 1980, p.42.
62. In his article 'Teacher Training in China', Gu Mingyuan describes in-service training under seven categories:

- (i) Short-term training courses offered during the summer and winter vacations.
- (ii) Full-time advanced studies.
- (iii) TV and correspondence courses.
- (iv) Evening in-service training offered by universities or teacher-training institutes and schools.
- (v) Lectures on pedagogy, psychology, and teaching methods.
- (vi) Group discussions.

63. Renmin Jiaoyu, No.9, Sept., 1980, p.64.
64. Banhao Shifan Jiaoyu, Fazhan Jiaoyu Kexue, pp.42-43.
65. FBIS - China Report (Political, Sociological & Military Affairs), No.105, 15 August, 1980, p.120. See Jiaoyu Yanjiu, No.1, January, 1981, p.24.
66. Renmin Jiaoyu, No.8, August, 1980, pp.20-21.
67. Guangming Ribao, 28 August, 1981, p.1.
68. Banhao Shifan Jiaoyu, Fazhan Jiaoyu Kexue, pp.49.
69. Renmin Jiaoyu, No.4, 4 April, 1979, p.30.
70. Jiaoyu Yanjiu, No.4, August, 1980, p.9.
71. FBIS - China Report (Political, Sociological & Military Affairs), No.105, 15 August, 1980, p.119.
72. Gu Mingyuan, 'Teacher Training in China', p.247.
73. FBIS - China Report (Political, Sociological & Military Affairs), No.105, 15 August, 1980, p.119.
74. China Daily, 27 November, 1981, p.3. See also Gu Mingyuan, 'Teacher Training in China', p.248.
75. Jiaoyu Yanjiu, No.4, August, 1980, p.11.
76. China Daily, 27 November, 1981, p.3.
77. Jiaoyu Yanjiu, No.4, August, 1980, p.11.
78. China Daily, 27 November, 1981, p.3.
79. China Daily, 27 November, 1981, p.3.
80. Gu Mingyuan, 'Teacher Training in China', p.250.
81. China Daily, 27 November, 1981, p.3.
82. There were 480,000 students in secondary teacher-training schools and 310,000 students in higher teacher-training institutes, giving a total of 790,000 students. Jiaoyu Yanjiu, No.4, August, 1980, p.7.
83. Jiaoyu Yanjiu, No.4, August, 1980, p.11.
84. For educational administration in China, see Schmidt, Thomas C., 'Organisation & Structure', in Montaperto, Ronald N. and Henderson, Jay, (eds.), China's Schools in Flux, N.Y., White Plains: M. E. Sharpe, Inc., 1979, pp.39-59.
85. Jiaoyu Yanjiu, No.4, August, 1980, p.8. The six higher teacher-training institutes affiliated to the Ministry are: Beijing Teacher Training University in Beijing, East China Teacher Training University in Shanghai, North Eastern Teacher Training University in Changchun, Central Teacher Training College in Wuhan, South Western Teacher Training College in Chongging, and Shanxi Teacher Training University in Xian.
86. Jiaoyu Yanjiu, No.4, August, 1980, p.8.

Notes and References   Pages 172 to 177

87. Ibid.
88. Jiaoyu Yanjiu, No.4, August, 1980, p.8.
89. Ibid., p.9.
90. Official directives issued 1977 are: 'Opinions on Strengthening In-service Training for Primary and Secondary School Teachers', Jiaoyu Yanjiu, No.4, August, 1980, p.11. 'On Speeding Up the Development of Teacher Education', Banhao Shifan Jiaoyu, Fazhan Jiaoyu Kexue, p.20. 'Plans for the Teaching of Pedagogy in Higher Teacher-Training Institutes and Schools of Pedagogy', Jiaoyu Yanjiu, No.6, June, 1981, p.96 and 'Tentative Training Programmes for Secondary Teacher-Training School', Guangming Ribao, 28 August, 1981, p.1.
91. Renmin Jiaoyu, No.5, May, 1981, pp.50-52, and No.4, April, 1979, pp.29-31.
92. Studies done on teacher training are Chan, Theodore, Teacher Training in Communist China Washington:U.S. Office of Education, 1960. Hu Shiao Chung, 'Education in the People's Republic of China 1949-1971: Focus on the Teaching Profession', PhD. Thesis, Graduate School of George Peabody College for Teachers, 1972. Chan, Sylvia and Price, R.F., 'Teacher Training in China: A Case Study of the Foreign Languages Department of Peking Teachers' Training College', Comparative Education, Vol.14, No.3, October, 1978, pp.243-252. Other related Studies are Kent, Ann, 'Red and Expert: The Revolution in Education at Shanghai Teachers' University, 1975-76', The China Quarterly, No.86, June, 1981, pp.304-321. Sieh, Marie, 'The School Teacher - Notes on Professional Tension in the Education System', in Fraser, Stewart E. (ed.), Education and Communism in China, London: Pall Mall Press, 1971. White, Gordon, Party and Professionals - The Political Role of Teachers in Contemporary China, New York: M.E. Sharpe, Inc., 1981.
93. This is the ratio used by Chinese educators. See Banhao Shifan Jiaoyu, Fazhan Jiaoyu Kexue, p.31. Educational Statistics of a Commune to which I have access shows an average ratio of 1 to 29. Price quotes a ratio of 1 to 28. Price, R.F., 'China: A Problem of Information?', Comparative Education Review, Vol. 25, No.1, February, 1981, p.91.
94. Banhao Shifan Jiaoyu, Fazhan Jiaoyu Kexue, p.31.
95. The number of secondary teacher-training schools in 1979 was 1,053. See Gu Mingyuan, 'Teacher Training in China', p.248. This number was decreased to 1,017 in 1981. See China Daily, 27 Nov., 1981, p.3.
96. To be fair, one training school for teachers in secondary vocational and technical schools - the Tianjin Technical Teachers College has been established in Tianjin recently. See Gu Mingyuan, 'Teacher Training in China', p.249.
97. Gu Mingyuan, 'Teacher Training in China', p.250.

Notes and References   Pages 178 to 183

98. An earlier version of this chapter appeared in Leung, C.K., and Chin, S. (eds.), China in Readjustment, Hong Kong: Centre of Asian Studies, 1983.

Chapter Seven

1. Chen Yuanhui (ed.), Lao Jiefang Qu Jiaoyu Jianshi, Beijing: Jiaoyu Kexue Chubanshe, 1982 passim.
2. See, e.g., 'Lun putong jiaoyu zhong de xuezhi yu kecheng' Jiefang Ribao (Yanan), 27 May, 1944.
3. Harper, P., Spare-Time Education For Workers In Communist China, Washington, D.C.: U.S. Dep't of Health, Education and Welfare, 1964.
   Chambers, D.I., 'Spare-Time Education in the PRC', Ph.D. Dissertation, University of Bristol, 1980, chs. 4, 5, 8.
4. Hu Yaobang, 'Create a new situation in all fields of socialist modernisation', The Twelfth National Congress of the CPC, Beijing: Foreign Languages Press, 1982, p.36ff.
5. See Brugger, W., Democracy and Organisation in the Chinese Industrial Enterprise, London: Cambridge University Press, 1976, pp.254-256.
6. Zang Boping, 'Tiaozheng, fazhan he tigao zhi gong jiaoyu', Jiaoyu Yanjiu, May, 1981, p.3.
7. Ibid., and the World Bank, China: Socialist Economic Development, Annex G: Education Sector, pp.10-14.
8. He Qi & Li Tiecheng, 'Lun gong jiao zhanxian de ganbu peixun', Jiaoyu Yanjiu, May, 1982, p.3. Emphasis added.
9. Shirk, S.L., 'Recent Chinese labour policies and the transformation of industrial enterprises in China', The China Quarterly, No.88, 1981, pp.576-579; author's interviews in various urban enterprises, March - April, 1982.
10. See Lo, Billie L.C., Research Guide to Education in China after Mao, Hong Kong: University of Hong Kong, 1982, pp.76-87.
11. Xinhua, 13 Jan., 1983, in BBC Summary of World Broadcasts Part 3, the Far East (FE), 22 Jan., 1983.
12. Yuan Baohua, 'Zai quanguo zhi gong sixiang zhengzhi gongzuo huiyi shang de jianghua', Jingji Ribao, 8 Jan., 1983, and the excellent collection of young employees' letters in Chinese Education, Vol.14, No.1, 1981.
13. Yuan Baohua, 'Tigao zhi gong jishu shuiping shi dangwu zhiji', Renmin Ribao, 12 Aug., 1978.
14. 'Zhong Gong Zhongyang, Guowuyuan guanyu jiaqiang zhi gong jiaoyu gongzuo de jueding', 20 Feb., 1981 in Zhonghua Renmin Gongheguo Guowuyuan Gongbao (ZRGGG), No.10, 1981, pp.295-300, from which all quotations in the remainder of this section are taken.
15. Guangming Ribao, 24 May, 1980, p.1.
16. See 'Quanguo zhi gong jiaoyu gongzuo zuotanhui zai Shanxi

Taiyuan juxing', Renmin Ribao, 29 Dec., 1981 and 'Quanguo Zhi Gong Jiaoyu Guanli Weiyuanhui deng wuge bumen dui qingzhuang wenhua jishu buke zuochu si tiao zhengce guiding', Renmin Ribao, 7 Feb., 1982.
17. Feb. 1981 'Decision', article 2.
18. The exact nomenclature of provincial bodies responsible for the administration of employee education varies considerably and is at present (1983) in a state of flux bound up with local government reform. In some provinces and directly administered cities educational bureaucracy is represented by both a Bureau of Education and a Bureau of Higher Education; in others by a single Bureau of Education. In some provinces an Employee Education Administration Committee co-exists with a Worker-Peasant Education Department/Committee, the latter subordinate to the provincial education bureau. In others, the Worker-Peasant Education Department/Committee has been dissolved and replaced by a provincial Employee Education Administration Committee, sometimes standing apart from the provincial bureau of education and responsible jointly to the national committee and relevant provincial people's congress.
19. Feb. 1981 'Decision', article 9 and 'Jiaoyu Bu Zhaokai zhi gong jiaoyu gongzuo huiyi', Guangming Ribao, 2 Oct., 1981.
20. Song Kanfu, 'Congfen fahui gong hui zuzhi zai gong jiaoyu zhong de jiji zuoyong', Zhi Gong Jiaoyu Yu Rencai Peiyang, Beijing: Jiaoyu Kexue Chubanshe, 1981, p.26; FE, 5 May, 1981, 28 July, 1983.
21. Xinhua Yuebao, Jan., 1983, pp.78-79.
22. Xinhua, 18 Jan., 1983, in FE, 27 Jan., 1983.
23. 'Guoying qiye zhi gong sixiang zhengzhi gongzuo gangyao', 20 June, 1983, Renmin Ribao, 28 July, 1983, FE, 30 July, 1983.
24. February 1981 'Decision', article 2.
25. 'Guoying qiye ... ', Renmin Ribao, 28 July, 1983, articles 15, 35-40.
26. 'Guanyu zhi gong jiaoyu jingfei guanli he kaizhi fanwei de zanxing guiding', ZRGGG, No.13, 1981.
27. 'Zhonghua Quanguo Zong Gong Hui, Zhongguo Renmin Yinhang, Caizheng Bu guanyu yange an "Gong Hui Fa" guiding ba jiao gong hui jingfei de tongzhi', 31 Dec., 1980, ZRGGG, No.1, 1981.
28. Interview with Worker-Peasant Education Bureau Officials, April 1982.
29. Compare Renmin Jiaoyu, May, 1981, pp.5-6 with Zhi Gong Jiaoyu Yu Rencai Peiyang, p.5 for differences.
30. This situation has changed recently, for World Bank funds are to be used to develop the Central Television University - Xinhua, 16 May, 1983, in FE, 24 May, 1983.
31. Xinhua, 29 Dec., 1982, and 25 Jan., 1983, in FE, 8 Jan., and 4 Feb., 1983.

Notes and References   Pages 190 to 197

32. Orleans, L.A., Every Fifth Child: The Population of China London: Eyre Methuen, 1972, p.139.
33. Wang Shou'an & Wang Xianrun, Zhi Gong Jiaoyu Jingji Gailun, Changchun: Jilin Renmin Chubanshe, 1981, p. 41.
34. Handwritten copy of selected curricula provided by the Deputy President Li Ruiyun, March 1982. Similar data were reported at other comparable institutions in Shanghai, Tianjin and Beijing in March- April 1982.
35. Zhao Yinhua, 'Nuli jiaqiang zheng gong duiwu jianshe', Qiye Guanli, Feb., 1983, p.3.
36. 'Guoying qiye ...', Renmin Ribao, 28 July, 1983, articles 16, 30-32.
37. Ibid., article 13.
38. Xinhua Yuebao, Jan., 1982, p.130.
39. Jiefang Ribao (Shanghai), 13 Jan., 1983, p.1 & 1 Mar., p.3.
40. See e.g. 'Cong zhi gong duiwu bianhua kan qiye zhengzhi sixiang gongzuo', Renmin Ribao, 1 Mar., 1982.
41. Wang Shou'an & Wang Xianrun, Zhi Gong Jiaoyu Jingji Gailun, p.39, and Xinhua Yuebao, Mar., 1982.
42. Wang Jing, 'Lun zhi gong jiaoyu de zhengguihua jianshe', Jiaoyu Yanjiu, May, 1981; Wang Shou'an & Wang Xianrun, Zhi Gong Jiaoyu Jingji Gailun, pp.11-15.
43. From interviews in China, March - April, 1982. For similar differences earlier in China, see Chambers, D.I., 'Spare-time Education in the PRC', pp.211-212, 240-249. On similar differences outside China, see Foster, P.J., 'The Vocational School Fallacy in Development Planning', in Anderson, C.A., (ed.), Education and Economic Development, London: Frank Cass, 1966, pp.142-166, and Simkins, T., Non-Formal Education and Development: some critical issues, Manchester: University of Manchester, 1977.
44. Xinhua, 25 May, 1983, in FE, 30 May, 1983.
45. See, e.g., 'Guowuyuan Bangongting zhuan fa Jiaoyu Bu guanyu zhi gong daxue, zhi gong yeyu daxue, gaodeng xuexiao jubende hanshou he ye daxue biyesheng ruogan wenti de qingshi de tongzhi', 1 Feb., 1983, ZRGGG, No.3, 1983.
46. Xinhua, 22 Jan., & 14 Mar., 1983, in FE, 4 Feb., & 18 Mar., 1983.
47. See Bruckner, L.I., 'Spare-Time Higher Education in Communist China with Emphasis on Higher Correspondence Education', Ed.D. Dissertation, Montana State University, 1970.
48. Interview with Guan Zhixiong, President of Beijing Broadcasting University, April, 1982.
49. For further details see McCormick, R., 'Central Broadcasting and Television University', The China Quarterly, No.81, 1980, pp.129-136.
50. Zhou Jianshu, 'Jiji fazhan gaodeng hanshou jiaoyu', Jiaoyu Yanjiu, May, 1982, p.15; Bruckner, L.I., 'Spare-Time Higher Education in Communist China with Emphasis on

Higher Correspondence Education'.
51. Hanshou Daxue Zai Qianjin, Shanghai: Renmin Chubanshe, 1975; 'Jiekai "Si Ren Bang" liyong hanshou jiaoyu fan Dang de heimu', Renmin Jiaoyu, Jan., 1978.
52. Tongji Daxue, 'Rumen xizhidi zhua hanshou jiaoyu', Zhi Gong Jiaoyu Yu Rencai Peiyang, p.141.
53. Education and Science, Beijing: Foreign Languages Press, 1983, p.96.
54. Zhou Jianshu, Jiaoyu Yanjiu, May, 1982, p.17.
55. Education and Science, p.101.
56. 'Guowuyuan pi zhuan Jiaoyu Bu guanyu "Gaodeng jiaoyu zi xue kaoshi shixing banfa" de baogao', 13 Jan., 1981, ZRGGG, No.1, 1981.
57. Interviews with Higher Education Bureau Officials, March, 1982; Zhongguo Baike Nianjian 1982, p.580.
58. Zhongguo Baike Nianjian 1982, p.580.
59. As this chapter was being written the State Council announced that the scheme was to be expanded to include non-degree equivalent courses in economic policy and enterprise management for cadres, Xinhua, 6 Aug., 1983 in FE, 10 Aug., 1983.
60. See Table 7.3.
61. 'Guowuyuan pi zhuan Jiaoyu Bu "Guanyu juban zhi gong zhongdeng zhuanye xuexiao de shixing banfa" de tongzhi', 9 Sept., 1982, ZRGGG, No.25, 1982 provides details of the structure, curriculum and management of the schools.
62. Personal observation during visits to machinery plants, March, 1982.
63. See Pu Xinwen et.al., 'Qingnian zhigong jiaoyu zhong de xinli yu jiaoxue wenti', Jiaoyu Yanjiu, June, 1981, pp.83-87 for discussion of these issues.
64. Yuan Baohua, 'Ba wo guo zhi gong jiaoyu ti dao yige sin de shuiping', Zhi Gong Jiaoyu Yu Rencai Peiyang, p.14.

Chapter Eight

1. Wang, Y.C., Chinese Intellectuals and the West, 1872-1949, Chapel Hill, North Carolina: University of North Carolina Press, 1966.
2. Xinhua News Agency, 1 September, 1982.
3. Ayers, William, Chang Chih-tung and Educational Reform in China, Cambridge, Mass: Harvard University Press, 1971.
4. Beijing Review, No.22, 30 May, 1983, p.XI.
5. See Beijing Review, 19 March, 1982, for a broader discussion of exchange beyond the boundaries of scholarly and educational institutions in an interview with Jiang Ming, Vice-Minister of the State Science and Technology Commission.
6. Interview at the Education Section of the Chinese Embassy in London, 22 April, 1983.

Notes and References

7. Xinhua News Agency, 1 November, 1982, p.18.
8. Joint Publications Research Service, No.79557, 1 December, 1981, p.74.
9. Reports on the valuable work done by western returned Chinese scholars appear frequently in the Chinese press. See for example Guangming Ribao, 15 September, 1981, Wenhui Bao, 25 September, 27 October, 1981. Wenhui Bao, 11 December, 1983, reported that 18,500 Chinese scholars and students had been sent abroad by the Chinese government since 1978, and another 7,000 had gone under private sponsorships, mainly to U.S.A. and Japan of those who had studied abroad, 7,000 had already returned by Dec., 1983.
10. Clough, Ralph, A Review of the U.S.-China Exchange Program, U.S.A.: Office of Research, International Communications Agency, 1981, pp.1, 45-46.
11. China Exchange News, No.10, No.4, December, 1982.
12. Clough, Ralph, A Review of the U.S.-China Exchange Program; Fingar, Thomas and Reed, Linda, Survey Summary: Student and Scholars from the People's Republic of China in the United States, 1 August, 1981, Washington, D.C.: U.S.-China Education Clearinghouse, 1981; Prewitt, Kenneth, (ed.) Research Opportunities in China for American Humanists and Social Scientists, New York: Social Sciences Research Council, 1982.
13. Clough, Ralph, A Review of the U.S.-China Exchange Program, p.7.
14. McLaren, Anne, 'Has Australia Lost out in Scholarly Exchange with China?', in The Australian Journal for Chinese Affairs, No.4, 1980, pp.91-103. This article develops this theme, which is reiterated by Sinologists in other western countries.
15. Clough, Ralph, A Review of the U.S.-China Exchange Program, pp.114-116.
16. Cheng Chi-yuan, Scientific and Engineering Manpower in Communist China 1949-1963, Washington, D.C.: U.S. Gov't Printing Office, 1965. Cheng gives a figure of 13,800 Chinese who received North American degrees up to 1962, in contrast to 2,500 in Britain, 3,000 in France and 3,500 in Germany, p223.
17. Lutz, Jessie, China and the Christian Colleges, Ithaca and London: Cornell University Press, 1971.
18. Clough, Ralph, A Review of the U.S.-China Exchange Program, pp.56-57. Sources of Financial Aid Available to Students and Scholars from the People's Republic of China, Washington, D.C.: Committee for Scholarly Communication with the People's Republic of China and National Association for Foreign Student Affairs, 1980.
19. Clough, Ralph, A Review of the U.S.-China Exchange Program, pp.46.
20. China Exchange News, Vol.11, No.2, June, 1983, pp.12-14.
21. New Horizons, Vol. LI, No.1, October, 1983, p.1-2.

22. Fingar and Reed, Survey Summary, pp.12-13 is the source of figures in Table One. A further study has been commissioned by the Committee for Scholarly Communication with the People's Republic of China, but its results are not likely to be out until 1985.
23. Guangming Ribao, 10 October, 1981, Wenhui Bao, 21 Nov., 1981, Xinhua News Agency, 29 May, 1982.
24. Informationen Austausch mit der Volksrepublik China, No.9, March, 1983, p.12.
25. Brandi-Dohrn, Beatrix, 'Rücklick auf fünf Jahre akademischen Austausch (1973-1978), in MITTELUNGEN des Koordinierungstelle für gegenwartsbezogene Ost- und Sudostasienforschung, No.33, July, 1980, pp.46-64.
26. Interview with Mr. Pollak, Westdeutsche Rektorenkonferenz, 23 March, 1983.
27. Informationen Austausch mit der Volksrepublik China, No.9, March, 1983, pp.13-16.
28. Ibid., pp.8-12.
29. Interview with Dr. Dierk Stuchenschmidt, DAAD, 23 March, 1983. The figures in Table 8.2 were kindly provided by Dr. Stuchenschmidt, as well as other information in this section.
30. Informationen Austausch mit der Volksrepublik China, No.5, February, 1982, p.17.
31. Kreissler, Francoise, 'L'Action Culturelle Allemande en Chine de la Fin du XIXè Siècle à la seconde Guerre Mondiale', unpublished doctorat du 3è cycle, Ecole des Hautes Etudes en Sciences Sociales, Paris, 1983, pp.63-125.
32. Peking Review, Vol.10, No.47, 17 Nov., 1967; Vol.11, No.20, 17 May, 1968.
33. Interview at the Germany Embassy in Beijing, 9 October, 1981.
34. Interviews at the DAAD and WRK, Bonn, March, 1983.
35. Interview with officials in the French Ministry of Foreign Affairs, and Ministry of Education, 7, 11 April, 1983.
36. Interview with Mr. Zhang Baoqing, Education Section of the Chinese Embassy in Paris, 22 March, 8 April, 1983. Mr Zhang kindly provided the information presented in Table 8.3.
37. The programme d'échanges culturels 1982-3 states that 250 Chinese would be sent to France for doctoral studies each year from Autumn 1982.
38. There is an indirect reference to this in section 7 of the programme d'échanges culturels 1982-3, p.3.
39. Visit to Shanghai No.2 Medical School, 28 Nov., 1980.
40. See Hayhoe, Ruth, 'Towards the Forging of a Chinese University Ethos: Zhendan and Fudan 1903-1919', China Quarterly, No.94, June, 1983, pp.323-341. for a historical account of the link between Fudan University and the French Jesuit Aurore (Zhendan) University.

41. Visit to Shanghai No. 2 Medical School, 28 Nov., 1980.
42. Visit to Wuhan University, 30 July, 1980.
43. Programme of Cultural, Educational and Scientific Exchanges Between Britain and China, 1980-1982, London: The British Council.
44. Mrs Beryl Barker of the British Council kindly gave information on both British Council services for Chinese scholars and students in Britain and its teacher-training programme in China. Interviews on 26 April and 15 August, 1983.
45. Mr. Wang Baizhe of the Education Section of the Chinese Embassy in London kindly gave details on Chinese scholars and students in Britain, 10 Sept., 1982, and 22 April, 1983. These are presented in Table 8.4.
46. This document is available from the Council of Ministers of Education, Canada (CMEC), 252 Bloor St. W., Suite 5-200, Toronto, Canada M5S 1V5. The writer had interviews with Dr. Lucian Perras, Director of CMEC, and Mr. Ben Wilson, Assistant Deputy Minister of Education, Ontario, both of whom were members of the Canadian delegation which drew up the memorandum.
47. Interview with Dr. Miles Wisenthal, International Development Office, Association of Universities and Colleges of Canada, Ottawa, 4 October, 1983.
48. Interview with Mr. Don McMaster, CIDA China Programme, Ottawa, 5 October, 1983.
49. China/Canada Management News: An Occasional Newsletter, No.1, Sept., 1983, International Development Office, 151 Slater, Ottawa.
50. This Table is based on statistics collated by the CMEC and presented in the report Canada/China Student Placement Program, 1 October, 1982.
51. Interview with Mr. Cheng Jianhua, Education Section of the Chinese Embassy in Ottawa, Canada, 7 October, 1983.
52. Education Sector Policy Paper, Washington: The World Bank, 1980, p.10.
53. China Exchange News, Vol.9, No.3, Sept., 1981.
54. Xinhua News Agency, 19 November, 1982, p.5.
55. Information on this project and further details on the other two was obtained through a visit to the World Bank in Washington, 21 October, 1983.
56. China Exchange News, Vol.9, No.4, December, 1981, p.20.
57. Informationen Austausch mit der Volksrepublik China, No.5, February, 1982, p.18.
58. CMEC Study of Originating Institutions of Chinese Scholars, September, 1983.
59. The list of institutions is given in China Exchange News, Vol.9, No.3, Sept., 1981. 5 are in Beijing, 4 in Shanghai, 2 in Tianjin, 2 in Nanjing, 2 in Hangzhou, 2 in Guangzhou, and 1 in Xiamen, all major East Coast cities.

STATISTICAL APPENDIX OF CONTEMPORARY EDUCATIONAL PROVISION

David I. Chambers

As the chapters in this book have indicated, Chinese education has undergone profound changes since 1976. For Western scholars, one welcome feature of this change has been the publication since 1980 of detailed quantitative indicators of performance at all levels of the educational system. Such data, coupled with those released or about to be released from the 1982 National Census, will provide a valuable insight into the problems and prospects of a rapidly changing education system.

This is not suggest that all major indicators are now available or that the data so far released by Chinese authorities are perfect. A 1979 publication containing comprehensive national data for the years 1949-1979 is unavailable to foreigners, provincial data are not yet published on a systematic basis and little distinction is made at the lower levels of education between initial and effective enrollments. Nevertheless, quantitative approaches to the study of Chinese education are no longer the 'impossible dream' which they were between 1959 and 1980.

The tables which appear below present a selection of data from the period 1976 - 1982. They are based upon material from the Chinese Encyclopaedic Yearbook, published annually since 1980*. Readers seeking to acquaint themselves with more detailed statistics may wish to consult Billie L. C. Lo, Research Guide to Education in China After Mao (Hong Kong University, 1983), which covers 1976 to 1981.

* Zhongguo Baike Nianjian (Beijing & Shanghai), cited hereafter as ZBN followed by year of edition.

Statistical Appendix

KINDERGARTEN SCHOOLS

	1976	1979	1980	1981	1982
Number	442,700	165,600	170,419	130,296	122,107
Enrollment (1,000's)	13,955	8,792	11,508	10,562	11,131
Teachers (1,000's)	514	295	411	401	415

PRIMARY SCHOOLS

	1976	1979	1980	1981	1982
Number (1,000's)	1,044	924	917	894	881
Enrollment (10,000's)	15,006	14,663	14,627	14,333	13,972
Teachers (1,000's)	5,288	5,382	5,499	5,580	5,505
New Admissions (10,000's)	*	*	2,942	2,749	2,672
Graduates (10,000's)	*	*	2,053	2,076	2,069

1976 and 1979: ZBN1980 pp. 535,536.
1980   : ZBN1981 p. 471.
1981   : ZBN1982 p. 568.
1982   : ZBN1983 p. 595.

* not available

Statistical Appendix

SECONDARY SCHOOLS

	1976	1979	1980	1981	1982
I: Ordinary					
Numbers	192,152	144,233	118,377	106,718	101,649
Enrollment (1,000's)	58,365	59,050	55,081	48,596	45,285
New Admissions (1,000's)	*	*	19,343	17,405	16,424
Graduates (1,000's)	*	*	15,810	16,403	13,427
II: Specialised					
Numbers	2,443	3,033	3,069	3,132	3,076
Enrollment (1,000's)	690	1,199	1,243	1,069	1,039
New Admissions (1,000's)	*	*	468	433	420
Graduates (1,000's)	*	*	410	605	446

1976 and 1979: ZBN1980 pp. 535,536.
1980 : ZBN1981 p. 471.
1981 : ZBN1982 p. 568.
1982 : ZBN1983 p. 595.

* not available

Statistical Appendix

UNIVERSITIES AND COLLEGES

	1976	1979	1980	1981	1982
Numbers	392	633	675	704	715
Enrollment (1,000's)	565	1,020	1,144	1,280	1,154
New Admissions (1,000's)	217	275	281	279	315
Graduates (1,000's)	149	85	147	140	457
Teachers (1,000's)	167	237	247	250	287

1976 and 1979: ZBN1980 pp. 535,536,538.
1980   : ZBN1981 p. 471.
1981   : ZBN1982 p. 568.
1982   : ZBN1983 p. 595.

Graduates figures for 1976 and 1979 from Zhongguo Tongji Nianjian 1983 (Chinese Statistical Yearbook 1983), p.521.

Note: This table excludes post-graduate study.

Statistical Appendix

ADULT EDUCATION STUDENT ENROLLMENT

(All figures in 1,000's)

Institution	1980	1981	1982
Broadcasting Universities	324	268	347
Worker-Peasant Universities & Colleges	455	491	351
Worker-Peasant Secondary Technical Schools	2,963	3,119	3,264
Worker-Peasant Spare-Time Secondary Schools	3,551	3,766	6,350
Worker-Peasant Primary Schools	16,461	9,736	7,566
of which:			
Literacy Classes	12,209	6,213	3,960

1980: ZBN1981 p. 481.
1981: ZBN1982 p. 579.
1982: ZBN1983 p. 603.

GLOSSARY

Chinese Term*		English Translation	Page
benke	本科	regular course	84
benke xuesheng	本科学生	regular undergraduate	125
boshi	博士	doctorate	248
budaoweng	不倒翁	wobbly man	191
bu ke	补课	remedial class	182
chuji zhongxue	初级中学	lower secondary schools	90
buxi xuexiao	补习学校	tutorial schools	91
daiye	待业	waiting for work	72
dang wei	党委	Party committee	187
dang xiao	党校	Party schools	186
dang zu	党组	Party group	187
daxue biyesheng	大学毕业生	university graduates	197
duanqi zhiye daxue	短期职业大学	short-term vocational university	124
fu jiaoshou	付教授	associate professor	129

*All contemporary terms are given in modern Chinese script, while the few traditional terms are written in the traditional, more complex script. Standard phonetic script (*pinyin*) has been used for the transliteration.

Glossary

Chinese Term		English Translation	Page
gaodeng shifan yuanxiao	高等师范院校	higher teacher-training institutes	125
gaodeng zhuanke xuexiao	高等专科学校	junior colleges	125
gaodeng zi xue kaoshi zhidao weiyuanhui	高等自学考试指导委员会	higher education self-study examination guidance committee	199
gongren daxue	工人大学	workers' university	195
guagou	挂钩	establish links	83
guan yi	官意	will of the officials	89
jiangshi	讲师	lecturer	129
jiaohua	教化	transform the manners (of the masses)	234
jiaoshi jinxiu xueyuan	教师进修学院	schools for teacher refresher courses	171
jiaoshou	教授	professor	129
jiaoyu geming	教育革命	revolution in education	105
jiaoyu xueyuan	教育学院	college of education	171
jiaoyuan	教员	teacher	129
jiben lilun	基本理论	basic theory	196
jinshi	进士	promoted scholar	29, 35
jigong xuexiao	技工学校	workers training school	91

Glossary

Chinese Term		English Translation	Page
jishu jichu ke	技术基础课	technical foundation courses	201
junzi	君子	superior man	32
juren	举人	recommended person	29, 35
lilun feng	理论风	theoretical wind	195
lun xun ke	轮训课	rotation courses	183
minban	民办	run by the people	33
minban jiaoshi	民办教师	rural teacher	257
min yi	民意	will of the people	89
minzu xueyuan	民族学院	minorities' colleges	151
mufu	幕府	secretariat	32
nongmin hukou	农民户口	rural residential status	257
putonghua	普通话	the common language	21
putong ke	普通课	ordinary (academic) courses	201
ru	儒	literatus	94
shi	士	scholar	94
shifan zhuanke xuexiao	师范专科学校	teacher-training schools	170

Glossary

Chinese Term		English Translation	Page
shijian feng	实践风	practice wind	195
shuoshi	硕士	master's degree	248
shuyuan	书院	college, scholarly society	30, 31 35, 232
sili daxue	私立大学	private university	120
sili xueyuan	私立学院	private college	120
sili xuexiao	私立学校	private school	120
tiaochu nongmen	跳出农门	escape from the country side	87
tiaojie xuexiao	调节学校	adjustment schools	91
wanquan zhongxue	完全中学	complete secondary schools	90
wusheng de mingling	无声的命令	silent commands	203
xiaowu weiyuanhui	校务委员会	university affairs committee	129
xitong	系统	system	183
xitong jiaoyu	系统教育	systematic education	191
xiucai	秀才	cultivated talent	29, 32
xuefenzhi	学分制	the credit system	127
xueshi	学士	bachelor's degree	248

Glossary

Chinese Term		English Translation	Page
yanjiusheng	研究生	research student	117
yi bufen	一部分	a part	182
yin di zhi yi	因地制宜	adapt policy to local conditions	183
yingmi biyesheng	影迷毕业生	graduate movie fan	197
yuan shui bujiu jin huo	远水不救近火	Distant water will not extinguish a fire close at hand.	195
yucai	育才	cultivate talent	234
zheng gong ganbu	政工干部	political work cadres	190
zhengguihua	正规化	regularise	192
zhengzhi sixiang baogaoyuan	政治思想报告员	political and ideological reporters	186
zhi gong daxue	职工大学	employee university	195
zhiye xuexiao	职业学校	vocational schools	91
zhongdeng shifan xuexiao	中等师范学校	secondary teacher-training school	170
zhongdeng zhuanke xuexiao	中等专科学校	secondary specialist schools	170
zhongdian gaodeng yuanxiao	重点高等院校	keypoint or priority higher education institutions	124
zhongdian xiaoxue	重点小学	keypoint primary school	56

Glossary

Chinese Term		English Translation	Page
zhongxin xiaoxue	中心小学	central primary school	56
zhujiao	助教	teaching assistant	129
zhuanke	专科	specialised courses	84
zhuanke xuesheng	专科学生	junior college students	125
zi xue	自学	self-study	199
zi xue daxue	自学大学	self-study university	199
zonghe gaozhong	综合高中	comprehensive upper secondary schools	90

THE CONTRIBUTORS

BRIAN HOLMES is Professor of Comparative Education and Head of the Department of Comparative Education in the University of London Institute of Education. He is also Dean of the Faculty of Education in the University of London and Dean and Professor of Education in the College of Preceptors. Professor Holmes has been at the Institute of Education since 1953, where his major interest has been to develop a paradigm within which research in Comparative Education can be undertaken. The main features of this paradigm have been drawn from the work of Sir Karl Popper and John Dewey. Of his many books <u>Problems in Education</u> (1965) and <u>Comparative Education: Some Considerations of Method</u> (1981) reflect his position as a comparative educationist.

RUTH HAYHOE is a Canadian who has taught Chinese students in Hong Kong and Shanghai for 13 years. She has recently completed her doctoral studies at the University of London Institute of Education on Chinese-western interaction in higher education.

BILLIE L.C. LO, a Hong Kong born Chinese, did her graduate studies in Comparative Education at the University of London Institute of Education. Ms. Lo was a Research Officer at the University of Hong Kong for three years, during which she compiled a <u>Reseach Guide to Education in China after Mao 1977-1981</u> (Centre of Asian Studies, University of Hong Kong, 1983).

STANLEY ROSEN teaches in the Political Science Department of the University of Southern California, and is the author of <u>Red Guard Factionalism and the Cultural Revolution in Guangzhou</u> (Westview, 1982). Dr. Rosen recently became the editor of the journal <u>Chinese Education</u>.

JÜRGEN HENZE is a researcher in the Comparative Education Centre of the Institute of Education at the University of Bochum. His publications include <u>Das Erziehungs- und Bildungswesen der VR CHINA seit 1969: Eine Bibliographie</u> (Hamburg, Institut für Asienkunde, 1978), and <u>Bildung und Wissenschaft in der Volksrepublik China zu Beginn der achtziger Jahre</u> (Hamburg, Institut für Asienkunde, 1983).

DAVID CHAMBERS has taught Chinese politics at the University of Bristol since 1971 and is a member of the advisory committee of <u>Chinese Education</u>. Dr. Chambers is currently completing a book-length study of the politics of Chinese education between 1958 and 1983.

INDEX

Academic Degrees Committee of the State Council   119
Academic freedom   41
Adult education   178-204
  administration   183-186
  aims & objectives   179-183
  curriculum   190-201
  enrollment   193-4
  types of institution   195-202
Agricultural education   19,21-23,46,67,72,87-90
                         222,225,228
Aims of education   8,13,23,33-34,36,40,45-6,74,104,11,156,-7,
                    174,179-83,206
All-China Federation of Trade Unions (ACFTU)   180,181,185,196,
                    188,192
American education   19,51
  influence on China   27,28,37-40,42,43,128,142
  see also USA, Scholarly exchange
Autonomy   9,11,24,30,40,57,129,132,174,214,217

Breshnev   25
Britain   20,22,206,219-221,227,229
British Council   219
Buddhism   11,30

Cai Yuanpei   37,41
Canada   206,221-224,227
Canadian International Development Agency (CIDA)   221-23
Centralisation/decentralisation   9,20,32-34,96,105-7,114,132,
                    189,213,219,223
Centre Nationale de la Recherche Scientifique (CNRS)   217
Chi Qun   195
Chiang Kai-shek   12,26
China Scientifique and Technical Association (CSTA)   185,192
Chinese Academy of Sciences (CAS)   117,192,208,217,219,221,247
Chinese Academy of Social Sciences (CASS)   117,219,221,247
Chinese Association for the Study of Ideological and Political
  Work among Employees   186
Chinese Communist Party   3,10,12,14,16,61,71,102,105,111,127,
        141,159,178,179,181,183,184,186,187,190,191,192,197,206
Chinese Communist Youth League (CCYL)   81,185,192
Coleman   152
Committee for Scholarly Communication with the PRC (CSCPRC)
                    210,211
Confederation of British Industry (CBI)   219
Confucianism   11,24,28,29-32,33,35,37,40,41,43,44,93,94,156,
                    205,256
Constitution   2,45-46
Correspondence education   14,148,184,192,197-9
Council of Ministers of Education, Canada (CMEC)   221,223

280

Index

Credit system   39,40,127
Cultural borrowing   27-8,128
Cultural Revolution
  see Great Proletarian Cultural Revolution (GPCR)
Curriculum   13,14,20,29,31,32,33,35-41,43
  adult education   190-202
  primary   52,54,60,63
  secondary   76,77,78,115
  teacher training   162-168
  tertiary   122,123,125-8

Daoist ideas   31
Decentralisation
  see centralisation
Degrees   119,125,208-9,248-9
  traditional   29,35,36,37
Deng Liqun   186,187
Deng Xiaoping   107,112,154,206
Deutscher Akademischer Austauschdienst (DAAD)   213,216
Dewey, John   38
Diversity/diversification   21,56,58,70,80,142,205,220,228
  of higher education   112,119-125
  of secondary education   66-7,89
Dual tasks of education   49-52

Economics of education
  see financing
  elite/elitism   12,16,17,20,21,22,31,32,60,93,179,205
  enrollment   17,18,23,36,37,42,57,58,65,66,71,72,73,75,82,89,
               90,91,97,102,105,108,111,113,114,116,117,
               117,118,125,126,127,132-3,151,193,194,217
Equality/inequality   3,8,17,22,45,69,80-86,93,107-8,142-5,152
  based on sex   60,80-1,144
  based on class   66-8,70,81,96
  based on regional differences   23,96,99,100,108,109,120,135,137
  related to ethnic and linguistic minorities   13,20,81,96,115,
               145-151
Equity   152,225
Europe   8,25,40,93
European education   8,17,22,24,153
  influence on China   27,28,40-43,44,142,206
  see also scholarly exchange
Examinations   16,34,69,74,76,79,80,88,154,166-7,181,226
  for study abroad   208,211,216
  self-study   200
  traditional   28,29,32,36,41,93-4,226
  university entrance   66,67,69,74,76,81,82,84,88,91,102,107,
               112-116

Fang Yi   111
Fees   59,87,88,123,124,188

281

Fei Xiaotong 84
Financing 86,137-141
  of adult education 187-89
  of keypoint schools 67,83,85-6
  of keypoint universities 124-25
  of rural education 19,48,57,59,86
  of scholars abroad 208,211,214,217,220,222,224-25
  of technical/vocational schools 74
First Five-year Plan 95,96,128,133
France 11,20,22,206,217-19,227
French education 15,40

Gandhi 15,16
Gang of Four 2,12,55,112,142,156,157,158,195
Gao Yi 166
Germany 11,12,22,41,206,213-16,227,229
Great Leap Forward 12,96
Great Proletarian Cultural Revolution (GPCR) 3,16,18,22,23,24,
    27,29,33,43-46,47,65,66,67,69-70,72,94,102-111,120,122,
    140,143,152,158,179,180,186,190,195,197,203,228
Guomindang Party 12,26,40,41,44
Gu Dachun 186

Hans, Nicholas 9,14,27
He Dongchang 200
Hierarchy 34,67,70,89,107,227
  tendencies towards 71,91,205,226
  traditional 35,94
Higher education 22,23-25,43,93-153
  access to 67,70,74,107-111,112,113,148-53
  administration 105-7,120-22,128-133,142
  broadcasting universities 196-7
  degrees 119,125,208-9,248-49
  financing 137-141
  graduate 117-119
  higher technical colleges 125,225
  keypoint 124-25,184,199,224-26
  planning 133-142
  private 120,122-24
  quality 22,45,84,93-96,142-44,152-53
  short-term vocational universities 124
  trade union universities 185
  universities 43-44,103-5,119
  workers universities 23,104
Higher institutions
  Beijing College of Chemical Engineering 131
  Beijing Foreign Languages Institute 221
  Beijing Institute of Technology 129
  Beijing Languages Institute 219
  Beijing Teacher Training University 123,163,166
  Beijing University 83,129

Index

    Central Broadcasting University 197,221
    Chinese People's University 198
    Fudan University 218-19
    Guangzhou Foreign Languages Institute 221
    Guangzhou Municipal Sparetime University 190
    Hunan Medical School 211
    Jiaotong University 129,130,221
    Qinghua University 83,107,123,132
    Shanghai Foreign Languages Institute 221
    Shanghai Number 2 Medical School 218
    Shanghai Teacher Training University 166
    Shansi Agricultural University 211
    Tongji University, College 198,214-16
    Wuhan Hydraulic and Electrical Engineering Institute 128
    Wuhan Medical College 215
    Wuhan University 218
    Xiamen University 124
Huang Yanpei 37,41

Ideological-political education 19,60-62,104,163-6,181,190-92,
                        206,229
Ideology 7,9,12-16,26-27
India 10,15,16
Illiteracy
  see literacy
Inequality
  see equality
Investment in education 137-141,178

Japan 8,11,25,27,37,42,225
  influence on Chinese education 27,35-37,41,206
Jiang Nanxiang 55
Job assignment 74,133-37

Kangda 102-104
Keypoint/priority institutions
  see financing, schools, higher education
Kruschev 16,23

Language policy 20-21
League of Nations 29,40,42
Lenin 12,13,24
Li Chi 52
Liang Qichao 26,37
Liang Shuming 42
Literacy/illiteracy 12-3,16-7,19,21,31,32,33,43,58,60,80,82,201
Liu Da 132
Liu Shaoqi 43,48,49

Ma Xulun 96
Makarenko 18

Manpower planning and utilisation   133,137,155
Mao Zedong   2,10,12,15,17,23,26,29,33,43,44,48,61,65,70,92,96,
          102,103,104,112
Marxism-Leninism   12,13,14,24,26,33,34,35,163,191,207
  see also ideological-political education
Mencius   156,256
Ministry of Education   48,50,54,57,71,74,105,107,115,117,120,
       135,137,167,172,173,174,175,184,189,192,197,199,200,
       203,207,208,211,212,215,219
  Foreign Affairs Office   207-8,217,226
Ministry of Finance   187,188,189
Ministry of Foreign Economic Relations and Trade   222
Ministry of Labour and Personnel   184
Ministry of Radio and T.V.   197
Minorities education   81,115,145-152
  language policy   20-21,151
  see also equality
Modernisation   15,21-3,24,25,29,45,46,48,49,61,92,93,113,179,
          181,205,206,207,220,226,228,229
  four modernisations   2,3,12,13,49,62,65,92,112,119,145,154,
          159,166
Monroe, Paul   38
Morals   31,35,46,52,53,61,94,156-57,191,226,229

National education conferences   2,107,113,154,159,166,169-170,
          172,189
National Employee Education Administrative Committee (NEACC)
          183-184
National Research Council, Canada (NRC)   221
National Women's Federation (NWF)   185

Orleans, Leo   190
Overseas Development Agency (ODA)   220

Parents   19,52,58,60,71,87,137
Parkhurst, Helen   38
Pedagogical principles   157,162
  problems   185,201
  studies   163,164-65,166
Pepper, Suzanne   128,132
Plato   14,24
Political education
  see ideological-political
  education
Population   36,42
  explosion   7
  demographic trends   10-11
Productive labour   13,19,24,35,44,45,53,62,66,69,103,164-65
Psychology   26,37,39,162,163,164-65

Index

Quality 3,45,51,52,54-6,60,71,76,93,112,113,133,142,143-8,152-
            153,154,155,160-61,167,197,203-4,224-226

Remedial education 182,201-202
Responsibility system 2,46,58,59,87,228
Royal Society 219
Rural-urban differences 10,13,15,16,18,19,22,42,46,60,62,63,
            70,72,86-89,205,227-28

Sadler, Michael 27
Scholar-official 11,20,22,24-25,29,30,31,94
Scholarly exchange 3,9,45,111,133,205-229
  Britain-China 209-213
  Canada-China 221-224
  Chinese policies of 206-209
  Curricular emphasis 208,212,215,217-18,220,222-23
  France-China 217-219
  Germany-China 213-216
Schools
  double-session 59
  half-day 33,58
  mobile 58
  part-farm part-study 51
  part-work part-study 51
  Party 178,186
  private 120,122,123
  rural people-run (minban) 33,47-8,57,58,59,62
  rural secondary 86-89
  state-run 52,123
  teacher-training 170
  traditional 30-31
  types of 15,33,44,48,56,58
  types of secondary 44,66-68,71,72,90-91,200-202
  urban academic 15,47,52-56,62
  winter 33,58
  work-study 18,47,51,69
Selection/recruitment 18,20,22,51,60
  for higher education 17,23,67,69-70,84,88,102,107,112-19,135
  for secondary education 69,76-80,82,88,90
  for study abroad 208,211-12,226
Self-study schemes 192,199-200
Sixth Five-year Plan 65,91,133,207
Social mobility 20,51,52,60,64,66-68,70,74,87,89,92,94,115,
            205,227,228
Social Sciences and Humanities Reseach Council of Canada
            (SSHRCC) 221
Socialisation 92
  of teachers 158-162
Soviet Union 9,22
Soviet education 13,14,16,17,18,19,20
  influence on China 16,42-43,95,96,128,142,152

285

Stalin 12
State Economic Commission (SEC) 183,191,192,219
State Planning Commission 135
State Science and Technology Commission (SSTC) 211
Stratification 51,62-63,72
Students
  abroad 35,38,45,205-229
  academic pressure on 55,62
  activism of 39,41-43,69-70,226
  drop-out rate 59,60,87,188,202
  female vs. male 60,80-81,144
  mobility 51-52,67,69,79,86-87,91
  research/graduate 117-119,247,249
  school entrance age 52
  streaming 54-56,72
Sun Yat-sen 11,12,26

Tao Xingzhi 42
Teacher Education 9,154-177
  administration 172-74
  curriculum 162-169
  in-service 167,171,172,175,176
  organisation 156
  perceptions of teaching 155
  quality 155,167-68
  recruitment 159-60,167
  role of the teacher 32,74,156-62,163
  structure 156,169-72
  teacher socialisation 155-56,158-62
  teaching practice 166
  types of institution 170-72,175
Teachers
  higher education 127,129,131,132,144
  ideal teacher 156-57,256-57
  little assistants 59
  rural 63-64,160
  salaries/income of 158-160,177,185
  traditional 31,47,156
Three People's Principles 12,26,39,40,44
Transition rates 71,82,83,84,108,110,111,116
Twiss, George 38
Two-line struggle 97
Two-track
  system 14,15,17,18,21-22,49,50-52,61,62,64,90,91
  theory 48
  tradition 47,62

United Nations 8
USA 9,22,40,206,209-213,223,227
  see also American education
University-level agreements 45,211,213-214,217,219-220,221-22

Index

Walking on two legs 15,48,88,190,204
Warnock, Mary 152
Westdeutsche Rektorenkonferenz (WRK) 213,216
World Bank 84,134,140,189,206,224-26,227

Yan Yangchu, James 42
Yanan 28,32-35,43,44,102-104
Yao Wenyuan 104
Yao Yilin 189
Yuan Baohua 183,202-203

Zang Boping 179
Zhang Chengxian 51
Zhao Yinhua 191
Zhou Enlai 2,107